SPORTS

ON THE NET

PLUG YOURSELF INTO...

THE MACMILLAN INFORMATION SUPERLIBRARY™

Free information and vast computer resources from the world's leading computer book publisher—online!

FIND THE BOOKS THAT ARE RIGHT FOR YOU!

A complete online catalog, plus sample chapters and tables of contents give you an in-depth look at **all** of our books, including hard-to-find titles. It's the best way to find the books you need!

- STAY INFORMED with the latest computer industry news through our online newsletter, press releases, and customized Information SuperLibrary Reports.

- GET FAST ANSWERS to your questions about MCP books and software.

- VISIT our online bookstore for the latest information and editions!

- COMMUNICATE with our expert authors through e-mail and conferences.

- DOWNLOAD SOFTWARE from the immense MCP library:
    - Source code and files from MCP books
    - The best shareware, freeware, and demos

- DISCOVER HOT SPOTS on other parts of the Internet.

- WIN BOOKS in ongoing contests and giveaways!

TO PLUG INTO MCP: ➜

GOPHER: gopher.mcp.com

FTP: ftp.mcp.com

WORLD WIDE WEB: http://www.mcp.com

SPORTS

ON THE NET

Bob Temple

que

SPORTS ON THE NET

Copyright© 1995 by Que® Corporation

Library of Congress Catalog No.: 95-67675

ISBN: 0-7897-0240-1

98   97   96   95   4   3   2   1

Interpretation of the printing code: the rightmost double-digit number is the year of the book's printing; the rightmost single-digit number, the number of the book's printing. For example, a printing code of 95-1 shows that the first printing of the book occurred in 1995.

Publisher: Roland Elgey

Associate Publisher: Stacy Hiquet

Publishing Director: Brad R. Koch

Director of Product Series: Charles O. Stewart III

Managing Editor: Sandy Doell

Director of Marketing: Lynn E. Zingraf

CREDITS

Publishing Manager
Thomas H. Bennett

Acquisitions Editor
Beverly Eppink

Acquisitions Coordinators
Ruth Slates
Andrea Duvall

Product Director
Stephen L. Miller

Production Editor
Jeff Riley

Copy Editors
Noelle Gasco
Nanci Sears Perry

Technical Editor
Mark Ward

Book Designer
Sandra Schroeder

Graphic Image Specialists
Brad Dixon
Jason Hand
Clint Lahnen
Michael Reynolds
Laura Robbins
Craig Small

Production Team
Claudia Bell
Anne Dickerson
Chad Dressler
Karen Gregor
Barry Jorden
Bob LaRoche
Beth Lewis
Steph Mineart
Darcy Myers
G. Alan Palmore
Kaylene Riemen

Indexer
Kathy Venable

TRADEMARK ACKNOWLEDGMENTS

WE'D LIKE TO HEAR FROM YOU!

As part of our continuing effort to produce books of the highest possible quality, Que would like to hear your comments. To stay competitive, we *really* want you, as a computer book reader and user, to let us know what you like or dislike most about this book or other Que products.

You can mail comments, ideas, or suggestions for improving future editions to the address below, or send us a fax at (317) 581-4663. For the online-inclined, Macmillan Computer Publishing now has a forum on CompuServe (type **GO QUEBOOKS** at any prompt) through which our staff and authors are available for questions and comments. In addition to exploring our forum, please feel free to contact us on CompuServe at 72410,2077 to discuss your opinions of this book.

Thanks in advance—your comments will help us to continue publishing the best books available on computer topics in today's market.

ABOUT THE AUTHOR

Bob Temple began his journalism career as a sports writer, and he's currently General Manager and Executive Editor of a group of weekly newspapers in the suburbs of Minneapolis-St. Paul. He keeps in touch with his first love—sports—by covering the Minnesota Twins, the Minnesota Vikings, and the Minnesota Timberwolves on a free-lance basis for the Associated Press. He has authored a fantasy football guide and several sports articles for magazines and newspapers. He can be reached at his CompuServe address (75212,607). Non-CompuServe members should address e-mail to INTERNET:75212.607@compuserve.com.

DEDICATION

For my wife Teri, who could live without sports and doesn't much care for computers but puts up with me just the same.

ACKNOWLEDGMENTS

Emily Temple was four years old and a definite "daddy's girl" when I began my work on this project—which ate up most of my weekends and many of my evenings. There were occasional tears when I'd have to work, but when it was all over, she was still daddy's girl.

Her twin brothers, Robby Temple and Sam Temple, were a pair of wild little one-year-olds during this period. They clearly didn't understand why I was so busy, but they know their daddy loves them, and they appear to love me, too.

Their full names appear because I want them to have *something* to show for this rather hectic time in their lives.

A lot of people had an impact—direct or indirect—on my ability to complete this project successfully. I can't possibly thank them all, but here's an attempt.

Thanks to my parents, who have always supported me.

Mark Neuzil, a friend, softball teammate, and author, provided some helpful and timely advice—and that was before I even started writing.

Eric Larson stepped up to the plate and delivered—his research assistance was top-notch.

Beverly Eppink, an Acquisitions Editor for Que, acquired me.

Ron Lesko of the Associated Press allowed me to adjust my Timberwolves coverage schedule so I'd have more time.

Que Corporation, of course, gave me this opportunity in the first place. They were also intelligent enough to assign the editing to Jeff Riley, who did an outstanding job on the book.

Finally, I'd like to thank Father James Whalen, who chaired the journalism department at my alma mater, served as my advisor, taught journalism ethics to more students than anyone in history, presided over my wedding, and can still send a shiver up my spine by saying, "Wake up, Temple!"

CONTENTS AT A GLANCE

TABLE OF CONTENTS

2 Sports Talk 25

II What's Out There 43

3 Pro Football 45

4 Pro Baseball 77

5 Pro Basketball   107

6 Pro Hockey · 135

10 College Sports   219

11 Hobbies and Recreational Sports 243

III Getting Connected   267

12 Internet Basics   269

13 Commercial Online Services   285

Index   **303**

Introduction

Does anyone else remember what it was like, not so many years ago, when PCs were a vision of the future, cable television was just getting started, and one of the most basic components of sports information—the boxscore—was unavailable in many daily newspapers?

It wasn't that long ago when even major newspapers didn't carry boxscores on all professional sports games. Baseball coverage on television consisted of the Saturday Game of the Week, plus a few local broadcasts every summer. NBA and NHL coverage was virtually nonexistent.

Now, all-sports cable and radio stations bring thousands of games into the majority of American homes. Satellite television makes it possible to see just about every game in every major sport.

Many people—maybe even someone special in your life—think that's more than enough sports for any one person. But oddly enough, as America's thirst for sports has grown, so has the number of games you now can watch and read about. That means more stats! More tidbits! More information than you'll probably ever need!

Sports fans have always found a way to use advances in technology as a means to satisfy their voracious appetites for sports news and information. As computers found their way into more and more American homes, owners were quick to find ways to use them to get—and share—sports information.

Today, an estimated 25 million people worldwide use the Internet—an international conglomeration of thousands of networks, all linked loosely together, yet all accessible.

Whether your interest lies in major professional sports, fantasy sports, sports trading cards or, say, Australian Rules Football, the Internet probably has some service you'd enjoy. Somewhere, out there in cyberspace, is a sports tidbit you don't know and a service through which you can find it.

How do you get it? Where is it? Who provides it? That's what this book is all about.

The answers to these questions can be as easy or as difficult as you want to make them. It all depends on your level of access to the Internet, your desire to find what you want, and—in some cases—how much you're willing to spend.

But before we can get too carried away with what's available on the Internet, it's important to get a basic understanding of the Internet itself—how to get to it, how to finesse your way through the various services, and so on.

What This Book Is About

Whether you have Internet access at work or home, whether you use a Macintosh or an IBM-compatible PC, *Sports on the Net* is designed to give you a complete guide to what's available on the Internet for sports fans. However, this book is much more than just a directory.

You don't need to be an experienced Internet user (or Internaut, or Internetie, as some people call themselves) to get the most out of this book. Although Internet vets will find a great deal of useful information on these pages, online rookies can use this book as not only a manual for sports possibilities, but as a beginner's tutorial for Internet service providers.

In other words, this book is designed to provide sports fans with a directory of sorts, a guide to where to find sports information and services, and a bit of a tutorial on how to use them. It's simple: If you want sports information, we'll show you where to go and what you'll find when you get there.

Here's a brief glimpse at the contents of the book, with short descriptions of each chapter:

Part I: Sports on the Net Basics

Part I provides a thumbnail sketch of what types of services are available to sports fans on the Internet.

- Chapter 1, "Sports News." This chapter provides an understanding of what types of sports news services can be found on the Internet and also provides information about commercial online services. It also tells you where that news comes from and who puts it there.
- Chapter 2, "Sports Talk." Bulletin board systems, newsgroups, and forums are widely used online. This chapter covers the wide variety of such "talk" groups, how they operate, where to find them, and how to use them.

Part II: What's Out There

This is the meat of the book. The nine chapters in this section are chock-full of places to go to find sports on the Internet. Each chapter concludes with a list of Internet addresses you can go to for each of these sports.

- Chapter 3, "Pro Football." This chapter covers professional football, including the Canadian Football League and even Australian Rules Football.
- Chapter 4, "Pro Baseball." Although recent surveys indicate football is the most popular spectator sport, baseball is probably the most popular Internet sport. Major League Baseball and the minor leagues are covered in this chapter.

- Chapter 5, "Pro Basketball." This chapter covers the NBA and other American professional leagues.
- Chapter 6, "Pro Hockey." The NHL, IHL, and AHL are all covered in this chapter.
- Chapter 7, "Other Pro Sports." We don't mean to demean, but we had to draw the line somewhere, so we've lumped these all together: Motor sports, golf, tennis, horse racing, soccer, and more.
- Chapter 8, "Fantasy Sports." Fantasy football and baseball are the most popular sports, but we also cover basketball, hockey, and others.
- Chapter 9, "Olympic and International Sports." This chapter tells you where to find information on the Olympics (past and future) and other international competitions such as the Goodwill Games, World Cup soccer, and more.
- Chapter 10, "College Sports." The Internet is full of information and services on college sports, and it's not just limited to men's football and basketball.
- Chapter 11, "Hobbies and Recreational Sports." If you're into skiing, golf, rock climbing, kayaking, or whatever, this is the chapter for you.

Part III: Getting Connected

Now that you know what's available to sports fans on the Internet, Part III shows you a variety of ways to get it. This section serves as a tutorial for Internet novices and a refresher for more experienced Internet users.

- Chapter 12, "Internet Basics." This chapter covers UseNet, e-mail, FTP servers, World Wide Web, Gopher, and other types of Internet servers.
- Chapter 13, "Commercial Online Services." This chapter covers dial-up services such as CompuServe, America Online, Prodigy, and others. We tell you the cost, the types of services provided, and the level of Internet access.

What This Book Is Not About

This book is not a manual on how to use the Internet. The Internet itself is the subject of a huge number of books, including *Easy Internet*, *Using the Internet*, and *Special Edition Using the Internet*, Second Edition (all published by Que).

You can't write a book like this without discussing how to get to the information and services on the Internet. But covering this topic and giving a full account of the Internet means producing a book that's too much for an author—or a reader—to handle.

Conventions Used in This Book

Because of the nature of this book, we didn't need to use as many conventions as other computer books. We've kept it as simple as possible.

This book is full of electronic addresses—often referred to as "places to go" on the Internet. Each address within the body of the text is listed in a special boldface type (**like this**) to set it apart from the rest of the text. We also provide icons next to these addresses that show you what type of address we've listed (see the following table). If you're not sure how to use an address, see Chapter 12, "Internet Basics." Addresses that appear in figure captions and in the lists at the end of most chapters are listed in a special type (`like this`).

Icon	Address Type
	America Online
	CompuServe
	Prodigy
	File Transfer Protocol (downloadable files)
	LISTSERVs (mailing lists)
	Gopher
	UseNet
	World Wide Web (WWW)

Keep in mind that the Internet is a strange and wonderful place where sites can come and go as they please because they are often run by individuals. So if you try to reach an address mentioned in this book and it no longer exists, don't get too frustrated. We've supplied you with many, many addresses, and there's bound to be another that suits your needs.

PART I

Sports on the Net Basics

1 *Sports News*
2 *Sports Talk*

Chapter 1

Sports News

Looking for sports news and information?
Look no further.

In this chapter

- *The sources for sports news*
- *How the Internet became a source of sports news*
- *What Associated Press Online has to offer*
- *Other sources of sports news on the Internet*
- *Statistics servers*

In other chapters

➤ *For more information on the commercial online services mentioned in this chapter, see Chapter 13*

➤ *For more information on how to use the addresses in this chapter, see Chapter 12*

Before we look at what specifically is available to sports fans on the Internet, we need to examine the types of sports information that can be found out there in cyberspace.

When you boil down the Internet to its bare essentials, you find there are two basic categories of sports sites:

- Sports news and information
- Sports talk

The news and information can be generated by a news-gathering organization or by individual fans. The talk generally comes from sports fans just like you.

Sports Information

Okay sports fans, here's today's stumper: Name the one thing a true sports fan can't live without.

The answer? Information.

To modify a saying from the immortal Yogi Berra, being a sports fan is 50 percent games, 50 percent news, and 50 percent statistics. (While the math may not make a lot of sense, Yogi is no mathematician. Besides, athletes constantly refer to "giving 110 percent," so I trust you'll indulge me.)

The point is this: the games, matches, meets, tournaments, and so on are great to watch and enjoy, but the nature of being a sports fan involves talking about them, reading about them, analyzing them, and so on.

The way sports fans go about getting their sports information hasn't changed that much over the past half-century. Although television has joined the fray previously dominated by newspapers and radio, sports fans continue to use the printed word more than any other source for sports news.

The games, matches, meets, tournaments, and so on are great to watch and enjoy, but the nature of being a sports fan involves talking about them, reading about them, analyzing them, and so on.

TIP

If you're looking for news about a particular sport, league, or team, consult the chapter that covers that topic. Chapters in Part II are divided by sport/interest, and they provide in-depth coverage of the wide variety of sites available to sports fans.

Some thought television's arrival, and the immediacy with which that medium could provide news and pictures to viewers all over the world, would signal the end of radio and a diminished role for newspapers. Certainly, when cable and satellite television became available, newspapers and radio stations were in jeopardy.

But each medium has found its own niche in the information industry. Newspapers, for example, came to realize that they were no longer the first source for game scores and shifted from the hard-news angle toward a softer, feature-oriented style of writing.

Radio continued to lead all of the traditional media because of the immediacy with which it can offer the latest news. Not only are the games of every major sports team carried on at least one radio station, but a radio station can immediately provide breaking news to its listeners.

Television can do the same, but for that medium to carry its full impact, it must have footage of the event—whatever it may be. That requires a camera crew to get to the scene, and so on.

Al Michaels

Al Michaels (see fig. 1.1) joined ABC Sports in 1976, but his place as one of the top sportscasters in the country wasn't assured until the 1980 Winter Olympics in Lake Placid.

It was then that Michaels said the words that would launch his career. As the clock ticked off the final seconds of the United States hockey team's improbable run to the gold medal, Michaels said, "Do you believe in miracles? YES!"

He was honored as Sportscaster of the Year that year and twice more, in 1983 and 1986. He has won two Emmy awards.

Today, his primary role is as host of ABC's *Monday Night Football*, which celebrated its 25th anniversary in 1994.

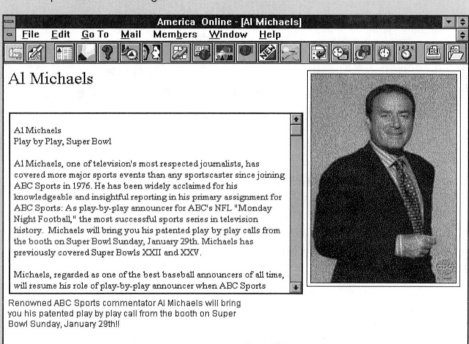

Figure 1.1
America Online members had access to a profile of Al Michaels around the time of the 1995 Super Bowl.

How Technology Affects the Written Word

When I cover a game for the Associated Press, I know going in that most fans who care will know the outcome of the game before they read what I write.

I try to provide the reader with something they can't get anywhere else. They heard the score on either radio or television, maybe even heard (or saw) part of an interview with a coach or key player.

So I have to figure out a way to highlight a particular aspect of the game—a key play, a trend—something that radio and TV might not have time to provide. Because the newspaper won't be on your doorstep until the next morning, I have time to further explore certain issues.

It's the same story with the Internet, or the information superhighway, or whatever you want to call it. Many who felt the Internet was *the* threat to media outlets believed it primarily threatened newspapers because it dealt with the written word and transmitted still-photographs. Although that may be true, it's also clear that it's only a matter of time before audio and video material will be easily transmitted and widely available to Internet users. That, of course, will threaten television.

The explosive growth of the World Wide Web in the past year has made the Internet a more attractive home for fans interested in a new and different means to obtain sports news and information. The Web offers the ability to download pictures and videos, audio clips, and more. New Web sports sites are springing up all the time.

The truth is, there will always be a place in our society for a printed newspaper to appear on your doorstep every day. There will always be a place for television and radio.

The Internet Becomes a Source of Sports News

The Internet is but another alternative, another way for people to get information—in this case, information about sports. The established media will react, adjust, and continue to thrive.

Daily newspapers have felt the threat, and the troubleshooters among them have reacted by making the Internet, and its commercial online service brothers, an even better place for the sports fan.

Many newspapers have begun operating Internet sites, and some of them are excellent. For the most part, they are used to provide even more in-depth coverage than that which is available in the newspaper, giving the serious sports fan a chance to find the information he or she needs.

In addition, wire services such as the Associated Press (for more information, see "What Is the Associated Press?" later in this chapter) have become Internet contributors or partners with commericial online service providers.

These services have long been providing news stories for use by newspapers, radio stations, and television stations. From a sports perspective, these services have been smart enough to know that their stories are reduced to a couple of paragraphs in most daily newspapers and a 5- or 10-second blip on television and radio sportscasts. By placing the full text of the stories on the Internet or providing it to a service provider such as Prodigy, wire services have reached an audience that wants to know more about out-of-town games and events.

Television networks and other outlets have also jumped in with both feet—witness ESPN's partnership with Prodigy and the ABC Sports partnership with America Online.

TIP

Specific aspects of the major commercial online service providers—Prodigy, CompuServe, and America Online—are included in every chapter of this book. If, however, you'd like to read an overview of each of these services, refer to Chapter 13, "Commercial Online Services."

These arrangements not only provide another outlet for the information generated by the networks, they serve as a continuous advertisement for their sports offerings through the traditional medium. For example, on Prodigy's ESPNet (see fig. 1.2), users can access program listings for a variety of ESPN shows.

It's unlikely that the Internet, or some other future online computer link, will become the primary source of sports news and information. After all, our world is a long way from the one that is inhabited by the Jetsons.

First Online Communication Is A Hit

TIME OUT

My first online communication was as basic as it gets. I sent a sports story from my laptop computer to the main computer at the Associated Press office in New York. Imagine my surprise back then—this was several years ago—when that computer talked back to mine, letting me know it had automatically received and filed my story!

Not long after that, I sent a magazine article to the magazine's editor, who captured it and saved it on his computer. Just as I was about to shut my computer off, the editor typed a note to me and I watched as the letters appeared on my screen. I was immediately hooked.

Figure 1.2 Jump: ESPNet

On Prodigy, sports fans can find pictures of their favorite ESPN hosts, along with program dates and times.

But it's getting closer every day, and the Internet is a viable outlet for sports news and information. In fact, it's a nearly endless source, with news coming from a wide variety of outlets all over the world.

When you're out there surfing, you'll find that some of these sources are extremely timely and very reliable; you might end up using them nearly every day. Others might not be updated for weeks or even months, or they might disappear from the Internet altogether, or they might provide inaccurate, incomplete, or incorrect information.

Associated Press Online

Perhaps the most reliable source of information on the Internet is provided by the Associated Press, which newspaper editors and the news directors of the electronic media have trusted for years.

What Is the Associated Press?

Simply put, the Associated Press (AP) is the largest news-gathering agency in the world. And more.

It is a wire service which, ironically, was a forerunner of today's online communications boom. For years, the AP has used telephone lines to transmit news to newspapers, radio stations, and television stations.

The Associated Press exists as a kind of support service for the sports staff at your local (and national) media outlet—be it a newspaper, television station, or radio station. When you pick up a copy of the newspaper, chances are that most of the national sports stories you read are provided by the AP.

The AP is a nonprofit organization that operates as a co-op news source. For example, newspapers that subscribe (by paying a fee) to the AP service have access to stories written by AP personnel. That service is provided in various levels, but most of the larger papers in the country pay for the full package.

In turn, the AP receives stories from its member newspapers, which it then can paraphrase in producing its own story. If you've ever read a story or heard a newscast that began, "The *Chicago Tribune* is reporting…," it is usually a story written by a *Chicago Tribune* reporter, and then transmitted to the Associated Press, which wrote its own story based on the *Tribune*'s story, giving credit to the original source.

This give-and-take relationship with newspapers across the globe makes the AP the most complete news source on the planet.

How AP Stories Are Written

In sports, the vast majority of Associated Press stories are written by AP writers, either full-time reporters or those with whom the service contracts on a free-lance basis.

It sounds hard to believe, but the AP has at least one writer at every major sporting event in the United States, every day. When Major League Baseball is in full swing and all 28 teams are active, those 14 games are all covered in person by the AP.

Associated Press writers and statistics personnel are responsible for producing game stories and boxscores on every contest. In fact, regardless of what *byline* (the name of the reporter who wrote the story) is at the top of the game story you read, the accompanying boxscore is almost always provided by the AP. Writers for the AP also produce feature stories and cover other breaking sports news, such as trades, contract negotiations, etc.

Immediately upon the conclusion of each game, the AP writer sends a story on the game, called a *lead*, to editors in New York. That story is then sent to every AP member media outlet, which uses it as it sees fit. Shortly thereafter, the writer sends a second story, including quotes from players and coaches, to editors who pass it along as well.

Depending on the importance of the game, the writer might also send either notes or follow-up stories on the teams involved in the game.

In each city, the AP functions like a daily newspaper, although no actual newspaper is produced by the AP. Associated Press sportswriters write stories to preview upcoming games, write feature stories on teams or individuals, write opinion columns, and cover breaking sports news stories.

Coming Online

So what does the AP have to do with you, the Internet user?

In recent years, some commercial online service providers—most notably CompuServe and Prodigy—have begun offering Associated Press Online to subscribers. It has quickly become one of the most often used, and most basic, sports information services available to fans.

Without a doubt, the question most asked by sports fans is, "What's the score?" Associated Press Online users have access to score updates of all professional and major-college games, roughly every half-hour. It's just the score, but anyone who's ever become frustrated waiting for a national television broadcast to air the scores of other games in progress understands that it's nice to know you can quickly find it by using Associated Press Online.

Once the game is over, it usually takes less than an hour or so for the game story and boxscore to appear in your Associated Press Online window. You're reading the real McCoy—not the usual scaled-down version of the story that probably will appear in tomorrow's paper.

One of the principal advantages that newspapers have had over television and radio stations is that newspaper reporters can afford to be more thorough. They can go in-depth on a particular story, but the electronic media must battle a limited amount of time. The AP on the Internet holds a similar advantage over daily newspapers.

If you live in a major city, your local newspaper probably produces an NBA page, or a couple of baseball pages, every day during their respective seasons. These pages generally include boxscores of games that took place the previous day and a brief story on each game.

Concerns About AP Access Have Disappeared

I have worked for the Associated Press as a free-lance sportswriter for seven years, and I am also the General Manager of a group of weekly newspapers. I have to admit, it was a little disconcerting when I first learned that anyone in America has access to Associated Press stories at roughly the same time as the editor of the newspaper (who still has to package the paper and send it on to be printed and distributed before newspaper readers have access to it). That's my personal bias, but I've come to appreciate this as just another outlet available to the consumer of this type of information.

That information was probably produced by the AP. But what most people don't know is that AP writers don't write two- or three-paragraph stories on these games. The stories are longer, but they're cut down by newspaper editors who must fit all the stories within a limited space on a page. Or the stories are sent by AP in its nightly "roundup" report, in which all of the game stories are shortened by AP for the same reasons.

Online, however, users get the whole story. Literally.

It used to be that most people identified with and followed only their local sports teams. But as access to information about teams in other cities has grown, people are often fans of teams in other cities.

It's frustrating when your local newspaper provides only a few paragraphs on these teams and your local television station provides only a score and maybe a quick highlight.

With Associated Press Online, users not only get full game coverage of their favorite teams—no matter what city they're located in—they also have access to feature stories and other information on their teams. Although a feature story on the Charlotte Hornets' latest winning streak might not find newsprint in the *Seattle Times*, it is available to people coast-to-coast on the Internet.

AP Sports Resources Online

Associated Press sports stories currently are available through a couple of

Internet sources and two of the major commercial online service providers.

Each provider offers nearly identical services as far as stories are concerned; the principal difference is the timeliness with which the stories are available to users.

 Nando X Sports Server

`http://www.nando.net/`
`sptsserv.html`

The News & Observer Publishing Co., which publishes the *Charlotte* (N.C.) *News & Observer* daily newspaper, has developed the most complete sports server available on the Internet.

This main address links users to a huge number of other services. From a sports news perspective, it links to "The Sports Page," which is essentially a clearinghouse of AP sports stories organized by topic. This service is updated continuously and carries the top 15 AP stories at any given moment. That makes it an excellent source of breaking sports information.

Say, for example, you've got a few minutes at work and you're dying to hear the latest on the baseball strike. You log onto the Internet and connect to the World Wide Web, jump to the Nando X Sports Server (see fig. 1.3), and click the Baseball Server (it appears in highlighted, underlined type called a *hypertext link*). There will be a number of subcategories listed, one of which (during the winter of 1994-95) includes breaking news on the strike (see fig. 1.4).

Figure 1.3 `http://www.nando.net/sptsserv.html`
The Nando X Sports Server includes a number of links to sports news and statistics.

There, you'll find a listing of headlines of the most recently transmitted AP stories, from which you can take your pick.

The Sports Page also links you to other sports, such as auto racing, professional golf, professional tennis, and more. Another link is the Sports Server Top 15, which is a listing of the 15 most

TIME OUT
Nando X Sports Server Highly Recommended

If you have full Internet access, I strongly recommend the Nando X Sports Server. As a CompuServe member, I was very happy with the Associated Press Online offerings for sports because they are continuously updated and the links are easy to manage.

However, when I came across the Nando X Sports Server while surfing the Internet, I found it to be an even easier source for the sports news I need. What I like best

about it are the subcategories provided under the major sport headings. With the Nando X Sports Server, you don't have to open a "Baseball" directory and run through the list of baseball stories looking for the specific topic you want. If all you want to read about is recent player signings, you can click on that menu. Thus, you don't have to fight through all the strike stories or other items to find what you want.

recent stories posted to the sports server, regardless of topic.

Other links include the following:

- The Baseball Server, which includes minor league baseball.
- The Basketball Server, which includes both college and professional hoops.
- The Football Server, which includes both college and professional football.

 Satchel Sports

`http://www.starwave.com/SatchelSports.html`

What's the score? The Satchel Sports home page can lead you to the answer to that question, and much more.

Satchel Sports (see fig. 1.5) offers a list of scores that is just about as up-to-the-minute as ESPN SportsCenter. It's probably the user's best source for that bit of basic—yet vital—sports information.

But Satchel Sports also links you to other services, including a list of that day's games (with links to a quick preview of each game in certain cases). There is a link to updated statistics and transactions. There is also a link to an archive of past sports stories, which appears to be from a number of different sources.

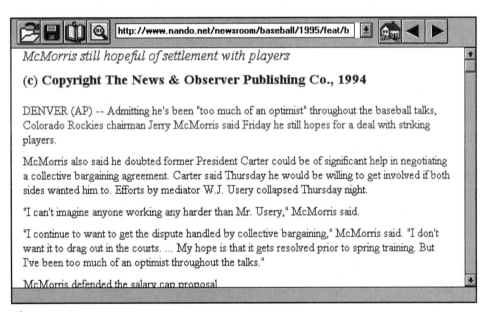

Figure 1.4 `http://www.nando.net/sptsserv.html`
Breaking sports news is continuously updated on the Nando X Sports Server.

Figure 1.5 `http://www.starwave.com/SatchelSports.html`
The Satchel Sports home page links you to current information and an archive of past game stories.

Satchel offers services comparable to those offered by Nando, although in most cases, Nando is more thorough. Satchel edges out Nando in the following two key areas, however:

- It offers coverage of the NHL, which Nando glosses over.
- Its up-to-the-minute scoreboard is better than anything Nando offers in that area.

 CompuServe

Go: **APO**

In CompuServe (see fig. 1.6), accessing the AP is as easy as it gets. The Associated Press Online menu provides you with a full range of news options. For our purposes, of course, we'll select Sports.

 Prodigy

Jump: **ESPNet**

Each sport has its own menu on Prodigy (see fig. 1.7), and Associated Press Online can be accessed through just about any of them. But the Prodigy lineup also includes a successful partnership with cable sports network ESPN.

By clicking on ESPN Inside Info, you access a wide range of information compiled by ESPN's research staff, plus columns from ESPN on-air hosts. ESPN baseball analyst Peter Gammons also writes a column that appears on the

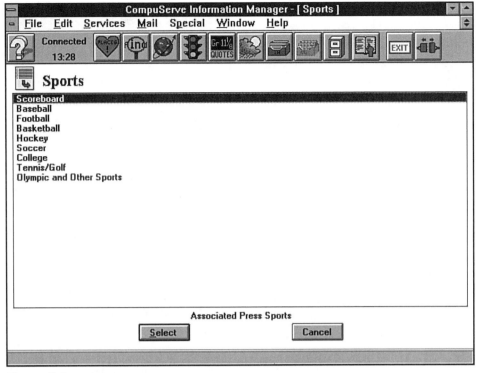

Figure 1.6 Go: AP0
CompuServe's Associated Press Online menu offers a full range of sports from which to choose.

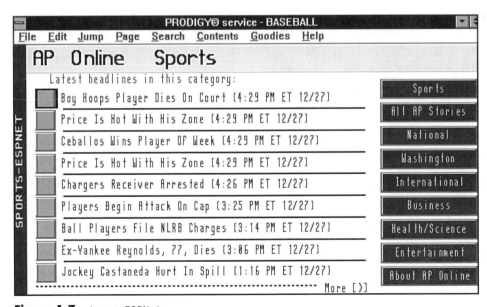

Figure 1.7 Jump: ESPNet
Prodigy's sports news offerings include Associated Press Online and much more.

baseball menu, and Fred Edelstein—an ESPN football analyst—writes a regular football column. ESPNet can be accessed from the main Prodigy sports menu.

Prodigy also uses Sports Ticker (as does America Online) to provide sports news updates in its "quick sports" area (Jump: quick sports), which is updated once an hour and includes the latest sports news briefs.

 UseNet

`clari.sports.*****`

This is not a real address. To read the AP copy on a particular sport, enter the sport name in place of the asterisks, such as **clari.sports.baseball**.

> **TIP**
>
> Specific UseNet addresses for each sport are listed in that sport's chapter. For example, if you're interested in reading AP football stories, see Chapter 3, "Pro Football," to find that address.

UseNet Clarinet is a solid source for AP stories, but the stories aren't available nearly as quickly as they are on the commericial online providers. Although CompuServe subscribers can read stories as quickly as an hour or less after the completion of a game, UseNet might not post the stories until more than a day later.

> **NOTE**
>
> Some service providers charge extra for the use of Clarinet newsgroups. Also, access to Clarinet is subject to whether your Internet provider actually carries it.

Other Online News Services

The Associated Press isn't the only news service available on the Internet or through commercial online service providers. There are others, and each has its own advantages and disadvantages.

Some of these providers, such as Sports Ticker on America Online, are very reliable and complete in the information they offer. Others, however, are less reliable and can contain some information from sources that may not be accurate.

The server you chose depends more on your personal tastes than anything else. On the Internet, there are several servers that provide links to sports news on the major professional sports.

 Yahoo Sports Server

`http://akebono.stanford.edu/ yahoo/Entertainment/Sports`

The Yahoo Sports Server offers a link to just about every sport imaginable, including professional, college, amateur, and recreational sports news.

It's a warehouse of other sports sites, including the Nando X Sports Server listed previously. This is an excellent starting point for sports fans who want to make their own path on the Internet.

 ### World Wide Web of Sports

`http://www.tns.lcs.mit.edu/`
`cgi-bin/sports`

The World Wide Web of Sports is also a good source of information on several sports. The home page is flashier than the Yahoo Sports Server, offering a graphic of each sport on its menu of topics.

This site offers information on professional, amateur, and recreational sports. It also provides links to information on sports that aren't represented in many of the other general sports sites (like rugby, cricket, and rowing).

 ### EINet Galaxy Sports Page

`http://www.einet.net/galaxy/`
`Leisure-and-Recreation/`
`Sports.html`

The EINet Galaxy Sports Page—much like the Yahoo site—links to all sorts of sports information.

For fans of major professional sports, the offerings include schedules, statistics, and transaction lists. However, this isn't a top site for game stories, feature stories, and similar material.

 ### Sports Ticker

Keyword: `Sports News`

The foundation of America Online's sports news coverage is provided by Sports Ticker, the organization whose primary purpose was once to give scoring updates to broadcast booths for announcers to pass along to their listeners or viewers.

Sports Ticker has grown, and so has its coverage. Sports Ticker's game and feature coverage on America Online (see fig. 1.8) now virtually mirrors that of Associated Press Online on CompuServe or Prodigy.

America Online's Sports Ticker coverage also includes notes on every team in each of the four major sports.

America Online also offers the Data Times News Reports (Keyword: **data times**), which includes reprinted stories from most of the major daily newspapers in the U.S. The stories usually don't appear until the day after they were published in the newspaper, but it's a great way to catch up on sports news stories that were published in other cities.

Once you're in the Data Times menu, double-click the sport of your choice and then double-click the team of your choice. You'll be given a menu of headlines of recent stories written about that team, usually written by beat reporters who cover the team on a regular basis.

Figure 1.8 Keyword: Sports News
America Online's sports news package is as diverse as it is thorough.

Statistics

Whether you need the statistics for your fantasy or rotisserie league or you're simply a stats junkie, the Internet has a site that will suit your needs.

The following list is only a tiny percentage of the statistics servers available on the Internet, but they are the top sites I have found.

 **America Online**

Keyword: **Sports News**

Of the three major commercial online service providers, America Online offers the best source of statistics, both on individual games and compiled for season-to-date (see fig. 1.9).

For season-to-date statistics, which are updated at least weekly, simply click the icon of the sport of your choice and choose Statistics from the menu provided. Included are league leaders and a team-by-team listing of every player in each sport.

For individual game statistics (provided by Sports Ticker), click the sport of your choice and make your selection from the menu provided, which is very clear and easy-to-use.

```
─  America Online - [FINAL NFC WEST TEAM-BY-TEAM STATS]   ▼ ▲
─  File  Edit  Go To  Mail  Members  Window  Help          ▲ ▼
```

```
San Francisco Forty Niners
──────────────────────────

PASSING
=======
                    G    ATT   CMP    PCT    YDS   TDS   INT

Steve Young        16    461   324   70.3   3969    35    10
Elvis Grbac        11     50    35   70.0    393     2     1
       TOTAL              511   359   70.3   4362    37    11


RUSHING
=======
                    G    ATT    YDS    AVG    TDS

Ricky Watters      16    239    877    3.7     6
William Floyd      16     87    305    3.5     6
Steve Young        16     58    293    5.1     7
Marc Logan         10     33    143    4.3     1
Derek Loville      14     31     99    3.2     0
Jerry Rice         16      7     93   13.3     2
Adam Walker         8     13     54    4.2     1
Dexter Carter      16      8     34    4.3     0
Elvis Grbac        11     13      1    0.1     0
John Taylor        15      2     -2   -1.0     0
       TOTAL             491   1897    3.9    23
```

Figure 1.9 Keyword: Sports News

America Online has the most complete statistics package among the three major commercial online service providers.

MLB Statistics

`etext.archive.umich.edu/pub/`
`Sports/Baseball/Majors/Stats`

This site includes league standings, individual leaders in all the major statistical categories, and complete stats for every big-leaguer. It is organized in an easy-to-read, team-by-team format that is updated weekly.

NBA Statistics

`wuarchive.wustl.edu/doc/misc/`
`nbastats/facts/stats`

This site provides complete NBA statistics, divided into league-leader categories and a team-by-team format that is updated weekly.

NFL Statistics

`ftp.vnet.net/pub/football/PRO/`
`STATS`

This site provides a very thorough source of NFL statistics that will make even the most devoted football fan happy.

NHL Statistics

`http://terrapin.umd.edu/`
`nhl.html`

This site provides a statistical home for the died-in-the-wool NHL fan.

TIP

If you're looking for statistics on a particular sport, check the chapter in this book devoted to that sport. At the end of each chapter, there is a list of sites with a brief description of what can be found there.

Chapter Summary

In this chapter, we have covered sports news and information, which are the basic types of sports offerings available on the Internet and commercial online services.

This chapter is the foundation for *Sports on the Net*. The remainder of the book—especially the chapters in Part II—contains a great deal more, specific information on the numerous sports sites on the Internet.

Chapter 2
Sports Talk

Office water coolers and taverns are still probably the primary sites for sports conversation, but the Internet is an active home for such discourse.

In this chapter

- *What are forums, newsgroups, and bulletin boards?*
- *Why sports fans use them*
- *How to talk on UseNet*
- *Using LISTSERV discussion lists*
- *Sports talk on Prodigy, CompuServe, and America Online*

In other chapters

→ *For specific information on a particular topic, check out the chapters in Part II*

→ *If you're not sure how to use an address in this chapter, see Chapter 12*

The first chapter of this book covered sports news and information. But what do sports fans do with that information once they have it?

I suppose there are a few who huddle in the privacy of their own homes, content with the knowledge of what they have accumulated, pouring over stories and statistics for their own personal use.

The rest of us—and the vast majority of sports fans on this planet—head out with it, either to the water cooler, the telephone, or the local bar. We use it to make pleasant conversation, we use it to argue. Whatever we use it for, the point here is we do something with our sports knowledge—we *talk* about it.

Whether it's a UseNet newsgroup, a discussion list, or some type of forum within CompuServe, there are plenty of places to go for sports talk online.

This chapter covers sports chatter and includes some ideas on places to go to participate. For more information on sports discussions on a particular sport or topic, consult the chapters in Part II that cover specific sports.

Forums, Newsgroups, and Bulletin Boards

The headline to this section implies that these are three types of Internet talk. But that's not the case.

These are—for the most part—identical forms of groups in which sports fans can meet and exchange information, discuss, argue, gloat, and so on. The only difference, really, is in the provider you use to get into these groups.

On UseNet, they are called newsgroups. On CompuServe, they are forums. Elsewhere, they are called bulletin board systems (BBSs).

Whether you use one of the major commercial online services or an Internet bulletin board or newsgroup, talking with other computer users is one of the most popular aspects of online communication.

What Are Bulletin Boards?

Bulletin board services are aptly named. Bulletin boards, in the traditional sense, are hunks of cork on which people pin up handwritten notes for others to read.

You've probably heard an outrageous quote from an athlete, and you've heard someone say, "That's going to find its way onto the bulletin board in the opponent's locker room."

On the Internet, it works basically the same way. People—regular folks just like you and me—post messages for other regular folks to read. These messages can be public or private, and they can be as general ("The 49ers are going to kill the Rams this week") or as specific ("The Rams' defensive backs can't cover Jerry Rice") as you and the millions of other users want them to be.

These notes can be passed on for posting, where they can be read by others for a period of days. In some cases, these can be "live" discussions with either a group of people or a single individual, where you type a sentence or two, others respond, you answer back, and so on—all without ever walking away from your terminal.

They can also be much more than home for your opinions and a place to read what others think. You can use them to play games, download software, view and download pictures, and more.

There are literally thousands of these, each dedicated to its own particular topic, and each a fount of information.

These bulletin boards have a variety of purposes. Some are set up by large companies as a means for their employees to communicate quickly and effectively. Many are set up for simple discussion in a specific area of interest, such as professional basketball.

Internet service providers and commercial online services simplify access to these types of discussions. Rather than calling another phone number to enter into a different newsgroup, you just have to click the mouse a few times.

Just as the messages themselves can be general or extremely specific, so can the bulletin boards themselves. Outside the world of sports, these newsgroups can be weird and wild places to go.

The same is true for sports fans with newsgroups as general as football or as specific as the Washington Redskins.

TIP

If you're trying to find a bulletin board on a specific topic, check out the chapters devoted to specific sports in Part II of this book. Each chapter includes information about bulletin boards.

Using the Internet to Talk Sports

The biggest question that those who aren't online ask those who talk sports on the Internet is "Don't you have any friends?"

The point of that remark is: Hey, if you have friends with similar interests, if you have a water cooler at work, why would you want to talk to people you don't even know on your computer?

Very little is new in the world of sports, but in the '90s, the sports world's biggest boom area is sports talk—the talk radio format, that is.

When WFAN in New York became the country's first 24-hour sports talk radio station, critics didn't think the format would survive.

It's not that people don't think there's a need for listeners to call these stations and talk to the hosts or ask questions. After all, at least it's a conversation— often with a knowledgeable party or an athlete or coach.

What they doubted, however, is that any-one would have an interest in *listening* to this type of radio format.

Online Chatter Can Be Lively

You can have a load of fun just turning on America Online's Grandstand before (or immediately after) any grudge-match game (especially in college football) and sitting back and reading the messages as they scroll up the screen. Sure, you'll see the typical "Notre Dame rules!" messages, but sometimes these people— who only in the rarest of occasions have any idea who their verbal sparring part-ner is—can really get into it.

Before you get carried away in any of these conversations, beware! If the lan-guage gets a little, shall we say, salty on one of the major commercial online services, you can lose your membership. These services have fairly strict code-of-conduct rules.

On the Internet, however, the rules are much more relaxed. In some cases, there are no rules at all.

Today, however, there are sports talk radio stations all over the place, in major cities and tiny towns—and, yes, they're making it.

Talking sports on the Internet isn't much different that calling a local all-sports radio station. You pick your topic, you dial up your online service provider, and you're off.

If the live conversation format of an all-sports radio station is your style, you can talk online live. If you'd rather read the messages of others, you can do that, plus leave one of your own.

You don't have to be friendless to like it, and you don't have to be embarrassed that you do it. Thousands, maybe even millions, of others aren't embarrassed. Once you've tried it, chances are you'll be hooked.

Sports fans use them for several reasons.

Some use them as an information source—a means to get little tidbits they can't find elsewhere, or perhaps even breaking news. A lot of people use them for fantasy sports purposes—to get information on who's starting, who's injured, who's got a bad attitude, and so on.

But most people use them for entertainment, as another way to get the most out of their interest in sports.

What Are UseNet Newsgroups?

There are bulletin boards all over the Internet map, but the most popular

---

TIME OUT

Don't Believe Everything You See On UseNet

The old saying, "Let the buyer beware," applies to UseNet newsgroups as well.

I was reading the UseNet group dedicated to my favorite football team, the Kansas City Chiefs, one evening when I came across a message from a fan who was wondering if Joe Montana was going to play in that week's game.

The first response to the message was from someone who claimed to be Chiefs general manager Carl Peterson, saying "Don't believe what you read in newspapers, Montana definitely will play."

While it's easy to believe that an NFL general manager might read a UseNet

group on his team, it was hard to believe one would offer such information online.

On UseNet, you can follow a string of messages in the order they were posted, so I kept reading the messages from these two users.

As it turned out, the fan was looking for information for his fantasy football team, and the man claiming to be Carl Peterson was a fantasy football rival—playing a little joke on a friend. He had gone so far as to establish a new Internet account for himself with a user name that looked official in order to pull off his joke.

place to go for sports talk is UseNet—created in 1979 by two Duke University graduate students to exchange information between their unix machines.

UseNet is a number of machines that exchange mail tagged with predetermined suject headers. The mail is referred to as an article and the subject is considered a newsgroup. UseNet newsgroups are broken into the groups shown in table 2.1.

How you use the newsgroups depends on how they are offered to you by your Internet service provider. Generally, once you pick the UseNet group you'd like, you can scroll through a list of message headings to choose those messages you'd like to read. Posting your own message usually involves merely clicking some sort of Post Message icon.

How to Talk on UseNet

UseNet is really a network of its own, and it's available in varying degrees to people with Internet access.

UseNet's newsgroups vary in form, function, and freedom. They're divided into several categories, and the category name makes up the first part of the UseNet address. The majority of the newsgroups are set up as bulletin boards for people to exchange messages, but those under the **clari.** category function as news sources. And while anyone is free to contribute anything to any of the other newsgroups, the amount of freedom varies in that

Table 2.1 UseNet Newsgroups	
Term	**What You'll Find**
`biz`	Business-related groups
`comp`	Computers, computer science, and software
`sci`	Scientific subjects
`misc`	Newsgroups that don't fall under any other category
`soc`	Social issues and socializing
`talk`	Debate-oriented, lengthy discussions
`news`	General news
`rec`	Groups aimed toward hobbies and recreational activities
`alt`	Alternative groups that have a more limited distribution than the other UseNet newsgroups and are not as formal as the other groups

some of the groups are moderated—that is, someone is reading *all* of the messages and seeing to it that the trash gets discarded before it gets posted. The moderator's goal is to maintain the topic and to keep the newsgroup focused.

If you look hard enough, you can probably find a sports newsgroup in just about any UseNet category, but the two in which sports newsgroups most commonly appear are the **rec.** and **alt.** categories.

The **rec.** groups are for recreational topics, but the sports newsgroups within it aren't solely dedicated to recreational sports.

There are hundreds of **rec.** groups, and sports fans can find just about anything they want there (see fig. 2.1).

If you're looking for a newsgroup devoted to a specific team, then the **alt.** groups are the place to be. These groups are devoted to alternative topics. Although that does mean there's an **alt.** group for Madonna fans, it doesn't mean that all messages posted to these newsgroups are R-rated.

UseNet addresses are included in the lists at the end of each chapter in Part II.

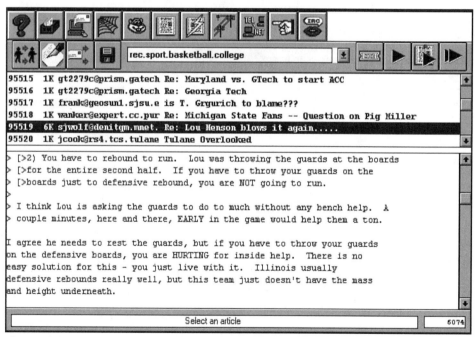

Figure 2.1 rec.sport.basketball.college
This UseNet group is for college basketball fans.

O.J. Simpson

The notoriety that O.J. Simpson achieved from being charged with the murders of Nicole Brown Simpson and Ronald Goldman has far exceeded his fame as a football player.

Simpson was a Heisman Trophy-winning running back at the University of Southern California and a record-setting National Football League runner, but all of that became lost in the summer of 1994.

From the discovery of the bodies to the low-speed chase to the trial itself, there has been more talk about O.J. Simpson in the span of one year than during his entire playing career.

It didn't take long for UseNet newsgroups to appear—some devoted to Simpson and at least one dedicated to discussion of prosecutor Marcia Clark. Plus, there has been a lot of Simpson talk in other Internet services and on the commercial online services.

The UseNet addresses for Simpson talk are **alt.fan.oj-simpson** and **alt.fan.marcia-clark**.

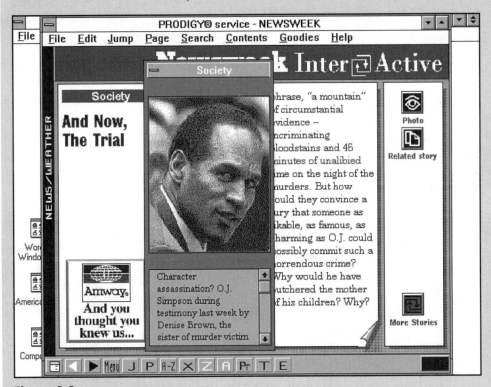

Figure 2.2 Jump: newsweek
O.J. Simpson (shown through Prodigy's Newsweek site) has received more attention over the past year than during his entire football career.

What Are Mailing Lists and LISTSERVs?

Another form of a bulletin board is the LISTSERV discussion groups, which come out of the Bitnet network and are based on e-mail. Simply put, a LISTSERV is a mailing list created by an Internet user to distribute messages via e-mail directly to the people who subscribe to it.

Originally, most of the "lists" were technical in nature, but they have come to include as many different topics as those included in UseNet newsgroups.

How They Work

It sounds a little technical, but using a LISTSERV is just as easy as getting into any other newsgroup or bulletin board.

It starts when you find the list you'd like to join. You send an e-mail to the LISTSERV, which places you on the list. The LISTSERV then acts like a top-notch NBA point guard—it distributes to everyone it can find.

Each time a message is sent to the list, the LISTSERV passes it on to every member of the list. Similarly, as a member of the list, you receive every message that anyone else sends to that list.

That's all well and good as long as your Internet service provider doesn't charge you for each e-mail message. But if you're on a commercial online service, for example, the charges can mount.

Most of the commercial online services charge for e-mail you send or receive. If you're using an e-mail address on one of the major commercial online services to receive LISTSERV mail and you subscribe to a LISTSERV that generates a lot of messages, you might find yourself drowning in e-mail charges.

Most lists now offer service in varying degrees. You can subscribe as a full member and get all of the messages sent to the list, or you can join to a lesser degree and get only a portion of the messages posted.

LISTSERVs To The Rescue

All Internet users need a little help once in a while, and that includes me. In the course of writing this book, the publisher sent some information on this LISTSERV database, which I had never encountered.

Needing a better source of LISTSERVs, I quickly called up this address,

`http//alpha.acast.nova.edu:80/listserv.html`, and it has become my primary source of information on LISTSERVs.

I point this out to remind you that it's virtually impossible to know all the hot spots on the Internet.

Many of these LISTSERVs can provide you with information on roughly how many messages flow out to subscribers on a monthly basis. That information is helpful because you can choose a LISTSERV based on how much mail you want to receive.

How to Find a LISTSERV

LISTSERVs are easy to use and fun to join, but they can be very difficult to find because few Internet service providers provide a tool that joins them all together.

We have included some LISTSERV addresses in the lists at the end of each chapter in Part II of this book. But if you'd like to develop your own list, there are a couple of ways to do that.

 Mailing Lists

http://alpha.acast.nova.edu:80/ listserv.html

This site (see fig. 2.3), located on the World Wide Web, is a database of LISTSERVs that contains nearly 6,000 mailing lists. Of course, the large number of mailing lists and the fact that it's updated weekly makes it an excellent source. But it also offers a feature that makes it the *best* source.

The database can be queried by subject. In other words, you can reduce it to a database that includes only sports-related LISTSERVs, or only tennis-related LISTSERVs, or whatever you please.

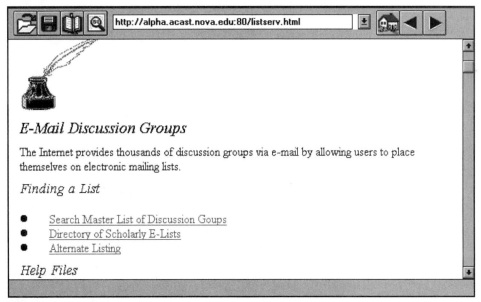

Figure 2.3 `http://alpha.acast.nova.edu:80/listserv.html`
This World Wide Web site contains perhaps the most complete database of LISTSERVs, and you can narrow the list to suit your needs.

 **Active LISTSERVs**

listserv@bitnic.educom.edu

This is a LISTSERV of LISTSERVs (see fig. 2.4). To obtain a list of current active LISTSERVs, simply e-mail this address and include the phrase **list global** in the body of the message. You automatically receive a listing of lists by return e-mail.

That's nice, of course, but there's no way to query that list down to limit it to only those lists about sports, or about hockey, or whatever your specific interest.

Subscribing

Okay. You've used one of the previous sources (or another you know of) and you've found a list or two to which you'd like to subscribe.

You'll note that every list has two addresses: a LISTSERV address and a list address. The LISTSERV address is the one to which you send your request to subscribe. Remember, the LISTSERV functions as the point guard. You have to let him know that you'd like to be on the court (so to speak) before he's going to give you the ball.

The second address is the list itself. It's to that address that you would send

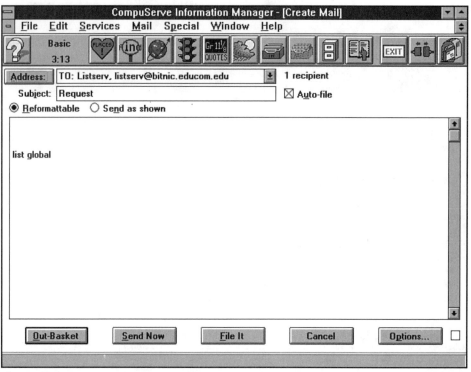

Figure 2.4 listserv@bitnic.educom.edu
By sending a message that looks like this to this address, you'll automatically receive a list of LISTSERVs.

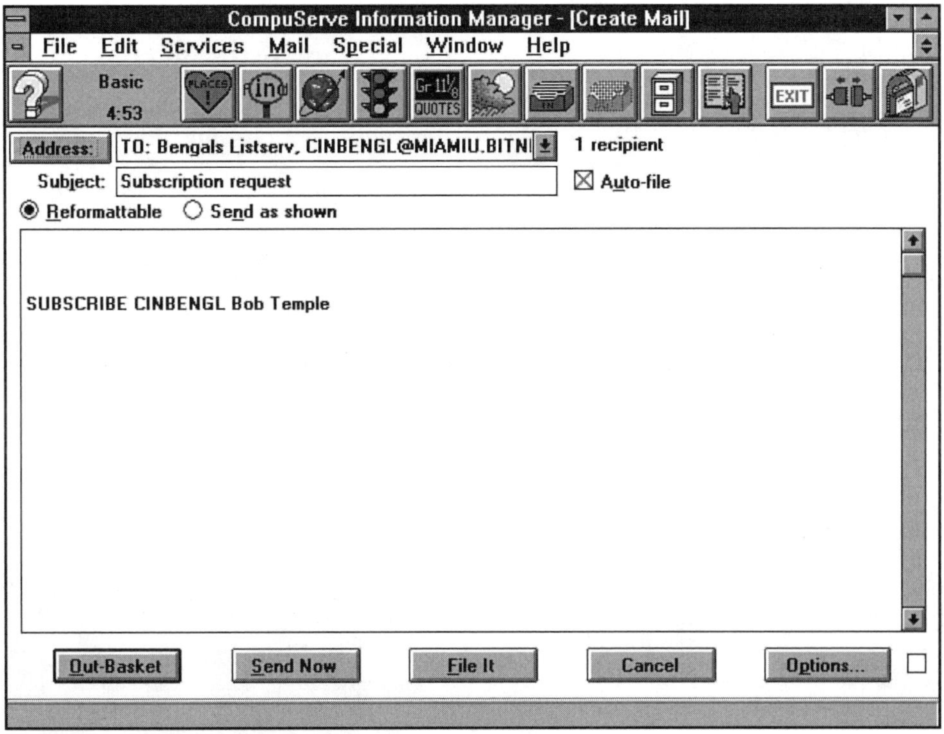

Figure 2.5 CINBENGL@MIAMIU.BITNET
If I were to subscribe to this list, which is devoted to fans of the Cincinnati Bengals, my e-mail message would look like this.

messages you would like forwarded to others on the list.

To subscribe, you send an e-mail message to the LISTSERV asking to subscribe. For most lists, that is accomplished very simply.

In the body of your e-mail message, type the following:

```
SUBSCRIBE listserv
yourfirstname yourlastname
```

Obviously, replace **yourfirstname** with your first name and **yourlastname** with your last name. It's important that this message be in the body of the e-mail, not in the

subject area. The LISTSERV name is that portion of the list's address that comes before the symbol **@**.

For example, there's a Cincinnati Bengals list with the address **CINBENGL@MIAMIU.BITNET**. To subscribe to that list, my message would look like the one shown in figure 2.5.

Some lists have different requirements for what you're supposed to include in the subscription request. In those cases, the correct wording for the request is generally noted in the database in which you first located the LISTSERV.

Some LISTSERVs automatically send a confirmation message back to you, welcoming you to the list and offering suggestions on how to use it or giving you commands you can use to optimize your service.

Many LISTSERVs are completely computerized, which usually means that you begin receiving messages from the list almost immediately. In cases where the LISTSERV isn't computerized—it's operated by humans—it might take a little longer.

Unsubscribing

If you've decided a particular list isn't suiting your needs, you need to unsubscribe. Much like subscribing, you need only to send an e-mail message to the LISTSERV with the following message:

```
SIGNOFF listserv
```

Again, whether subscribing or unsubscribing, make sure you send the e-mail message to the LISTSERV—not the list address—and ensure your request is in the body of the message, not in the subject.

Sports Talk on America Online, CompuServe, and Prodigy

You won't have any trouble finding places to express your viewpoints on the three major commercial online services.

 America Online

Keyword: **Grandstand**

America Online's Grandstand is an active home of sports talk. Its best feature is the live discussions of sports (see fig. 2.6), where the topics shift rapidly and the messages seem to fly up the screen. Once you're in the Grandstand, you're just a click away from a lively discussion that can range from electronic high-fives to a slew of insults in a matter of minutes.

> **TIP**
>
> If you're in the live-talk area, you've got to be fairly quick and keep a close eye on which of the other users posted which message. Often, two or more separate conversations on different topics can be going on at the same time.

America Online also occasionally brings in a player, coach, or other sports personality to be the headliner in an online conversation with members from coast to coast.

Live discussions are found by clicking Sports Rooms in the Grandstand menu. Regular bulletin boards also are available from the Grandstand menu (see fig. 2.7).

In the Grandstand menu, simply click Sports Boards and you will see a list of sports/topics. Double-clicking the topic of your choice brings you into that group.

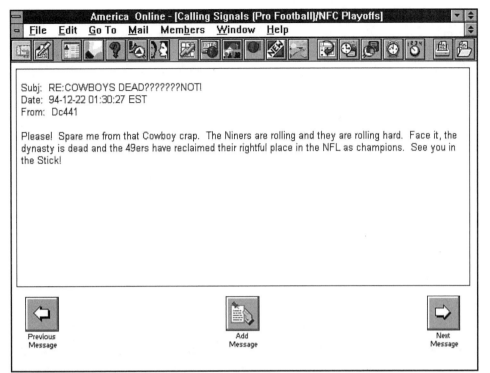

Figure 2.6 Keyword: Grandstand
America Online's sports bulletin boards and live discussions can be found in the Grandstand.

From there, you can post messages, read those of others, and more.

 CompuServe

Go: **Forums**

CompuServe offers separate forums (see fig. 2.8) on separate sports topics, and users can both post messages and engage in live conversations. These forums, however, are considered extended services and are subject to an extra charge.

Once you enter a CompuServe forum, clicking the Who's Here? icon provides you with a list of people who are in the forum at that moment. You can talk to the entire group, or you can invite another person into a one-on-one conversation on any topic you want by clicking the Invite icon. You'll know when someone is inviting you into such a conversation because a window appears on your screen with the message: **Would you like to join John Q. Public in a private conversation?** At that point, you click whichever response you prefer.

 **CompuServe**

Go: **CB**

CompuServe also offers a live-talk area, which it calls the CB Simulator. This is an extended service, meaning that additional charges apply (see Chapter 13, "Commercial Online Services," for more information).

Choose Access the General Band and you are brought to a Channel Selector screen (see fig. 2.9). The topics in each of these channels change regularly, but there is usually at least one devoted to sports topics.

If you click one of the channel numbers, the current topic of that channel is displayed in the upper-left corner of the window.

Once you find the channel you want, double-click the number to join the conversation.

 Prodigy

Jump: **sports bb**

Sports Bulletin Board (see fig. 2.10) is Prodigy's spectator sports forum. Whatever sport is on your mind, Prodigy has a place for you to meet and talk with

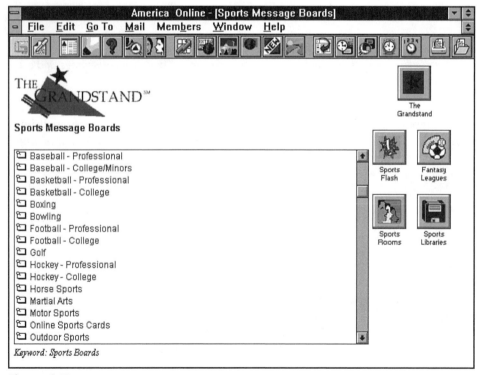

Figure 2.7 Keyword: Grandstand
America Online's Grandstand menu provides plenty of opportunity for discussion.

WinCIM - The Sports+ Forum - [Since 12/5/94 7:25 PM]

File   Edit   Services   Messages   Library   Conference   Special   Window   Help

Extended 1:24

Title	Topics	Msgs
Forum Feedback	35	56
Pro Football	167	1077
College Football	47	205
Pro Basketball	35	189
College Basketball	35	185
Baseball	39	339
Ring Things	29	73
Sport of Kings	14	38
Hockey	42	189
Soccer	29	120
Golf/Tennis	19	46
World Wide Sports	26	200
Other Sports	13	17
Fantasy BB Info	1	1
Fantasy BB Talk	6	18
FBB AL Transactions	0	0
FBB NL Transactions	0	0
Fantasy Football	58	106
HTH FB Transactions	9	21
OLL/Fantasy Sports	12	21
Fantasy Basketball	74	142
Fantasy Hockey	0	0
The Bullpen	0	0

Select   Mark   All   Close

Figure 2.8 Go: Forums
CompuServe's forums—sports and otherwise—are considered extended services and are subject to an extra charge.

other people from around the country.

From the Sports BB menu, click Choose a Topic. The next menu is a list of sports; each is a bulletin board to which you can post messages. Of course, you also can read the messages posted by others.

 Prodigy

Jump: **sports play bb**

This is Prodigy's home for athletes, both serious and recreational.

Discussions range from baseball and football to paintball and table tennis.

Prodigy often invites a celebrity guest in to "talk" to Prodigy members. In many cases, members who log on to the service are given a week's notice that a certain player will be online; they post their questions to that player as the week goes on. Then, at a specified time, the athlete responds to selected questions that were posted. Those responses are available for all members to read.

Chapter Summary

In this chapter, we've covered the types of sports talk that are available to sports fans, including bulletin boards and LISTSERVs. This chapter wraps up Part I of this book, which covers the types of sports information that is available on the Internet.

Part II gets more specific by exploring exactly what is available to Internet users.

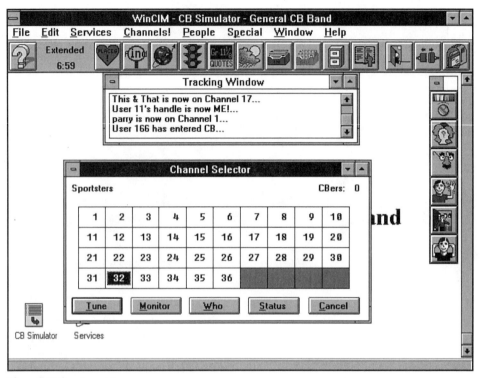

Figure 2.9 Go: CB

CompuServe's CB Simulator is a live-talk area offered by CompuServe.

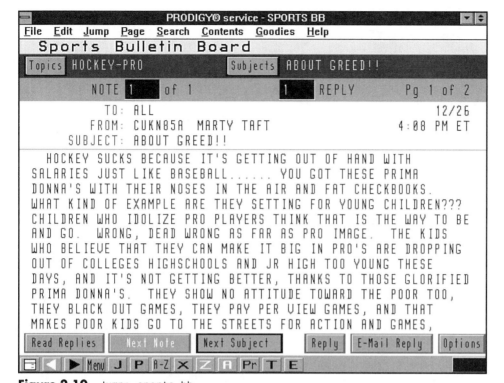

Figure 2.10 Jump: sports bb
Like its competitors, Prodigy's Sports Bulletin Board is divided by sport topic.

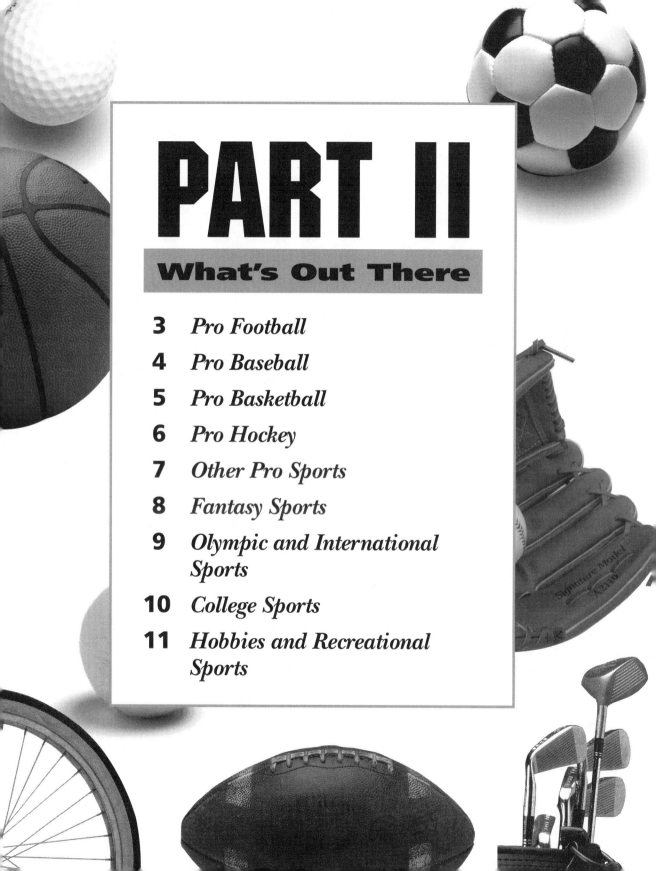

PART II

What's Out There

Chapter 3
Pro Football

If you're an NFL nut, this is the chapter for you. There's as much NFL information on the Internet as there is for any other sport.

In this chapter

- *Internet sources for Super Bowl information*
- *The top sources for football news and statistics*
- *Newsgroups and bulletin boards for football talk*
- *Sites to visit for information on your favorite team*
- *Other Internet sites of interest*
- *What commercial online services have to offer*

In other chapters

→ *For information on college football, check out Chapter 10*

→ *If you're not sure how to use the addresses listed in this chapter, see Chapter 12*

There's nothing quite like a gentle snowfall, a fire in the fireplace, loved ones gathered around, and…a football game on television.

Agree?

The only thing that might be better is a tailgate party with lots of friends, followed by a day at the stadium.

Are you ready for some football?

There's as much NFL information on the Internet as there is for any other sport.

In this chapter, we'll try to do justice to that wealth of information. We'll provide you with some great ideas for football sites and home pages to visit, and give you an idea of what is available at each of those places.

At the end of the chapter, we'll give you a list of Internet sites to visit, a list that includes the sites discussed in the text of the chapter, plus many, many more.

There is a special section devoted to the Super Bowl and the hype-filled week that precedes it. It's designed to give Internet newbies an idea of how a frenetic week like that is depicted online.

> **NOTE**
>
> This chapter is devoted to the National Football League. However, the list at the end of the chapter includes sites on the Canadian Football League and other professional football sites.

WHO'S HOT

Steve Young

When you stop and think about it, it's amazing that Steve Young had anything left to prove before Super Bowl XXIX.

After all, he had been one of the most prolific NFL players during the past three seasons. In most NFL cities, he would have been a hero even without the Super Bowl crown.

SAN FRANCISCO (Jan. 30) - Super Bowl XXIX MVP Steve Young acknowledges the cheers of fans during the victory parade. (Reuter Photo)

Figure 3.1 Keyword: ABC
Steve Young at the 49ers' Super Bowl victory parade, downloaded from America Online.

In San Francisco, however, Young was akin to Danny White in Dallas—he followed a superstar (Roger Staubach) and he was always falling short of winning The Big One.

Following Joe Montana was a heavy load for Young to carry.

He unburdened himself at Super Bowl XXIX, however, setting a record for touchdown passes and earning the Most Valuable Player award. Having won the Super Bowl and earned MVP trophies for both the Super Bowl and the regular season, Young is finally being recognized for what he is—the best quarterback in the NFL.

A Week in the Life of the Internet: Super Bowl Week

On January 15th, the San Diego Chargers upset the Pittsburgh Steelers in the AFC Championship Game. Later that day, the San Francisco 49ers jumped to a 21-0 lead in the first quarter, then held on for a victory that gave them the NFC Championship. Thus, the match-up for Super Bowl XXIX was set: the four-time Super Bowl champion 49ers against the first-time Super Bowl participant Chargers.

The first week after those games was relatively quiet on the Internet. Most of what was available were recaps of the conference title games. On UseNet, the network of newsgroups in which fans share their views with the world, the most exciting action was between 49er and Cowboy fans. They're still arguing over which team is better, even though the 49ers seemed to answer that question on the field.

On January 22nd, it was time to start thinking about the *Big Game.* Here's a look at seven days on the Internet, searching for Super Bowl tidbits.

 Super Bowl Guide

`http://www.imall.com/superbowl/`
`superbowl.html`

Were you going to the game in Miami? If so, this was the place to go for information on the game, the city, and more (see fig. 3.2).

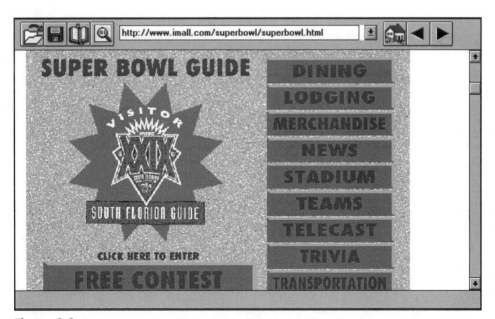

Figure 3.2 `http://www.imall.com/superbowl/superbowl.html`
The Super Bowl Host Committee's Home Page provided plenty of Super Bowl information.

This site was sponsored by Miami's Super Bowl Host Committee. It was one of five such sites on the World Wide Web—each designed to help make going to the game fun.

TIP

Sites like the one shown in figure 3.2 pop up on the World Wide Web for just about every major event held in the United States. For example, there are a couple of excellent sites already on the Internet for people who are considering attending the 1996 Summer Olympics in Atlanta. For information on those sites, check out Chapter 9, "Olympic and International Sports."

This site contained some general information for the football fan, like news related to the game and the competing teams, a trivia archive, and some information on the Super Bowl telecast.

But it was designed mostly for the fan who had tickets to the game. There was information on dining in and around Miami, lodging, transportation, and the like.

For the collector—or the ticketholder who wants proof that he or she was at the Super Bowl—there's a link to information on Super Bowl merchandise.

 Talking to the Participants

Jump: `football`

No one knows more about what's really going on during Super Bowl week than the players themselves.

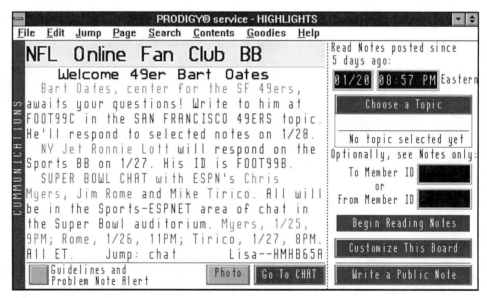

Figure 3.3 Jump: `football`
Prodigy offered a chance to talk to players during Super Bowl week.

Prodigy, which consistently offers a chance to "talk" online with various personalities, had a strong lineup for Super Bowl week. Leading the list was San Francisco center Bart Oates (see fig. 3.3), who had already won a Super Bowl ring with the New York Giants.

Prodigy members could post messages to Oates throughout the week and his responses appeared online the day before the game. In addition, New York Jets safety Ronnie Lott—a four-time Super Bowl winner with the 49ers—did the same, responding to selected messages on the Friday before the game.

Prodigy also offered live, online chats with ESPN personalities Chris Myers, Jim Rome, and Mike Tirico.

 Inside Info

Keyword: **ABC**

Having a membership to America Online during Super Bowl week was like knowing the manager of the Rolling Stones. You got backstage passes, great seats, the works.

Super Bowl XXIX was carried by ABC, and America Online just happens to have a link with ABC available to members. As the Super Bowl approached, that link offered all kinds of great information on the game, the broadcast, the teams, and all the goings-on of the hectic week before. On the other hand, if Super Bowl hype gets you down, this would have been a great place to avoid.

Included in the package was a day-by-day account of all the happenings of

Super Bowl week (see fig. 3.4), plus other special sites dedicated to the game. Like Prodigy, America Online offered "Online Super Bowl Guests."

The Super Bowl itself isn't enough for you? You need extra things to do, besides eating pizza and drinking beer?

On game day, this area went interactive.

The icon Enter QB1 (see fig. 3.5) offered fans a chance to test their football knowledge against others from across the country. Fans could select from a menu of plays before each play of the real game and those who did the best job of forecasting the real teams' moves during the game won prizes.

ABC also provided real-time game statistics that scrolled up the screen as the game was being played, keeping fans up-to-date on everything they needed to know.

The Instant Highlights icon was available to the multimedia types who were watching the game. That's right—it was instant replay, only you were in control of which plays were shown over and over and over.

Fans Have the Final Word

As the two-week hiatus between the conference title games and the Super Bowl wound to a close, the point spread for the game continued to grow. The 49ers were nearly 20-point favorites.

On sports radio talk shows, televisions, and newspapers around the country,

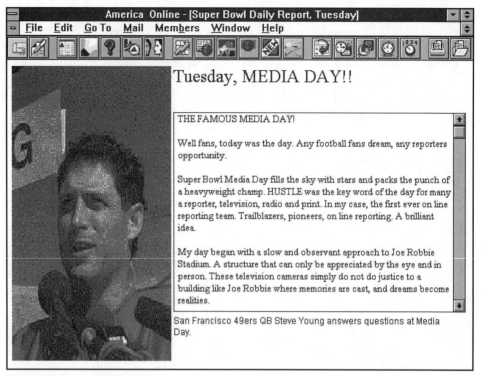

Figure 3.4 Keyword: ABC
America Online's ABC Sports link offered inside information on Super Bowl week.

the question wasn't which team would win, but by how much the 49ers would triumph.

Those who talked a good game, saying they thought the Chargers had a chance, seemed to be doing it just to be different—to stand out in the crowd.

Surely, somewhere there were those who honestly believed the Chargers were going to win. What better place to look than the UseNet newsgroup devoted to Chargers' fans?

 UseNet Newsgroups

`alt.sports.football.pro.`
`sd-chargers`

Of course, these newsgroups are available to anyone, anywhere. There were more than a few messages from 49er fans, just letting the Chargers faithful know that their team didn't have a chance.

But, in the midst of all that, there were Chargers fans who kept the faith (see fig. 3.6). Those hopes were crushed, of course, in the first few minutes of the actual game.

Getting the News and Stats

The NFL probably generates more news—that is, coverage other than game stories—than any other professional sport because there's a full week of dead time between games.

During that time, reporters around the country are engaged in a constant search for news—who's hurt, who's in the doghouse, who's going to be starting.

The Internet and commercial online services have great sources for NFL news.

NOTE

For more information on what the commercial online services have to offer to football fans, check out the "Commercial Online Services" section later in this chapter.

Football on the Internet is like hype before the Super Bowl—there's so much of it, it's hard *not* to find it.

Among the numerous NFL sites out there on the Internet are several that are very thorough and filled with links to outstanding NFL information.

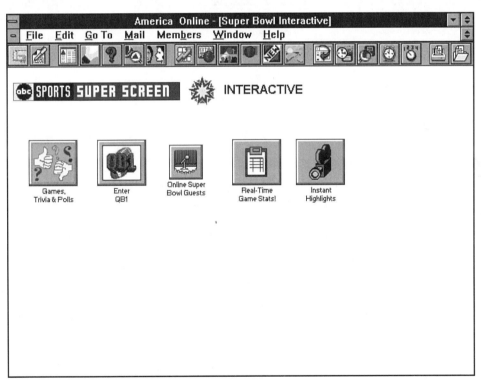

Figure 3.5 Keyword: ABC
America Online's Super Screen Interactive main menu.

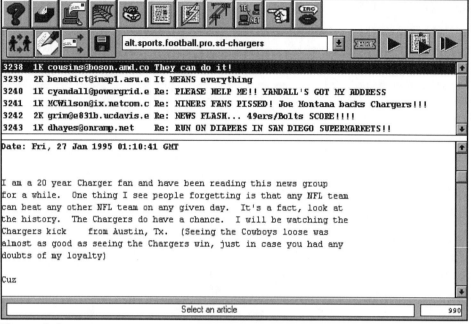

Figure 3.6 `alt.sports.football.pro.sd-chargers`
A Chargers fan expressed his views on the big game.

 Satchel Sports

`http://www.starwave.com/nfl/`
`toc.html`

You'll find Satchel Sports sites all throughout this book because Satchel offers one of the two most complete sports collections (along with Nando X) currently available on the Internet.

Satchel Sports uses Sports Ticker (see fig. 3.7) as its primary news provider, and the complete package is very thorough—yet not too complex.

During the season, you can find links to game stories, boxscores, upcoming schedules, game previews, injury reports, and so on. Also—and you'll find this mentioned in other chapters as well—Satchel's up-to-the-minute

scoreboard is a great place to drop by on Sunday afternoon for the scores and scoring updates.

The Satchel Sports NFL Server is a perfect example of how top-notch Internet sites react as major events approach.

As the 1994 season and the playoffs concluded, Satchel carried the following links for its users:

- Top stories
- News
- Playoff game recaps
- Playoff boxscores
- Playoff schedule
- Team reports
- Final standings
- Statistics

- Team schedules and final results
- Transactions
- Playoff previews
- Rosters
- An "Inside the NFL" column

The last item is a regular column written by a Sports Ticker writer and includes tidbits and inside NFL information.

Hawaii's NFL Home Page

`http://maxwell.uhh.hawaii.edu/football/football.html`

The state of Hawaii doesn't have a team in any major professional sport— in fact, the NFL's Pro Bowl is the only professional sports game played within Hawaii's borders. But Hawaii is home to an excellent NFL server (see fig. 3.8).

This home page even goes beyond the NFL by providing links to information on the Canadian Football League and its championship game, the Grey Cup.

There are NFL links to game coverage and recaps of the regular season—plus schedules, standings, and statistics.

This site also offers something that isn't found anywhere else: archives on the Super Bowl and the NFC and AFC championship games. The Super Bowl archive contains the Super Bowl records of every team that has participated, plus each conference's record in the big game. The championship game archives contain information on how each team has fared in those games.

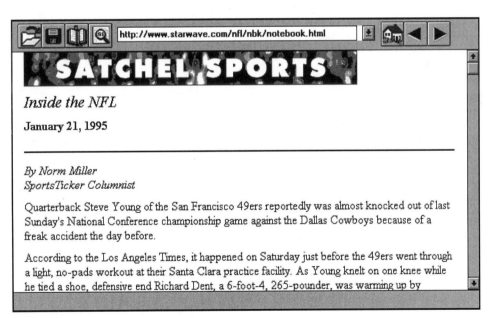

Figure 3.7 `http://www.starwave.com/nfl/toc.html`
Satchel's NFL site has a huge number of links, including to this "Inside the NFL" column.

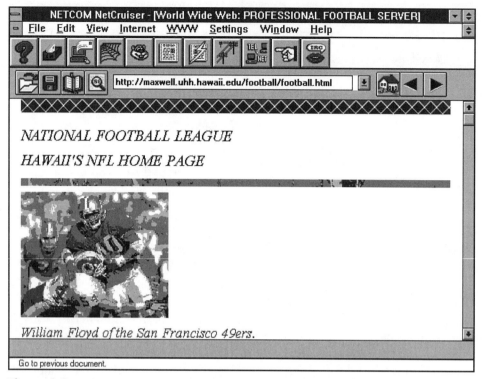

NATIONAL FOOTBALL LEAGUE

HAWAII'S NFL HOME PAGE

William Floyd of the San Francisco 49ers.

Figure 3.8 `http://maxwell.uhh.hawaii.edu/football/football.html`
Hawaii's NFL Home Page is an excellent source for NFL and CFL news.

 NFL News and Other Info

`http://lux.labmed.washington.`
`edu/~shoe/dallas/info/`
`football_news.html`

You're not going to find game stories and boxscores at this site. However, the NFL is a lot more than game stories and boxscores. Here you'll find some interesting statistics and other tidbits that will help you enjoy the NFL even more (see fig. 3.9).

This site includes links to the following information:

- A list of current starters
- Team winning percentages
- A list of free agents and where they signed
- Current rosters
- A schedule for the upcoming season
- An archive of mailing lists for NFL teams
- A list of UseNet newsgroups

 Statistics Sources

`http://www.cs.cmu.edu:8001/afs/`
`cs/user/vernon/www/nfl.html`

This is a great place to go for NFL statistics, especially for team statistics.

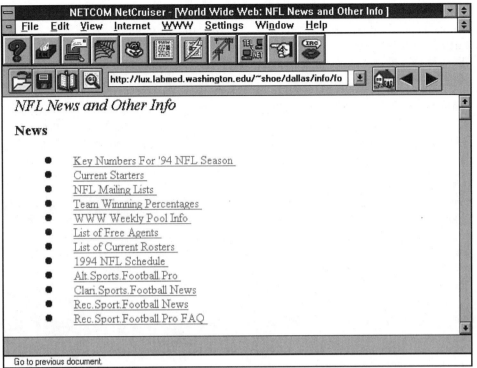

Figure 3.9 `http://lux.labmed.washington.edu/~shoe/dallas/info/`
`football_news.html`
This is a great site for the out-of-the-ordinary NFL information.

What You See Isn't What You Get

Appearances are not always what they seem. That smiling athlete you see in the network television interviews and commercials might be nothing more than a carefully crafted image. Image *isn't* everything.

A perfect example occurred one Sunday afternoon last season as reporters moved about the post-game visitor's locker room, interviewing players.

One print reporter asked the quarterback if he could talk for a minute. The player responded with a two-minute screaming fit about how meaningless and disgusting reporters are.

Less than five minutes after it ended, a television reporter approached the quarterback and the photographer turned on his camera. Once the lights were on, the quarterback was the nicest man on the planet.

Besides the most basic team statistic—the league standings—you'll find all kinds of stats here that you often hear play-by-play announcers cite during their broadcasts time and time again.

Team rankings by points scored, points allowed, and the ever-present "power rankings" are available—as is the personal point-system ranking of the person who operates this site.

There are several other interesting links as well.

 ### Nando X NFL Server

`http://www.nando.net/football/1994/nfl/nfl.html`

Nando X offers a complete line of sites on all of the major pro sports. For the NFL, Nando's coverage is top-of-the-line stuff (see fig. 3.10).

This site includes links to recent game stories, summaries, past game stories, statistics, boxscores, and more from the Associated Press. As the Super Bowl approached, it included a "News and Views" section devoted to the big game—plus updated injury reports.

TIP

Nando X also maintains a home page for every NFL team and the page can be accessed from the main NFL home page. These team-specific home pages are covered in "Information on Your Favorite Team" later in this chapter.

Figure 3.10 `http://www.nando.net/football/1994/nfl/history/nflimages.html` *Nando's NFL site provides you with a link to "Images of the Game," which are photos from the Associated Press.*

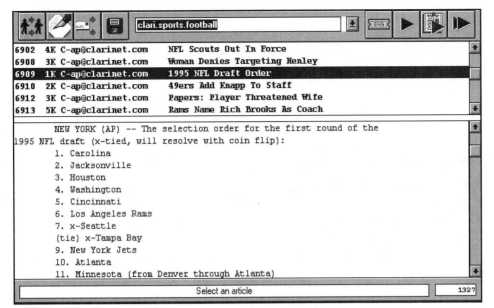

Figure 3.11 `clari.sports.football`
UseNet's Clarinet is a strong source for NFL news.

NFL Server

vnet.net/pub/football/PRO

This FTP site is an archive of NFL information past and present. There is an archive on the 1993, 1994, and even the 1995 seasons—plus records, point spreads, rosters, schedules, and team addresses.

UseNet's Clarinet

clari.sports.football

This is a menu full of wire service copy on the NFL (see fig. 3.11). It includes the Associated Press' NFL coverage, which consists of game previews, game stories, injury reports, standings, statistical leaders, breaking NFL news, and feature stories.

> **NOTE**
>
> Some service providers charge extra for the use of Clarinet newsgroups. Also, access to Clarinet is subject to whether your Internet provider actually carries it.

UseNet Newsgroups for Football Talk

UseNet includes newsgroups on every NFL team, including the two expansion teams. Through these newsgroups, fans can post messages, read messages, and respond to messages within the newsgroup.

The address of each NFL team is available in the team-by-team list at the end of this chapter.

For general NFL talk, UseNet's `rec.sport.football.pro` is the place to be.

Information on Your Favorite Team

The previous section discussed Internet sites that are relatively general in nature. Now we get specific.

Sites devoted to specific teams make up a large portion of the football information available in cyberspace, and there are more team-specific sites for NFL teams than for any other league.

In fact, sites devoted to the Jacksonville Jaguars and Carolina Panthers popped up in 1994—a full year before those teams were to take the field for their first games and well before either team had a coach or player under contract.

These sites are designed for fans to get the latest information on their teams' exploits.

World Wide Web

The World Wide Web (WWW) is the best place to go for team-specific information. As you will see, the Nando X Sports Server operates a site for every NFL team. Other servers offer team reports or notes columns on each team.

Other sites are managed by fans. Although the information at these sites isn't as reliable as professionally managed sites, the sites are fun to visit. Some of these fan-run sites, however, are extremely well-produced.

 Nando X Team Sites

`http://www.nando.net/football/1994/nfl/fbhome/`

Nando X is the only server to offer a complete home page for each NFL team (see fig. 3.12). The expansion teams in Carolina and Jacksonville had not yet been added at this writing, but by the time you read this book, they'll probably exist.

Each home-team page fits into a formula that is very complete. Each contains league-wide information such as standings and league statistical leaders.

Team-specific information includes the following:

- A team schedule
- A recap of the most-recent game
- Statistics from the most-recent game
- Feature stories and between-game reports from throughout the season
- An archive of the current season's game reports
- A preview of the next game
- A running column of notes and quotes on the team

The address listed above takes you to the main Nando team-page server. Figure 3.10 shows the New York Giants' page, which is accessed by adding `nyg.html` to the address. Addresses for every NFL team are available in the list at the end of this chapter.

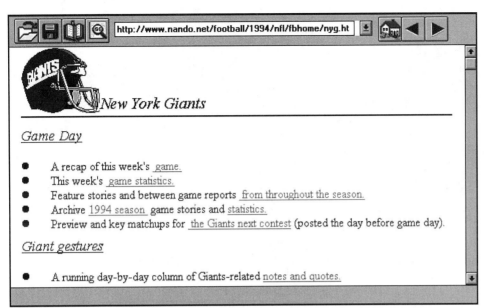

Figure 3.12 `http://www.nando.net/football/1994/nfl/fbhome/nyg.html`
This is the Nando X home page for the New York Giants.

 Other Web Sites

`http://www.freenet.ufl.edu/`
`~jburk/jags/`

This is a site that has popped up within the last year, devoted to the expansion Jacksonville Jaguars (see fig. 3.13).

> **NOTE**
>
> This section isn't a complete list of this type of site. We've chosen this site as a solid example of what this type of site typically contains—addresses for individually run World Wide Web sites on NFL teams are located in the team-by-team list at the end of this chapter.

Because of the status of this franchise, this page is a little different than most sites. But it contains just about everything a Jaguars fan could want.

Since the team was just beginning to sign players and formulate a roster at this writing, this site included a roster of players signed to date and a lot of information on the then-forthcoming expansion draft, including two lists of players who were available—divided by team and by position.

It also included a franchise timeline, which provided important dates in the team's development. There was also a "JagsNews" section, a schedule for the team's first season, and responses to frequently asked questions about the franchise.

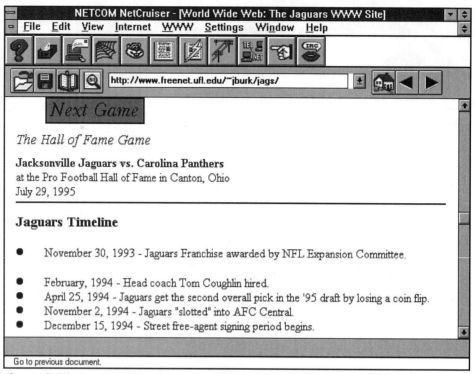

Figure 3.13 `http://www.freenet.ufl.edu/~jburk/jags/`
A home page for fans of the Jacksonville Jaguars.

Other Internet Sites of Interest

LISTSERVs are, in effect, mailing lists for fans of a specific team or sport. Fans subscribe to the mailings lists and receive, via e-mail, any messages that are posted by other members of the list. In addition, fans can post their own messages, which will then be forwarded to the other members of the group.

Mailing lists currently exist for the following teams:

> Buffalo Bills
> Cincinnati Bengals
> Cleveland Browns
> Dallas Cowboys
> Denver Broncos
> Detroit Lions
> Green Bay Packers
> Indianapolis Colts
> Kansas City Chiefs
> Los Angeles Raiders
> Minnesota Vikings
> New England Patriots
> Philadelphia Eagles
> Pittsburgh Steelers
> San Diego Chargers

LISTSERV addresses for these teams are available in the team-by-team list at the end of this chapter.

You won't have to do too much hunting to find these sites (especially since we're providing you with the addresses). Although they're by no means "hidden," they aren't generally part of the main NFL coverage on the Internet. In other words, they're a little out of the ordinary.

 NFL Quarterback Ratings

`http://www.cdg.ucar.edu/cscor/ gary/NFL.html`

There is probably no statistic more confusing in the entire world of sports than the NFL's complicated quarterback rating system. Even the sportswriters who write about it don't understand what it really means.

Well, there's a site on the Internet— this one—doesn't go out of its way to explain it to you, but it does show you what the ratings are (see fig. 3.14).

You can choose any week of the NFL season and see how the quarterbacks rated. The same is true for the post-season. And, of course, the year-to-date ratings are also available.

 Tom Jackson's Pro Football Update

`http://www.awa.com/arena/ jackson/`

Tom Jackson, the former Denver Broncos linebacker who is now a studio host for ESPN's coverage of the NFL, produces a pro football update that can be accessed from this site. Be forewarned, however, that it comes with a cost.

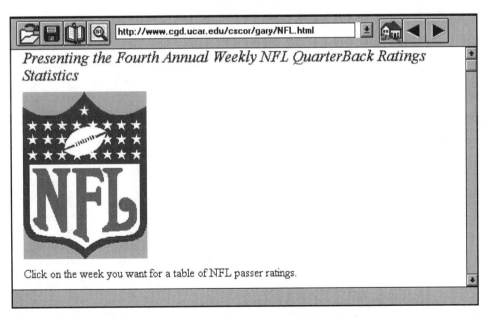

Figure 3.14 `http://www.cdg.ucar.edu/cscor/gary/NFL.html`
This site provides you with the weekly NFL Quarterback Ratings.

Commercial Online Services

Each major commericial online service offers solid NFL packages for its members.

Two major commercial online services carry team-specific information, but it's not as detailed as most of the team home pages on the World Wide Web.

 Prodigy

Jump: `football`

Prodigy has the best and most thorough coverage of NFL teams among the commercial online services (see fig. 3.15).

Prodigy's football coverage is provided by the Associated Press and by ESPN. Among the advantages of subscribing is a column by Fred Edelstein, a contributor to ESPN's NFL coverage.

The NFL Fan Club includes articles, bulletin boards, and more. And, of course, Prodigy provides the usual game stories, boxscores, and so on.

From the main football menu, click NFL and you'll be able to choose from the following options:

- Scores
- Schedule and Previews

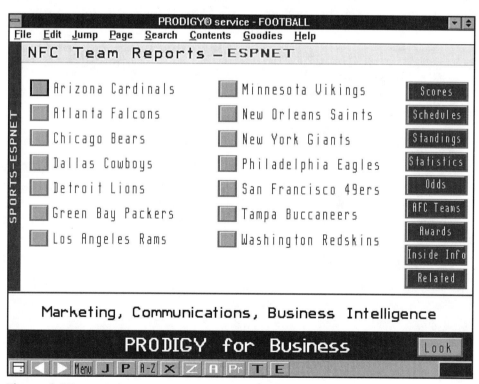

Figure 3.15 Jump: `football`
Prodigy offers thorough reports on every NFL team.

- Standings
- Statistics
- Latest Odds
- AFC Team Reports
- NFC Team Reports
- Player Awards
- NFL Online Fan Club
- NFL Bulletin Board
- AP Online

If you're interested in getting specific information on your favorite team, click either AFC Team Reports or NFC Team Reports and you'll be led to a list of teams. Pick your team and you'll be presented with the following choices:

- Injury Reports
- Notes
- Roster
- Statistics
- Recap (of the team's last game)
- Fan Club

That's right, you can even join a Prodigy fan club for your favorite team.

 America Online

Keyword: **football**

America Online (see fig. 3.16) carries team-by-team notes, provided by Sports Ticker, that are very useful for fans of teams outside of their home cities. That is, your local daily newspaper probably carries the same information on your home team, but if you're a fan of teams in other cities, America Online's notes can be a lifeline of sorts.

America Online provides game stories, boxscores, complete statistics for every NFL team, and more.

The main football menu is very clear—simply make your selection from the menu provided.

Double-click Football from the menu provided. On the main football menu (refer to fig. 3.16), you'll find the notes listings for the teams, which are divided by conference.

 CompuServe

Go: **APO**

The Associated Press provides CompuServe's sports news and information.

From the main Associated Press Online menu, choose Sports and then choose Football from the next menu.

It's a very basic package of game stories and other news, previews, injury reports, standings, and so on.

The Associated Press football package includes game previews, game stories, injury reports, standings, statistical leaders, feature stories, and breaking news.

Chapter Summary

In this chapter, we have taken a look at some of the hottest sites on the Internet for NFL fans. If you're interested in college football, you should check out Chapter 10, "College Sports."

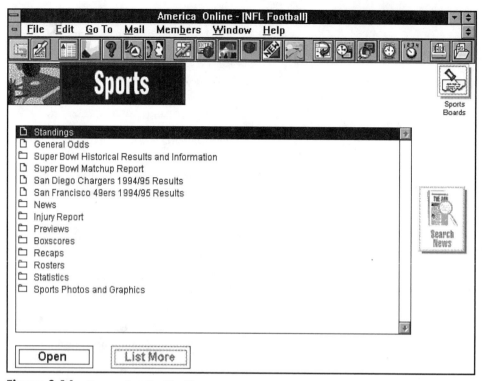

Figure 3.16 Keyword: `football`
America Online's football menu provides plenty of information on every NFL team.

The List

A complete list of addresses follows, including general football sites and a team-by-team list of NFL franchises. If you're not sure how to use an address, see Chapter 12, "Internet Basics."

General Football Sites

Canadian Football League home page:

WWW address: `http://www.ee.umanitoba.ca/CFL/`

Draft, 1994 NFL:

WWW address: `http://www.mit.edu:8001/services/sis/NFL/draft/draft_1994.html`

Eric Richard's NFL Server:

WWW address: `http://www.netgen.com/sis/sports.html`

Football Information Page:

WWW address: `http://www.armory.com/~lew/sports/football`

FTP Server for the NFL:

FTP address: `vnet.net/pub/football/PRO`

Gate Cybersports NFL home page:

WWW address: `http://sfgate.com/sports/sports/nfl/index.html`

Hawaii's NFL Home Page:

WWW address: `http://maxwell.uhh.hawaii.edu/football/football.html`

Nando X NFL Server:

WWW address: `http://www.nando.net/football/1994/nfl/nfl.html`

NFL home page:

WWW address: `http://www.cs.cmu.edu:8001/afs/cs/user/vernon/www/nfl.html`

NFL Information Finger Server:

Gopher address: `xmission.com:79/0rob`

NFL news and other information:

WWW address: `http://lux.labmed.washington.edu/~shoe/dallas/info/football_news.html`

NFL Pool, The Weekly:

WWW address: `http://www.hal.com/~markg/NFL/`

NFL Quarterback Ratings, The Weekly:

WWW address: `http://www.cdg.ucar.edu/cscor/gary/NFL.html`

NFL schedule:

WWW address: `http://www.cis.ksu.edu/~chiefs/nflstat.html`

NFL team home pages:

WWW address: `http://tns-www.lcs.mit.edu/nfl.html`

Satchel Sports NFL Server:

WWW address: `http://www.starwave.com/nfl/toc.html`

Super Bowl Host Committee home page:

WWW address: `http://www.imall.com/superbowl/superbowl.html`

Tom Jackson's Pro Football Update:

WWW address: `http://www.awa.com/arena/jackson/`

Team-by-Team List

Arizona Cardinals

Local home page:

WWW address: `http://www.nd.edu/StudentLinks/mecheves/cards/cards.html`

Nando X home page:

WWW address: `http://www.nando.net/football/1994/nfl/fbhome/arz.html`

Team-by-Team List

Newsgroup:

UseNet address:
`alt.sports.football.pro.`
`phoe-cardinals`

Satchel Sports home page:

WWW address: `http://`
`www.starwave.com/nfl/sch/`
`t-ari.html`

Atlanta Falcons

Nando X home page:

WWW address: `http://`
`www.nando.net/football/`
`1994/nfl/fbhome/atl.html`

Newsgroup:

UseNet address:
`alt.sports.football.pro.`
`atl-falcons`

Satchel Sports home page:

WWW address: `http://`
`www.starwave.com/nfl/sch/`
`t-atl.html`

Buffalo Bills

Local home page:

FTP address: `ftp.netcom.com/`
`pub/dkvalent/Buffalo_Bills/`
`bills.html`

Nando X home page:

WWW address: `http://`
`www.nando.net/football/`
`1994/nfl/fbhome/buf.html`

Newsgroup:

UseNet address:
`alt.sports.football.pro.`
`buffalo-bills`

Satchel Sports home page:

WWW address: `http://`
`www.starwave.com/nfl/sch/`
`t-buf.html`

The Bills mailing list:

To subscribe, send e-mail to:
LISTSERV address: `buffalo-`
`bills-request@netcom.com`

To post messages send e-mail to:
`buffalo-bills@netcom.com`

Carolina Panthers

Local home page:

WWW address: `http://`
`www2.ncsu.edu/eos/users/`
`r/rdarnese/www/pant.html`

Newsgroup:

UseNet address:
`alt.sports.football.pro.`
`car-panthers`

Panthers' FTP site:

FTP address: `vnet.net/pub/`
`football/PRO/PANTHERS`

Chicago Bears

Nando X home page:

WWW address: `http://`
`www.nando.net/football/`
`1994/nfl/fbhome/chi.html`

Newsgroup:

UseNet address:
`alt.sports.football.pro.`
`chicago-bears`

Satchel Sports home page:

WWW address: `http://`
`www.starwave.com/nfl/sch/`
`t-chi.html`

Cincinnati Bengals

Nando X home page:

WWW address: `http://`
`www.nando.net/football/`
`1994/nfl/fbhome/cin.html`

Newsgroup:

UseNet address:
`alt.sports.football.pro.`
`cinci-bengals`

Satchel Sports home page:

WWW address: `http://`
`www.starwave.com/nfl/sch/`
`t-cin.html`

The Bengals mailing list:

To subscribe, send e-mail to:
LISTSERV address:
`listserv@miamiu.acs.muohio.edu`

To post messages, send e-mail to:
`cinbengl@miamiu.acs.muohio.edu`

Cleveland Browns

Local home pages:

WWW address: `http://`
`oucsace.cs.ohiou.edu/`
`personal/kmahoney/Browns/`
`browns.html`

WWW address: `http://`
`lady.wariat.org/1/sports/`
`Browns`

Nando X home page:

WWW address: `http://`
`www.nando.net/football/`
`1994/nfl/fbhome/cle.html`

Newsgroup:

UseNet address:
`alt.sports.football.pro.cleve.browns`

Satchel Sports home page:

WWW address: `http://`
`www.starwave.com/nfl/sch/`
`t-cle.html`

The Browns mailing list:

To subscribe, send e-mail to:
LISTSERV address:
`aj755@cleveland.freenet.edu`

To post messages, send e-mail to:
`sports@wariat.org`

Dallas Cowboys

Local home page:

WWW address: `http://`
`lux.labmed.washington.edu/`
`~shoe/dallas/fball.html`

Team-by-Team List

Nando X home page:

WWW address: `http://`
`www.nando.net/football/`
`1994/nfl/fbhome/dal.html`

Newsgroup:

UseNet address:
`alt.sports.football.pro.`
`dallas-cowboys`

Satchel Sports home page:

WWW address: `http://`
`www.starwave.com/nfl/sch/`
`t-dal.html`

The Cowboys mailing list:

To subscribe, send e-mail to:

LISTSERV address:
`dansmith@skopen.dseg.ti.com`

To post messages, send e-mail to:

`cowboys@emmitt.dseg.ti.com`

Denver Broncos

Nando X home page:

WWW address: `http://`
`www.nando.net/football/`
`1994/nfl/fbhome/den.html`

Newsgroup:

UseNet address:
`alt.sports.football.pro.`
`denver-broncos`

Satchel Sports home page:

WWW address: `http://`
`www.starwave.com/nfl/sch/`
`t-den.html`

The Broncos mailing list:

To subscribe, send e-mail to:

LISTSERV address:
`listserv@lists.colorado.edu`

To post messages, send e-mail to:

`broncolist@lists.colorado.edu`

Detroit Lions

Local home page:

WWW address: `http://`
`www.nd.edu/StudentLinks/`
`dbarstis/Lions/lionspage.html`

Nando X home page:

WWW address: `http://`
`www.nando.net/football/`
`1994/nfl/fbhome/det.html`

Newsgroup:

UseNet address:
`alt.sports.football.pro.`
`detroit-lions`

Satchel Sports home page:

WWW address: `http://`
`www.starwave.com/nfl/sch/`
`t-det.html`

To subscribe to the Lions list, which is at the same address as the one that follows:

LISTSERV address:
`bhenry@autodesk.com`

Green Bay Packers

Local home page:

WWW address: `http://www.netnet.net/green-bay-packers.html`

Local home page:

WWW address: `http://www.cs.cmu.edu:8001/afs/cs/user/vernon/www/packers.html`

Nando X home page:

WWW address: `http://www.nando.net/football/1994/nfl/fbhome/gbp.html`

Newsgroup:

UseNet address: `alt.sports.football.pro.gb-packers`

Packers archive:

Gopher address: `fullfeed.fullfeed.com/11/packers`

Satchel Sports home page:

WWW address: `http://www.starwave.com/nfl/sch/t-gnb.html`

The Packers mailing list:

To subscribe, send e-mail to:

LISTSERV address: `packers-request@fullfeed.com`

To post messages, send e-mail to:

`packers@fullfeed.com`

Houston Oilers

Nando X home page:

WWW address: `http://www.nando.net/football/1994/nfl/fbhome/hou.html`

Newsgroup:

UseNet address: `alt.sports.football.pro.houston-oilers`

Satchel Sports home page:

WWW address: `http://www.starwave.com/nfl/sch/t-hou.html`

Indianapolis Colts

Nando X home page:

WWW address: `http://www.nando.net/football/1994/nfl/fbhome/ind.html`

Newsgroup:

UseNet address: `alt.sports.football.pro.indy-colts`

Satchel Sports home page:

WWW address: `http://www.starwave.com/nfl/sch/t-ind.html`

The Colts mailing list:

To subscribe, send e-mail to:

LISTSERV address: `colts-request@storm.cadcam.iupui.edu`

Team-by-Team List

To post messages, send e-mail to:

colts@storm.cadcam.iupui.edu

Jacksonville Jaguars

Jaguars' FTP site:

FTP address: vnet.net/pub/
football/PRO/JAGUARS

Local home page:

WWW address: http://
www.freenet.ufl.edu/~jburk/
jags/

Newsgroup:

UseNet address:
alt.sports.football.pro.
jville-jaguars

Kansas City Chiefs

Local home pages:

WWW address: http://
www.cis.ksu.edu/~chiefs/
chiefs.html

WWW address: http://
www.interstate.net/chiefs/

Nando X home page:

WWW address: http://
www.nando.net/football/
1994/nfl/fbhome/kan.html

Newsgroup:

UseNet address:
alt.sports.football.pro.
kc-chiefs

Satchel Sports home page:

WWW address: http://
www.starwave.com/nfl/sch/
t-kan.html

The Chiefs mailing list:

To subscribe, send e-mail to:

LISTSERV address: chiefs-
request@mccall.com

To post messages, send e-mail to:

chiefs@mccall.com

Los Angeles Raiders

Local home page:

WWW address: http://
www.super.org:8000/
adamfox/raiders/main.html

Nando X home page:

WWW address: http://
www.nando.net/football/
1994/nfl/fbhome/rai.html

Newsgroup:

UseNet address:
alt.sports.football.pro.
la-raiders

Satchel Sports home page:

WWW address: http://
www.starwave.com/nfl/sch/
t-lar.html

The Raiders mailing list:

To subscribe, send e-mail to:

LISTSERV address: `raiders-request@super.org`

To post messages, send e-mail to:

`raiders-fans@super.org`

Los Angeles Rams

Nando X home page:

WWW address: `http://www.nando.net/football/1994/nfl/fbhome/ram.html`

Newsgroup:

UseNet address: `alt.sports.football.pro.la-rams`

Satchel Sports home page:

WWW address: `http://www.starwave.com/nfl/sch/t-los.html`

Miami Dolphins

Local home page:

WWW address: `http://www.ai.mit.edu/~curt/dolphins.html`

Nando X home page:

WWW address: `http://www.nando.net/football/1994/nfl/fbhome/mia.html`

Newsgroup:

UseNet address: `alt.sports.football.pro.miami-dolphins`

Satchel Sports home page:

WWW address: `http://www.starwave.com/nfl/sch/t-mia.html`

Minnesota Vikings

Local home page:

WWW address: `http://cadserv.cadlab.vt.edu/woyak/VIKINGS/vikings.html`

Nando X home page:

WWW address: `http://www.nando.net/football/1994/nfl/fbhome/min.html`

Newsgroup:

UseNet address: `alt.sports.football.pro.mn-vikings`

Satchel Sports home page:

WWW address: `http://www.starwave.com/nfl/sch/t-min.html`

The Vikings mailing list:

To subscribe, send e-mail to:

LISTSERV address: `Deborah.Greene@Corp.Sun.COM`

To post messages, send e-mail to:

`Vikings@twins.corp.sun.com`

Team-by-Team List

New England Patriots

Local home page:

WWW address: `http://research.ftp.com/~solensky/patriots.html`

Nando X home page:

WWW address: `http://www.nando.net/football/1994/nfl/fbhome/nep.html`

Newsgroup:

UseNet address: `alt.sports.football.pro.ne-patriots`

Satchel Sports home page:

WWW address: `http://www.starwave.com/nfl/sch/t-nwe.html`

The Patriots mailing list:

To subscribe, send e-mail to:

LISTSERV address: `majordomo@world.std.com`

To post messages, send e-mail to:

`patriots@world.std.com`

New Orleans Saints

Nando X home page:

WWW address: `http://www.nando.net/football/1994/nfl/fbhome/nos.html`

Newsgroup:

UseNet address: `alt.sports.football.pro.no-saints`

Satchel Sports home page:

WWW address: `http://www.starwave.com/nfl/sch/t-nor.html`

New York Giants

Local home page:

WWW address: `http://info.med.yale.edu/Adriene/NYGiants/giants.html`

Nando X home page:

WWW address: `http://www.nando.net/football/1994/nfl/fbhome/nyg.html`

Newsgroup:

UseNet address: `alt.sports.football.pro.ny-giants`

Satchel Sports home page:

WWW address: `http://www.starwave.com/nfl/sch/t-nyg.html`

New York Jets

Nando X home page:

WWW address: `http://www.nando.net/football/1994/nfl/fbhome/nyj.html`

Newsgroup:

UseNet address:
`alt.sports.football.pro.`
`ny-jets`

Satchel Sports home page:

WWW address: `http://`
`www.starwave.com/nfl/sch/`
`t-nyj.html`

Philadelphia Eagles

Nando X home page:

WWW address: `http://`
`www.nando.net/football/`
`1994/nfl/fbhome/phi.html`

Newsgroup:

UseNet address:
`alt.sports.football.pro.`
`phila-eagles`

Satchel Sports home page:

WWW address: `http://`
`www.starwave.com/nfl/sch/`
`t-phi.html`

The Eagles mailing list:

To subscribe, send e-mail to:

LISTSERV address:
`rsmith@sol.cms.uncwil.edu`

To post messages, send e-mail to:

`eagles@mars.cms.uncwil.edu`

Pittsburgh Steelers

Local home page:

WWW address: `http://`
`www.cs.cmu.edu:8001/afs/cs/`
`user/vernon/www/steelers.html`

Nando X home page:

WWW address: `http://`
`www.nando.net/football/`
`1994/nfl/fbhome/pit.html`

Newsgroup:

UseNet address:
`alt.sports.football.pro.`
`pitt-steelers`

Satchel Sports home page:

WWW address: `http://`
`www.starwave.com/nfl/sch/`
`t-pit.html`

Steelers' FTP site:

FTP address: `vnet.net/pub/`
`football/PRO/STEELERS`

The Steelers mailing list:

To subscribe, send e-mail to:

LISTSERV address: `steelers-`
`request@andrew.cmu.edu`

To post messages, send e-mail to:

`steelers@andrew.cmu.edu`

Team-by-Team List

San Diego Chargers

Local home page:

WWW address: `http://www.cs.cmu.edu:8001/afs/cs/user/vernon/www/chargers.html`

Local home page:

WWW address: `http://www.armory.com/~lew/sports/football/chargers.html`

Nando X home page:

WWW address: `http://www.nando.net/football/1994/nfl/fbhome/sdc.html`

Newsgroup:

UseNet address: `alt.sports.football.pro.sd-chargers`

Satchel Sports home page:

WWW address: `http://www.starwave.com/nfl/sch/t-sdg.html`

The Chargers mailing list:

To subscribe, send e-mail to:

LISTSERV address: `bolt-backers-request@andrew.cmu.edu`

To post messages, send e-mail to:

`Bolt-Backers@andrew.cmu.edu`

San Francisco 49ers

Local home page:

WWW address: `http://www.armory.com/~lew/sports/football/49ers`

Local home page:

WWW address: `http://cyber.sfgate.com/examiner/49ers/49ershome.html`

Nando X home page:

WWW address: `http://www.nando.net/football/1994/nfl/fbhome/sf9.html`

Newsgroup:

UseNet address: `alt.sports.football.pro.sf-49ers`

Satchel Sports home page:

WWW address: `http://www.starwave.com/nfl/sch/t-sfo.html`

Seattle Seahawks

Nando X home page:

WWW address: `http://www.nando.net/football/1994/nfl/fbhome/sea.html`

Newsgroup:

UseNet address: `alt.sports.football.pro.sea-seahawks`

Satchel Sports home page:

WWW address: `http://`
`www.starwave.com/nfl/sch/`
`t-sea.html`

Tampa Bay Buccaneers

Local home page:

WWW address: `http:///`
`www.hamline.edu/`
`~sfitchet/bucshome.html`

Nando X home page:

WWW address: `http://`
`www.nando.net/football/`
`1994/nfl/fbhome/tbb.html`

Newsgroup:

UseNet address:
`alt.sports.football.pro.`
`tampabay-bucs`

Satchel Sports home page:

WWW address: `http://`
`www.starwave.com/nfl/sch/`
`t-tam.html`

Washington Redskins

Local home page:

WWW address: `http://`
`www.email.net/www/`
`bkayton/skins.html`

Nando X home page:

WWW address: `http://`
`www.nando.net/football/`
`1994/nfl/fbhome/was.html`

Newsgroup:

UseNet address:
`alt.sports.football.pro.`
`wash-redskins`

Satchel Sports home page:

WWW address: `http://`
`www.starwave.com/nfl/sch/`
`t-was.html`

Chapter 4

Pro Baseball

Although Major League players called it quits in the summer of 1994, there was plenty of action on the Internet.

In this chapter

- *Internet sources on the baseball strike*
- *The best places to find baseball news and statistics*
- *Sites to check out for information on your favorite team*
- *Newsgroups and bulletin boards for baseball talk*
- *Other Internet sites of interest*
- *What commerial online services have to offer*

In other chapters

→ *If you're looking for college baseball sites, see The List at the end of Chapter 10*

← *For more information on the LISTSERVs discussed in this chapter, see Chapter 2*

→ *If you're not sure how to use an address in this chapter, see Chapter 12*

What else can possibly be said about pro baseball? In 1994, our grand ol' game suddenly wasn't a game at all. America's pastime appeared to be well past its prime.

The players' strike that ended the 1994 season and brought about the cancellation of the World Series turned many fans against the game that once was their passion. If history is any indication, however, fan support of the game will return to its pre-strike levels—it may even increase after a short time.

Much like their pro hockey brethren, baseball owners and players didn't know a good thing when they saw it in 1994. For example, consider the following:

- Three players were in position to make a run at Roger Maris' season record for home runs and yet another was eyeing a .400 batting average.
- A new divisional alignment put traditional patsies like the Cleveland Indians in contention for a playoff berth.

However, the players walked out in August. And the owners let them.

That left fans to argue over who might have won the World Series—an argument settled on one Internet site (more on that later).

Much of the baseball activity on the Internet shut down after the strike started. Only the strongest sites and the most dedicated site managers continued to update their sites on a daily or weekly basis.

But so much of the baseball information on the Internet is team-specific—that is, it's dependent on having teams to discuss—that there wasn't a whole lot of activity.

The sites remained, however, with the vast majority serving as resources for summarizing the season that was—*and wasn't.*

> **NOTE**
>
> Baseball is a lot more than the Major Leagues. In the list at the end of this chapter, you will find some sites that cover minor league baseball.

The Baseball Strike

While many sites on the Internet shut down for the duration of the strike, or at least went on hiatus, the labor strife actually spawned a few new ones.

Fans, after all, needed something to do, some place to go. More importantly, they needed a place to vent their anger, or to have someone tell them *how* to vent their anger.

Many found that the Internet was the perfect place for all that.

While UseNet newsgroups were full of strike talk, there were some very interesting sites that popped up on the World Wide Web for fans frustrated by the first cancellation of the World Series in nearly a century.

This is typical of the Internet, where site operators are quick to respond to changes in the landscape and provide Internet users with something new to enjoy.

The sites included in this section may no longer exist by the time this book hits the shelf. This section is designed to give fans an idea of the type of sites that pop up during unusual situations.

Nando X Strike Coverage

The Nando X Sports Server is the most complete baseball source on the Internet, and when the players went on strike, Nando came through with four new sites.

Baseball Strike 1994

`http://www.nando.net/baseball/`
`bbstrike.html`

The above address carried the most comedic value. As figure 4.1 shows, it carried some "baseball strike pacifiers" for fans who wanted to kick some dirt on home plate in anger.

The photos of chief negotiators Donald Fehr (the players' representative) and Richard Ravitch (the owners' representative) were superimposed on makeshift dartboards. The site encourages frustrated fans to download the photos, print them out, tack them to a wall, and buy a set of darts.

The site also had a serious side, carrying Associated Press stories on the strike. There were stories on what the end of the season meant to fans and players, biographies of the negotiators, and more. It was the Associated Press' complete strike package.

 ## Fans Site

`http://www.nando.net/baseball/`
`bbs/boycott.html`

Are the fans finally mad enough at the baseball powers that be to do something about it? This site asks the questions, and offers some talk of a boycott by fans.

 ## Negotiation Updates

`http://www.nando.net/newsroom/`
`baseball/strike.html`

Figure 4.1 `http://www.nando.net/baseball/bbstrike.html`
These "baseball strike pacifiers" helped fans vent their anger.

White Sox Win World Series, End Drought

Baseball fans were left without a World Series in the fall of 1994, so the Nando sports network finished it off for them. Through the use of a computerized baseball game, Nando actually finished the season for fans, and wrapped it all up by playing the playoffs and the World Series.

The result will only make the long-suffering baseball fans in Chicago more angry—the White Sox defeated the Atlanta Braves four games to two to end the second-longest World Series championship drought in Major League history. The real White Sox haven't won the World Series since 1917; only the Chicago Cubs, who haven't won it since 1908, have gone longer without a title.

The address for this site is **http://www.nando.net/baseball/strike/recreate/recreate.html**

This site includes summaries of all the simulated games—a daily summary of the games that would have been played, including the playoffs, had the season not ended.

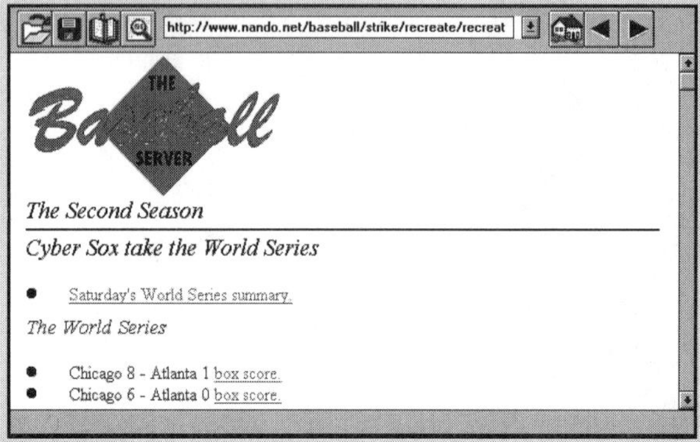

Figure 4.2
In Nando's Second Season, the White Sox beat the Braves in six games to win a simulated World Series in 1994.

And what a season it would have been, according to this site.

The San Francisco Giants' Matt Williams hit his 62nd homer on the season's final day, eclipsing Roger Maris' record of 61 set in 1961. Williams also led the National League with 144 RBIs, while San Diego's Tony Gwynn fell short in his quest for .400, hitting .382.

In the American League, Cleveland's Albert Belle narrowly missed the triple crown. He led the cyber-American League with a .372 batting average and 153 RBIs, but was third in homers behind Ken Griffey, Jr. and Frank Thomas.

Cleveland made the playoffs as a wild-card team and upset the New York Yankees, winners of 108 regular-season games, in the first round. The White Sox defeated the Seattle Mariners, which became the first team to win a division title with a losing record—taking the AL West at 76-84. The White Sox then toppled the Indians to go on to the World Series.

The Braves became the first wild-card team to make it to the World Series. They finished second to the Dodgers in the NL West, and then upended NL East champion Montreal (which won 103 games) in the first round. The Dodgers topped NL Central champion Cincinnati before losing to the Braves.

I provided you with the result of the pseudo World Series because such knowledge doesn't ruin the impact of the site. Any true baseball fan—and anyone who's honestly angered by the strike—has simply got to read the World Series Summary link. It's absolutely hilarious.

The title of this site says it all. This is the place fans turned for all the Associated Press updates on the strike negotiations, the teams' plans to play the 1995 season with replacement players, and so on.

Other Strike Resources

Nando X wasn't the only outlet for fans. UseNet's baseball newsgroups were virtually alive with strike talk, and there were other sources on the Internet to keep baseball fans talking about—or at least thinking about—the game.

 Sawdon's Baseball Page

`http://www.cs.cmu.edu:8001/afs/`
`cs.cmu.edu/user/wsawdon/www/`
`baseball.html`

Sawdon's Baseball Page turned itself into a strike haven during the fall of 1994, and it carried into 1995 as well.

It became a collection of quotes from baseball's past (see fig. 4.3), each of which shed a little light on the game's current labor situation.

The site includes a revealing quote from Shoeless Joe Jackson in W.P. Kinsella's book, "Shoeless Joe." It also includes quotes taken from previous labor battles in the game, from such luminaries as former Commissioner A. Bartlett Giamatti, previous negotiators, and more. Most of them foreshadow the 1994 strike and remind fans that previous strikes and lockouts failed to resolve much of anything.

It can be some depressing reading when you consider that the quotes are associated with dates that clearly

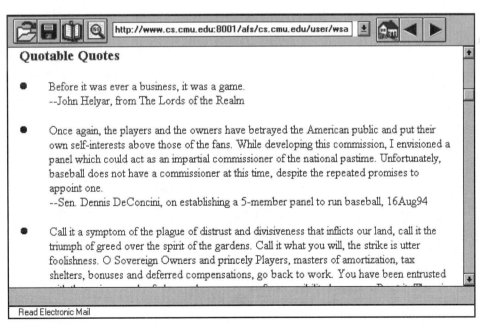

Figure 4.3 `http://www.cs.cmu.edu:8001/afs/cs.cmu.edu/user/wsawdon/www/`
`baseball.html`
A site that sheds new light on the players' strike.

indicate that the issues of 15 years ago (and longer) are still the issues that are discussed today. It is, however, also very enlightening.

 ## UseNet Newsgroups

```
rec.sport.baseball
rec.sport.baseball.analysis
rec.sport.baseball.data
```

Each of the previous newsgroups was full of talk of the baseball strike. Fans across the country couldn't decide who to blame—was it the millionaire players who were at fault or the millionaire owners?

The debate raged through last September, slowed for a while, and then reignited when the season and post-season were officially cancelled. Once October came to a close, the debate calmed again.

Getting the News and Stats

When there are games, there are statistics. There is also news about the games, coverage of the winners and losers, talk about who's hot and who's not, and so on.

The Internet is there to handle it all—as long as there is some of it to handle.

Internet Sources

Much like the other major professional sports, you'll find a lot of baseball activity on UseNet and within the Nando network. But there are several other interesting baseball sites that have a lot to offer the fan. When it comes to quality, baseball sites don't take a back seat to sites devoted to other sports.

Internet Is More Than Fun And Games

When I first logged on to the Internet, I did it mostly for the fun of it. While I still use it for fun, I've also found it to be helpful in my work covering baseball for the Associated Press.

During a game in the 1994 season, I couldn't recall a statistic I needed for a story I was writing. I had my Internet service provider's software loaded on the laptop I use at game sites, so I logged on to the Internet and surfed until I found the statistic I needed.

Doing that, of course, I had to be careful that the site I was using for the stat was one I trusted to provide accurate information. Once I did that, I had the stat I needed to help make my story strong.

Jason Kint's Baseball Web

http://pear.wustl.edu/~jekint/
baseball.html

Jason Kint's Baseball Web (see fig. 4.4) covers the game admirably, with links to several subtopics that fans will find enjoyable.

For multimedia types, it offers links to two areas: "The Sounds of Baseball" and a "Portfolio of Baseball Graphics."

For those trying to contact their favorite team, it offers links to mailing list information and team addresses, plus a list of radio and television affiliates that carry the games.

It also offers scores and standings for coverage of the games themselves, plus a strong statistics package.

There also is a link to several archives of baseball information.

 ## Nando X Baseball Server

http://www.nando.net/baseball/
bbmain.html

Nando's strike coverage is detailed in the "Nando X Strike Coverage" section earlier in this chapter, but the server also provides great coverage of the sport when there are games being played.

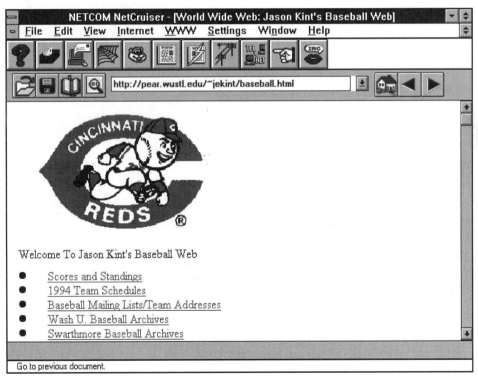

Figure 4.4 http://pear.wustl.edu/~jekint/baseball.html
Jason Kint's Baseball Web is a strong site for baseball fans.

Nando's regular offerings include game stories and boxscores on every Major League game, plus the following list of links:

- A minor league report
- Daily American League and National League starting pitchers
- Links to team-by-team reports
- Complete standings
- Transactions
- Statistics and streaks

 Video Highlights

`http://tnswww.lcs.mit.edu/cgibin/sports/mlb/highlights`

This is the perfect site for the owner of the top-of-the-line multimedia computer.

Each day, this site carries brief video highlights—which originate from the cable network CNN—of the previous day's games. It's not recommended for people with slower modems and lower-end monitor and sound systems.

To best use this site, you'll need at least 8M of RAM, a multimedia monitor, and a 14,400-bps modem.

 Satchel Sports Major League Baseball

`http://www.starwave.com/mlb/toc.html`

All of Satchel Sports' servers include one link that few, if any, of the other such servers include—an up-to-the-minute scoreboard of games in progress.

Once the games conclude, a game summary and boxscore—both provided by Sports Ticker—are available. This site also links you to updated statistics, transactions, and an archive of past games.

Of special interest should be "Inside Baseball," a notebook of tidbits from around the Major Leagues.

 Baseball FTP Archive

`etext.archive.umich.edu/pub/Sports/Baseball`

This is a great statistics archive for serious baseball fans and Rotisserie League players (see fig. 4.5). Each week it provides updated season statistics for each Major League team, compiled and presented in an easy-to-follow format.

The statistics are as complete as they come, including individual stats on every Major League player.

 UseNet Newsgroups

`rec.sport.baseball`
`rec.sport.baseball.analysis`
`rec.sport.baseball.data`

UseNet newsgroups are popular among baseball fans, particularly those devoted to specific teams.

Also in UseNet newsgroups, which are generalized, several issues are debated.

Whether it's labor unrest, the new divisional alignment, expansion, or the designated hitter rule, baseball fans can get their fill of others' opinions in any of these groups.

 Schedules

`http://www.cs.rochester.edu/`
`cgibin/ferguson/mlb`

The complete Major League schedule can be a complex web of road trips and two-, three-, and four-game series. This site simplifies it all.

It enables you to conduct searches in several different ways. You can call up the complete schedule of just one team, or you can bring up a list of all the games between, for example, the Red Sox and the Orioles.

Information on Your Favorite Team

Baseball, more than any other professional sport, lends itself perfectly to the team-specific Internet site.

With games played virtually every day, there are plenty of things a good Internet site proprietor can offer to fans. Baseball's constant pace of game after game also helps separate the good sites from the bad—the good ones are those that can keep up with the mountain of results, statistics, and so on.

Until this past fall, there were three basic types of team-specific sites on the Internet:

- The UseNet newsgroup
- A site offered by a network that provides sites on all the league's teams

`ftp://etext.archive.umich.edu/pub/Sports/Baseball/Maj`

KansasCity

	NAME	AB	HIT	2B	3B	HR	SLG	RUN	RBI	BB	SO	O
1	Joyner	332	104	17	3	8	.455	49	54	43	37	.3
2	Gaetti	304	89	14	2	12	.470	49	55	18	60	.3
3	Jose	332	97	23	1	10	.458	52	50	35	69	.3
4	McRae	408	113	20	6	4	.385	67	39	47	63	.3
5	Hamelin	285	77	22	1	22	.586	58	58	51	58	.3
6	Lind	265	71	13	2	1	.343	31	26	16	32	.3
7	Gagne	344	90	20	3	7	.398	35	47	27	73	.3
8	MacFarlane	294	74	15	3	13	.456	52	45	35	66	.3
9	Koslofski	4	1	0	0	0	.250	2	0	2	1	.5
10	DHenderson	198	49	14	1	5	.404	27	31	16	28	.3
11	Shumpert	173	42	6	2	8	.439	26	23	13	35	.2
12	Coleman	410	98	13	11	2	.339	57	29	27	70	.2
13	Howard	81	19	4	0	1	.321	9	13	11	22	.3
14	Mayne	136	32	4	0	2	.309	17	17	10	27	.2
15	Brooks	61	14	2	0	1	.311	5	14	2	10	.2
16	Miller	11	2	0	0	0	.182	1	0	0	1	.1

Figure 4.5 etext.archive.umich.edu/pub/Sports/Baseball
Complete Major League statistics are available at this site.

- Individual sites started by a fan of the given team

In the fall of 1994, however, the Seattle Mariners became the first pro sports franchise to operate a site on their team. (For more information, see "The Official Mariners Web" below.)

> **NOTE**
>
> This section doesn't provide a complete listing of team-specific sites. We'll highlight some of the more interesting ones in an effort to provide an example of how these sites are run. There is a complete list of team-specific sites at the end of the chapter.

World Wide Web

The World Wide Web (WWW) is the perfect home for baseball sites. It provides hypertext links and it's easy to transfer complex files such as photos, sounds, and video clips.

The Web provides at least one home page on every Major League team.

 The Official Mariners Web

`http://www.mariners.org/`

The Mariners haven't been the most successful franchise on the field since they joined the league in 1977. With only one season in which they won more games than they lost, the Mariners haven't appeared in the playoffs or even seriously threatened to do so.

But the organization is currently in first place in one area—technology.

The Mariners opened a site on a network operated by the Seattle-based Semaphore Corp. But soon thereafter, the Mariners and Semaphore decided to set up a joint network between them, with the Mariners' site as the flagship. That switch brought about the new address for the site above (see fig. 4.6).

The Mariners were smart enough to forsee not only an avenue for increased interest in the product on the field, but a huge resource for marketing the team's merchandise both in the U.S. and abroad.

Baseball teams—like their counterparts in other sports—tend to follow the lead of other baseball teams, so this type of marketing will likely become more common in the years to come. After all, merchandising has become an increasingly important aspect of the game, with many teams changing their uniforms, hats, and logos in pursuit of more revenue.

In its first few months, the Mariners' site hasn't become merely an advertising vehicle. It's a solid mix of news and information on the team and other tidbits that fans can't get anywhere else.

Where else can you get in touch with the manager or other members of a team's front office? At this site, you can.

You can also get team news, a complete schedule for the coming season, player and team information, game reports, historical information, statistics, and photos. (And, of course, merchandise.)

There also is a Mariners Trivia Challenge that challenges the knowledge of the team's most ardent followers. In the future, fans may even be able to order tickets from the site.

Nando X Team Sites

`http://www.nando.net/baseball/`
`bbs/bbhome/`

Nando X goes well beyond any other baseball server by providing a home page on each team in the Major Leagues.

They're all set up in similar fashion and they all offer the same basic services. Fortunately, those basic services are just about everything any fan would want.

Included are game summaries and boxscores, each provided by the Associated Press. In addition, there is a running column of notes and quotes, statistics (for that specific team, as well as league leaders), standings, schedules, team history and information, and photos.

The address listed above leads you to the main Nando team server. The example in figure 4.8 shows the Colorado Rockies' site. To get there, add `col.html` to the end of the above address. Each Nando team address is included in the list at the end of this chapter.

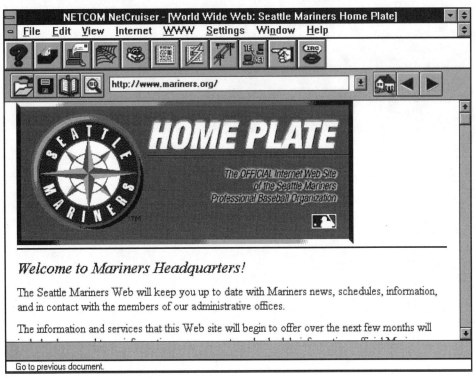

Figure 4.6 `http://www.mariners.org/`
The Mariners operate this site for their fans.

Ken Griffey, Jr.

Ken Griffey, Jr. has been involved in a lot of baseball firsts.

He was the first player to play on the same team with his father, the first player to play in the same outfield with his father, and the first player to hit a home run in the same game as his father.

He's also one of the best young stars in the game today.

Today, Griffey is believed to be the first Major Leaguer to have his own home page on the World Wide Web (see fig. 4.7). Of course, Griffey is not actually running the page—the Mariners set it up as part of their new network.

At this writing, the site doesn't have a whole lot of Griffey information. But the fact that it exists at all is a testament to his importance to the Mariners—and to Major League baseball.

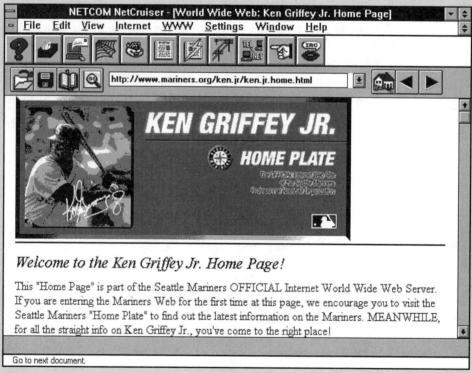

Figure 4.7 http://www.mariners.org/ken.jr/ken.jr.home.html
Ken Griffey Jr. is believed to be the first Major Leaguer with his own home page.

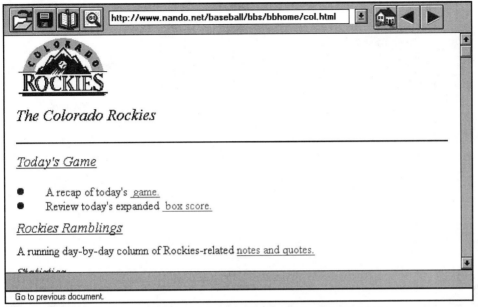

Figure 4.8 `http://www.nando.net/baseball/bbs/bbhome/col.html`
Here's the Colorado Rockies' home site on Nando X.

 Phillies Home Page

`http://storm.cadcam.iupui.edu/`
`phils/phils.html`

The site depicted in figure 4.9 is a perfect example of a locally produced home page on a specific team. These sites are typically set up by a fan—or even several fans—of a specific team, and the sites are operated in a variety of ways. Some are very professional and objective, others are "homer" sites where the operator is disgusted with losses and overjoyed with victories.

There are pros and cons to both types of sites. The locally produced sites are great places to look for opinionated writing and home-team slanted recaps of the games. They generally can't,

however, match the objectivity and the depth of the coverage that's typically provided by sites that are part of an online sports network.

There are many of these sites on the Internet—about half of the teams in the Major Leagues have one or more of these sites devoted to them. Because they aren't run by an established organization (for the most part), they can be transient. They might move from network to network, or disappear altogether without leaving a trace. Most, however, are in it for the long haul.

At the site shown in figure 4.9, Phillies fans can find standings, statistics, a team schedule, the team logo, and news about the team.

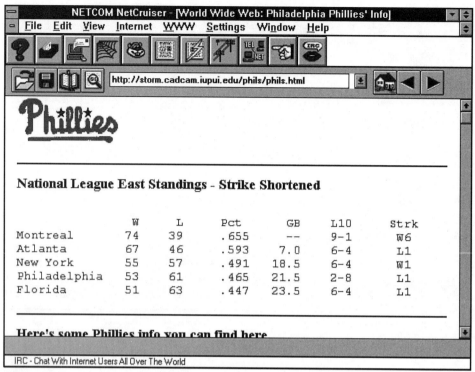

Figure 4.9 `http://storm.cadcam.iupui.edu/phils/phils.html`
A local home page for the Philadelphia Phillies.

Places to Go for Baseball Talk

The UseNet network contains a series of newsgroups that operate as bulletin boards for fans of specific teams to meet and discuss issues about their teams.

Subscribing to one of these groups is usually easy, especially if your Internet service provider includes a graphical interface in which you click a Subscribe button. Most providers now have these interfaces.

Once you've subscribed, you can read messages posted by others, respond to them, or post your own message on another topic.

Although these online "discussions" aren't live, they can be lively. Anything you'd hear on a sports-talk radio program is just as likely to be found on one of these UseNet newsgroups—fans calling for the coach's head, trade rumors bouncing back and forth, suggestions on changes in the lineup, and talk about hot players in the minor leagues. In general, it's talk about what's wrong—or what's right—with the home team.

Most of the Major League teams now have UseNet newgroups devoted to them. It probably won't be long before every team does. At this writing, the teams shown in Table 4.1 have UseNet newsgroups devoted solely to them.

Complete addresses for these UseNet newsgroups are also included in the team-by-team list at the end of this chapter.

Table 4.1 UseNet Newsgroups for Major League Teams

Team	Address
Atlanta Braves	`alt.sports.baseball.atlanta-braves`
Baltimore Orioles	`alt.sports.baseball.balt-orioles`
Boston Red Sox	`alt.sports.baseball.bos-redsox`
California Angels	`alt.sports.baseball.calif-angels`
Chicago White Sox	`alt.sports.baseball.chi-whitesox`
Cleveland Indians	`alt.sports.baseball.cleve-indians`
Detroit Tigers	`alt.sports.baseball.detroit-tigers`
Houston Astros	`alt.sports.baseball.houston-astros`
Kansas City Royals	`alt.sports.baseball.kc-royals`
Los Angeles Dodgers	`alt.sports.baseball.la-dodgers`
Montreal Expos	`alt.sports.baseball.montreal-expos`
New York Mets	`alt.sports.baseball.ny-mets`
New York Yankees	`alt.sports.baseball.ny-yankees`
Philadelphia Phillies	`alt.sports.baseball.phila-phillies`
San Francisco Giants	`alt.sports.baseball.sf-giants`
Seattle Mariners	`alt.sports.baseball.sea-mariners`
St. Louis Cardinals	`alt.sports.baseball.stl-cardinals`
Texas Rangers	`alt.sports.baseball.texas-rangers`
Toronto Blue Jays	`alt.sports.baseball.tor-bluejays`

4

PRO BASEBALL

Other Sites for Baseball Talk

Mailing lists are a form of bulletin boards in which fans of a given team correspond via e-mail. These lists are operated several ways, but generally, when a message is sent to the list by one of the members, it's then immediately forwarded to the e-mail addresses of all of the members on the list.

> **NOTE**
>
> LISTSERVs are covered in depth in Chapter 2, "Sports Talk."

Baseball has more mailing-list services, called LISTSERVs, than any other sport. LISTSERV addresses are included in the list at the end of the chapter.

The messages sent through LISTSERVs are essentially similar to those that are posted to UseNet newsgroups. Fans discuss their feelings about their team, their ideas about lineup/personnel changes, and so on.

At present, LISTSERVs exist for the following teams:

Atlanta Braves
Baltimore Orioles
Boston Red Sox
Chicago White Sox
Cincinnati Reds (not currently taking new subscribers)
Cleveland Indians
Kansas City Royals

Minnesota Twins
Montreal Expos
New York Mets
New York Yankees
Oakland Athletics
Philadelphia Phillies
Pittsburgh Pirates
San Francisco Giants
Seattle Mariners
Texas Rangers
Toronto Blue Jays

Other Internet Sites of Interest

In this section, we'll cover sites that are out of the mainstream of baseball coverage.

 ### Chris Berman's Nicknames

`wiretap.spies.com/00/Library/`
`Media/Games/berman.nik`

Chris Berman, one of the original studio hosts at ESPN, has made a name for himself in part for his ability to spice up his sportscasts with witty nicknames for the players in the highlights.

This Gopher site (see fig. 4.10) is a list of those names. Berman spouts off these nicknames constantly, and regularly makes up new ones. This list was compiled from messages posted to the UseNet newsgroup **rec.sport.baseball**, so it's possible some of Berman's quips have been overlooked.

Baseball Archive

`http://wuarchive.wustl.edu/pub/baseball/`

In addition to typical offerings like statistics, this site offers a complete list of radio and television affiliates for each team and e-mail addresses for each team.

Commercial Online Services

The major commercial online services such as Prodigy, CompuServe, and America Online all offer some type of baseball coverage through their various associations with news services.

The graphical interfaces and easy-to-follow menus make these services popular with baseball fans.

 Prodigy

Jump: `baseball`

Prodigy's baseball coverage is deep and thorough. It is offered through both the Associated Press and ESPN (see fig. 4.11).

At Prodigy's main baseball menu, you can choose several options. Clicking the AL/NL button brings you to the core of Prodigy's baseball offerings.

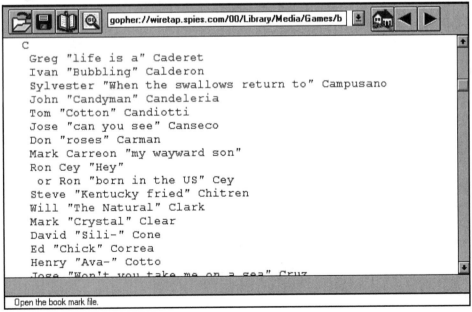

Figure 4.10 `wiretap.spies.com/00/Library/Media/Games/berman.nik`
A lengthy list of Chris Berman's funny nicknames.

This menu offers the following options:

- Scores
- Schedule and Starting Pitchers
- Standings
- Stats
- Team Reports
- Today's Stars
- Current Streaks

The Baseball Manager and Player Track buttons on the main menu are for those who participate in Rotisserie League baseball.

The Inside Info button leads you to a menu of headlines about several sports. The information is provided by ESPN.

The final choice is the AP Online button, which leads you to game stories, boxscores, baseball news, and more—all provided by the Associated Press.

Prodigy also carries a regular column by ESPN baseball analyst Peter Gammons, a former Boston Globe columnist who has the inside scoop on pro baseball. The column can be accessed from the main baseball menu.

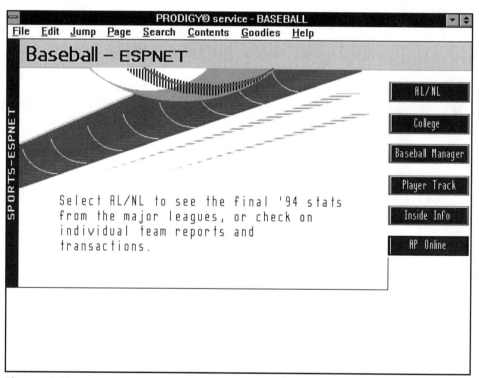

Figure 4.11 Jump: baseball

Prodigy's main baseball menu provides several information options.

America Online

Keyword: `baseball`

America Online's baseball coverage is typical of its coverage of all major sports leagues.

It includes Sports Ticker's stories, boxscores, standings, team-by-team notes, statistics, and more. It's a very thorough package that is presented in a user-friendly manner.

 CompuServe

Go: `apo`

CompuServe, like Prodigy, also offers Associated Press Online's coverage of Major League Baseball, but not much else.

The stories, standings, boxscores, and league statistical leaders are all on par with the other providers, but CompuServe doesn't offer team-by-team notes or the other extras.

Chapter Summary

This chapter covered the top sites on the Internet for baseball fans and provided some examples of team-specific sites that can be found.

On the following pages, you'll find a list of all of these sites plus much, much more, including a complete list of team-by-team sites.

The List

A complete list of addresses follows, including general baseball sites and a team-by-team list of Major League franchises. If you're not sure how to use an address, see Chapter 12, "Internet Basics."

General Baseball Sites

Archives

FTP Baseball Archive, including weekly stats updates:

> FTP address:
> `etext.archive.umich.edu/ pub/Sports/Baseball`

Swarthmore Baseball Archives:

> WWW address: `http:// eucalyptus.cc.swarthmore.edu/ pub/baseball/`

Washington University (St. Louis) Baseball Archives:

> WWW address: `http:// wuarchive.wustl.edu/pub/ baseball/`

World Wide Web (WWW) Virtual Library:

> WWW address: `http:// www.atm.ch.cam.ac.uk/ sports/baseball.html`

General Baseball Sites

Discussion Groups

Baseball discussion groups:

UseNet addresses:
```
rec.sport.baseball
rec.sport baseball.analysis
rec.sport.baseball.data
```

Foreign-Language Info

A baseball home page in German:

WWW address: `http://www.informatik.uni-freiburg.de/~leineweb/Baseball.html`

General Info

The Internet Baseball Information Center:

WWW address: `http://www.gems.com/ibic/`

Highlights

Highlights of the previous day's games:

WWW address: `http://tns-www.lcs.mit.edu/cgi-bin/sports/mlb/highlights`

Home Pages

Jason Kint's Baseball Page:

WWW address: `http://pear.wustl.edu/~jekint/baseball.html`

Nando X:

WWW address: `http://www.nando.net/baseball/bbmain.html`

Satchel Sports:

WWW address: `http://www.starwave.com/mlb/toc.html`

Sawdon's Baseball Page:

WWW address: `http://www.cs.cmu.edu:8001/afs/cs.cmu.edu/user/wsawdon/www/baseball.html`

Minor League Info

Nando X Minor League Baseball Server:

WWW address: `http://www.nando.net/baseball/bbminor.html`

News Stories

Game stories:

UseNet address:
`clari.sports.baseball.games`

News:

UseNet address:
`clari.sports.baseball`

Other

ESPN's Chris Berman's baseball nicknames:

Gopher address: `wiretap.spies.com/00/Library/Media/Games/berman.nik`

Rotisserie League Fans

The Baseball FTP site:

FTP address: `eucalyptus.cc.swarthmore.edu/pub/baseball/fanta-roto`

Schedules

Interactive schedule:

WWW address: `http://www.cs.rochester.edu/cgi-bin/ferguson/mlb`

Regular-season schedules:

Gopher address: `umslvma.umsl.edu:71/11/BASEBALL`

Servers

Nando X Baseball Server:

WWW address: `http://www.nando.net/baseball/bbserv.html`

Satchel Sports Major League Baseball Server:

WWW address: `http://www.starwave.com/mlb/toc.html`

Statistics

Scores and standings:

WWW address: `http://www.artsci.wustl.edu/`

Gopher address: `xmission.com:79/0robc`

Strike Info

The 1994-95 baseball strike:

WWW address: `http://www.nando.net/baseball/bbstrike.html`

Proposed fan boycott:

WWW address: `http://www.nando.net/baseball/bbs/boycott.html`

Team-by-Team List

Atlanta Braves

Nando X home-team page:

WWW address: `http://www.nando.net/baseball/bbs/bbhome/atl.html`

Newsgroup for discussion of the team:

UseNet address: `alt.sports.baseball.atlanta-braves`

Schedule:

WWW address: `http://www.starwave.com/mlb/sch/t-atl.html`

The Braves mailing list:

To subscribe, send e-mail to:
LISTSERV address: `listserv@gisatl.fidonet.org`

To post messages, send e-mail to:
`braves-l@gisatl.fidonet.org`

Team-by-Team List

Baltimore Orioles

Nando X home-team page:

WWW address: `http://www.nando.net/baseball/bbs/bbhome/bal.html`

Schedule information:

FTP address: `dsys.ncsl.nist.gov/pub/dwhite/os/orioles.html`

Schedule:

WWW address: `http://www.starwave.com/mlb/sch/t-bal.html`

Newsgroup for discussion of the team:

UseNet address: `alt.sports.baseball.balt-orioles`

The Orioles mailing list:

To subscribe, send e-mail to:

LISTSERV address: `oriole-fans-request@strdev.jhuapl.edu`

To post messages, send e-mail to:

`oriole-fans@strdev.jhapl.edu:`

Boston Red Sox

Nando X home-team page:

WWW address: `http://www.nando.net/baseball/bbs/bbhome/bos.html`

Local home page:

WWW address: `http://research.ftp.com/~solensky/bosox.html`

Newsgroup for discussion of the team:

UseNet address: `alt.sports.baseball.bos-redsox`

Schedule:

WWW address: `http://www.starwave.com/mlb/sch/t-bos.html`

The Red Sox mailing list:

To subscribe, send e-mail to:

LISTSERV address: `bosox-request@world.std.com`

To post messages, send e-mail to:

`Bosox@world.std.com:`

California Angels

Nando X home-team page:

WWW address: `http://www.nando.net/baseball/bbs/bbhome/cal.html`

Newsgroup for discussion of the team:

UseNet address: `alt.sports.baseball.calif-angels`

Schedule:

WWW address: `http://www.starwave.com/mlb/sch/t-cal.html`

Chicago Cubs

Nando X home-team page:

WWW address: `http://www.nando.net/baseball/bbs/bbhome/cub.html`

Newsgroup for discussion on the team:

UseNet address: `alt.sports.baseball.chicago-cubs`

Schedule:

WWW address: `http://www.starwave.com/mlb/sch/t-chc.html`

Chicago White Sox

Nando X home-team page:

WWW address: `http://www.nando.net/baseball/bbs/bbhome/cws.html`

Newsgroup for discussion of the team:

UseNet address: `alt.sports.baseball.chi-whitesox`

Schedule:

WWW address: `http://www.starwave.com/mlb/sch/t-chw.html`

The White Sox mailing list.

To subscribe, send e-mail to:
LISTSERV address:
`cid@athena.mit.edu`

To post messages, send e-mail to:

`white-sox@mit.edu`:

Cincinnati Reds

Nando X home-team page:

WWW address: `http://www.nando.net/baseball/bbs/bbhome/cin.html`

Schedule:

WWW address: `http://www.starwave.com/mlb/sch/t-cin.html`

Cleveland Indians

Nando X home-team page:

WWW address: `http://www.nando.net/baseball/bbs/bbhome/cle.html`

Local home pages:

WWW address: `http://ace.cs.ohiou.edu/personal/kmahoney/Indians/indians.html`

WWW address: `http://lady.wariat.org/1/sports/Indians`

Newsgroup for discussion of the team:

UseNet address: `alt.sports.baseball.cleve-indians`

Schedule:

WWW address: `http://www.starwave.com/mlb/sch/t-cle.html`

Team-by-Team List

An all-Cleveland sports teams mailing list:

To subscribe, send e-mail to:

LISTSERV address:
`aj755@cleveland.freenet.edu`

To post messages, send e-mail to:

`sports@wariat.org`

Colorado Rockies

Nando X home-team page:

WWW address: `http://www.nando.net/baseball/bbs/bbhome/col.html`

Schedule:

WWW address: `http://www.starwave.com/mlb/sch/t-col.html`

Detroit Tigers

Local home pages:

WWW address: `http://rs560.cl.msu.edu/~cookm/tigers/tigers.html`

WWW address: `web.cps.msu.edu/~woodruff/tigers/tigers.html`

Nando X home-team page:

WWW address: `http://www.nando.net/baseball/bbs/bbhome/det.html`

Newsgroup for discussion of the team:

UseNet address: `alt.sports.baseball.detroit-tigers`

Schedule:

WWW address: `http://www.starwave.com/mlb/sch/t-det.html`

Florida Marlins

Nando X home-team page:

WWW address: `http://www.nando.net/baseball/bbs/bbhome/fla.html`

Schedule:

WWW address: `http://www.starwave.com/mlb/sch/t-fla.html`

Houston Astros

Nando X home-team page:

WWW address: `http://www.nando.net/baseball/bbs/bbhome/hou.html`

Newsgroup for discussion of the team:

UseNet address: `alt.sports.baseball.houston-astros`

Schedule:

WWW address: `http://www.starwave.com/mlb/sch/t-hou.html`

Kansas City Royals

Nando X home-team page:

WWW address: `http://`
`www.nando.net/baseball/`
`bbs/bbhome/kcr.html`

Newsgroup for discussion of the team:

UseNet address: `alt.sports.`
`baseball.kc-royals`

Schedule:

WWW address: `http://`
`www.starwave.com/mlb/sch/`
`t-kan.html`

The Royals mailing list:

To subscribe, send e-mail to:
LISTSERV address:
`royals-request@mccall.com`

To post messages, send e-mail to:
`royals@mccall.com`:

Los Angeles Dodgers

Nando X home-team page:

WWW address: `http://`
`www.nando.net/baseball/`
`bbs/bbhome/lad.html`

Local home pages:

WWW address: `http://`
`www.armory.com/`
`~lew/sports/baseball/`
`dodgers.html`

WWW address: `http://`
`www.ugcs.caltech.edu/`
`~magyar/baseball.dodgers.html`

WWW address: `http://`
`www.cs.washington.edu/`
`homes/ugrads/shoe/dodgers/`
`bball.html`

Newsgroup for discussion of the team:

UseNet address: `alt.sports.`
`baseball.la-dodgers`

Schedule:

WWW address: `http://`
`www.starwave.com/mlb/sch/`
`t-los.html`

Milwaukee Brewers

Nando X home-team page:

WWW address: `http://`
`www.nando.net/baseball/`
`bbs/bbhome/mil.html`

Schedule:

WWW address: `http://`
`www.starwave.com/mlb/sch/`
`t-mil.html`

Minnesota Twins

Nando X home-team page:

WWW address: `http://`
`www.nando.net/baseball/`
`bbs/bbhome/min.html`

Schedule:

WWW address: `http://`
`www.starwave.com/mlb/sch/`
`t-min.html`

Team-by-Team List

The Twins mailing list:

To subscribe, send e-mail to:

LISTSERV address: `Deborah.Greene@Corp.Sun.COM`

To post messages, send e-mail to:

`fans@twins.Corp.Sun.COM`:

Montreal Expos

Nando X home-team page:

WWW address: `http://www.nando.net/baseball/bbs/bbhome/mon.html`

Newsgroup for discussion of the team:

UseNet address: `alt.sports.baseball.montreal-expos`

Schedule:

WWW address: `http://www.starwave.com/mlb/sch/t-mon.html`

The Expos mailing list:

To subscribe, send e-mail to:

LISTSERV address: `majordomo@cc.gatech.edu`

To post messages, send e-mail to:

`expos@cc.gatech.edu`:

New York Mets

Nando X home-team page:

WWW address: `http://www.nando.net/baseball/bbs/bbhome/nym.html`

Newsgroup for discussion of the team:

UseNet address: `alt.sports.baseball.ny-mets`

Schedule:

WWW address: `http://www.starwave.com/mlb/sch/t-nym.html`

The Mets mailing list:

To subscribe, send e-mail to:

LISTSERV address: `majordomo@cc.gatech.edu`

To post messages, send e-mail to:

`mets@cc.gatech.edu`:

New York Yankees

Nando X home-team page:

WWW address: `http://www.nando.net/baseball/bbs/bbhome/nyy.html`

Newsgroup for discussion of the team:

UseNet address: `alt.sports.baseball.ny-yankees`

Schedule:

WWW address: `http://www.starwave.com/mlb/sch/t-nyy.html`

The Yankees mailing list:

To subscribe, send e-mail to:

LISTSERV address: `jk5x+@andrew.cmu.edu`

Oakland Athletics

Nando X home-team page:

WWW address: `http://
www.nando.net/baseball/
bbs/bbhome/oak.html`

Schedule:

WWW address: `http://
www.starwave.com/mlb/sch/
t-oak.html`

The Athletics mailing list:

To subscribe, send e-mail to:

LISTSERV address:
`athletics-request@maredsous.
eng.sun.com`

To post messages, send e-mail to:

`athletics@maredsous.
eng.sun.com:`

Philadelphia Phillies

Local home page:

WWW address: `http://
strom.cadcam.iupi.edu/
phils.html`

Nando X home-team page:

WWW address: `http://
www.nando.net/baseball/
bbs/bbhome/phi.html`

Newsgroup for discussion of the team:

UseNet address: `alt.sports.
baseball.phila-phillies`

Schedule:

WWW address: `http://
www.starwave.com/mlb/sch/
t-phi.html`

The Phillies mailing list:

To subscribe, send e-mail to:

LISTSERV address:
`psyhank@vm.ouguelph.ca`

Pittsburgh Pirates

Nando X home-team page:

WWW address: `http://
www.nando.net/baseball/
bbs/bbhome/pit.html`

Schedule:

WWW address: `http://
www.starwave.com/mlb/sch/
t-pit.html`

The Pirates mailing list:

To subscribe, send e-mail to:

LISTSERV address:
`pirates-request@cats.ucsc.edu`

To post messages, send e-mail to:

`pirates@cats.ucsc.edu:`

San Diego Padres

Nando X home-team page:

WWW address: `http://
www.nando.net/baseball/
bbs/bbhome/sdp.html`

Team-by-Team List

Schedule:

> WWW address: `http://www.starwave.com/mlb/sch/t-sdg.html`

San Francisco Giants

Nando X home-team page:

> WWW address: `http://www.nando.net/baseball/bbs/bbhome/sfg.html`

Candlestick Park information (including ticket info):

> WWW address: `http://www.armory.com/~deadslug/candlestick_park.html`

Newsgroup for discussion of the team:

> UseNet address: `alt.sports.baseball.sf-giants`

Schedule:

> WWW address: `http://www.starwave.com/mlb/sch/t-sfo.html`

The Giants mailing list:

> To subscribe, send e-mail to:
> LISTSERV address: `giants-request@medraut.apple.com`

> To post messages, send e-mail to:
> `giants@medraut.apple.com:`

Seattle Mariners

Official Mariners home page (produced by the team):

> WWW address: `http://www.mariners.org/`

Nando X home-team page:

> WWW address: `http://www.nando.net/baseball/bbs/bbhome/sea.html`

FTP site:

> FTP address: `ftp.kei.com/pub/mariners`

Newsgroup for discussion of the team:

> UseNet address: `alt.sports.baseball.sea-mariners`

Schedule:

> WWW address: `http://www.starwave.com/mlb/sch/t-sea.html`

The Mariners mailing list:

> To subscribe, send e-mail to:
> LISTSERV address: `seattle-mariners-request@kei.com`

> To post messages, send e-mail to:
> `seattle-mariners@kei.com:`

St. Louis Cardinals

Nando X home-team page:

WWW address: `http://www.nando.net/baseball/bbs/bbhome/stl.html`

Newsgroup for discussion of the team:

UseNet address: `alt.sports.baseball.stl-cardinals`

Schedule:

WWW address: `http://www.starwave.com/mlb/sch/t-stl.html`

Texas Rangers

Nando X home-team page:

WWW address: `http://www.nando.net/baseball/bbs/bbhome/tex.html`

Newsgroup for discussion of the team:

UseNet address: `alt.sports.baseball.texas-rangers`

Schedule:

WWW address: `http://www.starwave.com/mlb/sch/t-tex.html`

To subscribe to the Texas Rangers News Service (this is not a LISTSERV):

E-mail address: `cs1442au@decster.uta.edu`

Toronto Blue Jays

Nando X home-team page:

WWW address: `http://www.nando.net/baseball/bbs/bbhome/tor.html`

Newsgroup for discussion of the team:

UseNet address: `alt.sports.baseball.tor-bluejays`

Schedule:

WWW address: `http://www.starwave.com/mlb/sch/t-tor.html`

The Blue Jays mailing list:

To subscribe, send e-mail to:

LISTSERV address: `jays-request@hivnet.ubc.ca`

To post messages, send e-mail to:

`jays@hivnet.ubc.ca:`

Chapter 5
Pro Basketball

This chapter is devoted to basketball fans, especially fans of the National Basketball Association.

S ince Magic Johnson and Larry Bird entered the NBA in the late 1970s, the NBA has grown more in popularity and influence than any other major professional league.

The NBA has also done more than any other league to promote itself, both within the U.S. and internationally. Though Johnson, Bird, and Michael Jordan have retired from the league, the NBA has built a foundation that is not likely to be torn down.

The NBA's rise resulted in a lot of Internet activity. NBA sites—be they for statistics, team-related information, news stories, or whatever—have been popping up all over the Internet. Many have stuck and have become popular sites where Interneties regularly visit.

NOTE

Of course, there are a lot of other basketball leagues besides the NBA, and a lot of people are interested in them. Don't worry, we haven't forgotten about you. If you're a college basketball junkie, check out Chapter 10, "College Sports." If you have an interest in European basketball leagues or international basketball competitions, take a look at Chapter 11, "Olympic and International Sports."

Getting the News and Stats

How'd the Lakers do last night? How many points did Shaq score? Did Charles Barkley play, or is his back still bothering him?

These are typical questions basketball fans ask on a daily basis, and traditionally the daily newspaper or ESPN were the best places to get the answers.

The Internet offers another way to get answers to these and many other questions.

Getting information from a credible source is essential for the true basketball fan, and there are several credible sources that contribute to the Internet.

Internet Sources

UseNet, a network within the Internet that consists mainly of newsgroups, also serves as a clearinghouse for professionally written stories—news, features, sports, and so on. These stories are generally produced by wire service reporters (most often from the Associated Press) and consist of game recaps, feature stories, and breaking news on such things as trades and injuries. The Associated Press and its online resources are discussed in depth in Chapter 1, "Sports News."

 Nando Sports Basketball Server

```
http://www.nando.net/
sports/bkb/1994/nba/
nba.html
```

This World Wide Web (WWW) home page, known as the Nando Sports Basketball Server (see fig. 5.3), contains a massive number of links to a variety of NBA-related sites and services.

As figure 5.3 shows, the first link connects you to "The NBA Today." This site serves as an excellent quick-reference first thing in the morning because it concentrates on trends and upcoming league action. Included is capsule-type coverage—usually known as "Briefs" in newspapers—on a number of topics, including "Who's Hot," and "Who's Not." Also included are previews of that day's games, a chance to look at who's playing who, and what to look for if you are going to be watching one of these games. There is also a "Tidbits" section, which includes the type of information found in a notebook column in a newspaper.

Charles Barkley

When Charles Barkley (see fig. 5.1) entered the NBA as a rookie with the Philadelphia 76ers, he did so with the nickname "The Round Mound of Rebound." He was supposed to add inside toughness and aggressiveness to a 76ers team sorely in need of both.

Throughout his career, he has been outspoken to the point of annoying both referees and team personnel. As his career has grown, he has polished both his game and his act to become a perennial all-star and someone who is respected—not loathed.

In the process, his nickname has also improved. He is now known as "Sir Charles." A Dream Teamer who now plays for the Phoenix Suns, Barkley has only one thing missing from his resume—an NBA championship.

The picture shown in figure 5.1 was downloaded from the Suns' home page at **http://www.nd.edu/ StudentLinks/mecheves/suns/ suns.html**.

Figure 5.1 http://www.nd.edu/StudentLinks/mecheves/suns/ suns.html
Charles Barkley has evolved from the "Round Mound of Rebound" to "Sir Charles."

The best sites for basic news coverage of the NBA are in UseNet's Clarinet and the World Wide Web (for more information on the World Wide Web, see "The World Wide Web" later in this chapter).

If you want to learn about yesterday's action or the games from another day during the current season, this home page also links you to an archive that contains that type of information. Once in the archive, you need merely to select a date and you'll find yourself immersed in stories on the games played on that date.

This home page also links you to "Today's Games," which contains score updates on games still in progress and more complete coverage of games that have ended.

Some Interesting Tidbits About AP Stories

For the past seven years, I've served as an Associated Press (AP) sportswriter. For the last two, I've covered the NBA, specifically the home games of the Minnesota Timberwolves. Writing for AP is strange in that I rarely get a chance to see my work in print. The stories I write (see fig. 5.2) appear in newspapers all over the country, but almost never in those in the Minneapolis-St. Paul area because the two daily papers here have their own beat reporters covering the Timberwolves.

So when I first gained access to the Internet, I quickly found the UseNet newsgroup on NBA basketball and immediately came across a story I had written on a Timberwolves game. It was a pleasant surprise.

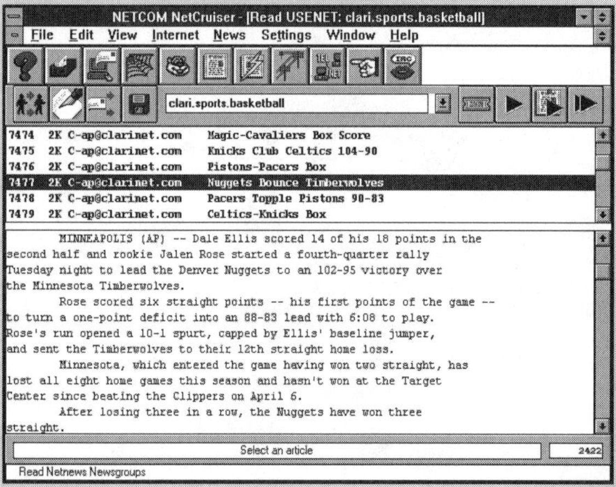

Figure 5.2 `clari.sports.basketball`
This is a story I wrote last December on a Timberwolves-Nuggets game (plucked from UseNet).

This site also serves as a link to a large number of other sites, including sites on specific teams. A complete list of basketball sites appears at the end of this chapter. This chapter also includes "Information on Your Favorite Team," which covers team-specific sites.

 Eric Richard's Basketball Server

`http://www.mit.edu:8001/`
`services/sis/NBA/NBA.html`

This basketball home page provides a number of links, but many of them remain a work-in-progress. The last few accesses I made to this site before publication indicated that it was not fully up and running. It maintains an archive of the most recent NBA draft and other information. More services are planned.

 The Gate Daily NBA Report

`http://sfgate.com:80/sports/`
`basketball/index.html`

Produced out of the San Francisco Chronicle newspaper, this basketball home page is a link to several NBA-related sources similar to those provided by the Nando X server.

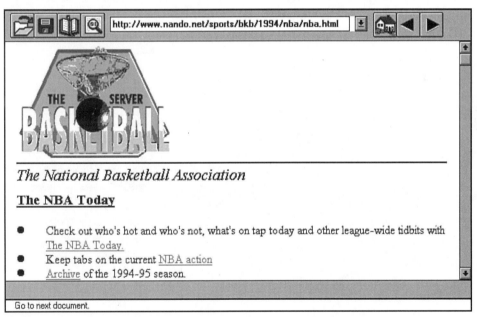

Figure 5.3 `http://www.nando.net/sports/bkb/1994/nba/nba.html`
The Nando Sports Basketball Server is an amazingly complete source for basketball information.

A newspaper strike caused this site to go untouched for some time. When the all the employees are at work, this is a strong source.

 Satchel Sports NBA Server

http://www.starwave.com/nba/toc.html

If you're getting ready to hit the sack but want to get a quick update on the games of the day, the Satchel Sports NBA home page (see fig. 5.4) links you to several useful sites. Included is a site that lists the day's games, including up-to-the-minute scores of games in progress.

Other information available includes statistics and transactions, plus an archive of past stories on NBA games.

 UseNet's Clarinet

clari.sports.basketball

This UseNet newsgroup is full of wire service stories on recent games, plus features, basketball news, and statistical references such as league standings, league leaders in several statistical categories, and game boxscores. Game stories and boxscores can appear at this address within an hour of the end of the game, but occasionally can take up to a full day.

> **NOTE**
>
> Some service providers charge extra for the use of Clarinet newsgroups. Also, access to Clarinet is subject to whether your Internet provider actually carries it.

TIME OUT

So What The Heck's A Notebook Column?

As a veteran sportswriter, I tend to lapse from time to time into what is called *journalese*—a journalist's lingo. A perfect example of that is the reference to the notebook column in the previous discussion of the Nando X basketball server.

A notebook column is a compilation of smaller news items that are likely to be of interest to fans, but are not meaty enough to become full stories on their own.

Typically, when reporters cover a game, they're responsible for writing a game story and a notebook. The notebook usually runs under a separate headline (for example, "Mavs Up Next For Wolves") and each note carries its own subhead (for example, "Quote of the Day," and "Injury Update"). A typical notebook column contains information on minor injuries, statistical items, and perhaps a quote or two.

Information on Your Favorite Team

Whether you're a season-ticket holder, an avid television watcher, the owner of a team jacket or cap, or merely someone who likes the games, there's probably one or two teams you identify with more than others.

> **NOTE**
>
> A complete team-by-team list of Internet sites appears at the end of this chapter.

On the Internet, you've got plenty of tools for finding information on your favorite team or, for that matter, the team you hate the most. There are newsgroups, bulletin boards, and World Wide Web home pages on just about every NBA franchise.

The World Wide Web

The World Wide Web (WWW) is growing by leaps and bounds every day, and it can be difficult to keep up with its progress. It has quickly become the most prolific source of sports-related sites, and it's an easy-to-use tool.

On the Web, you can find professionally operated sites that are updated daily (if not more often) and include links to just about everything you might want to know about your team. You can also find sites operated by individual fans, who may or may not be providing accurate information and, worse yet, may not even be on the Internet a week from now.

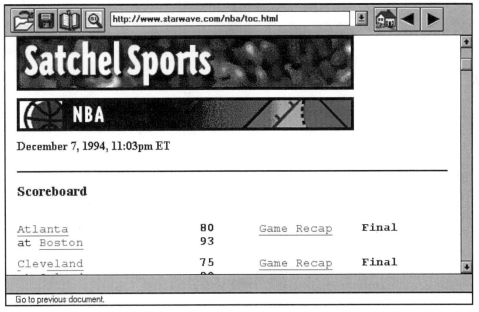

Figure 5.4 `http://www.starwave.com/nba/toc.html`
The Satchel Sports home page includes a link to an up-to-the-minute NBA scoreboard.

But that's okay. These sites provide a dynamic view of the NBA and its teams. While they can offer outstanding team coverage, news, and statistics, they also can give you interesting notes, tidbits, and even gossip (in some rare cases).

There is at least one site on the Web dedicated to every NBA team. These sites have simple interfaces that make moving site-to-site about as easy as it gets on the Internet.

Nando Sports Basketball Server

The Nando Sports Basketball Server includes a home page for every NBA team. Each page includes links to an extensive source of information on each team. The offerings include the following:

- Game stories
- Feature articles
- Archives of past game stories
- Boxscores and statistics
- Updated columns of notes and quotes
- Current team statistics and rosters
- Schedules for the current season
- Elements of teams' histories and other information

Also, each team site includes a link to current NBA standings and league leaders.

This is an excellent source of information and it is handled in a newsy, objective style. Other Internet sites that are produced by fans or other interested

parties in the home city generally have more of a "homer" feel to them.

In the next section, we've listed the addresses for each NBA division, which serve as links to the teams within that division. For the exact address of your favorite team, consult the list of addresses at the end of this chapter.

 NBA Atlantic Division

`http://www.nando.net/sports/`
`bkb/1994/nba/nbaatl.html`

East Coast basketball fans will find a home at the site that provides links to the seven teams in the NBA's Atlantic Division (see fig. 5.5).

The site includes the Boston Celtics, Miami Heat, New Jersey Nets, New York Knicks, Orlando Magic, Philadelphia 76ers, and Washington Bullets.

> **NOTE**
>
> The Nando Sports Basketball Server has a professional feel to it, while the other Internet sites that are locally handled generally are more fan-oriented. That is, when reading the team updates, you get a strong impression the writer is rooting for that particular team. Those sites are covered in the "Other Web Sites" section later in this chapter.

NBA Central Division

`http://www.nando.net/sports/`
`bkb/1994/nba/nbacent.html`

The preceding link to the teams in the NBA's Central Division includes the Atlanta Hawks, Charlotte Hornets, Chicago Bulls, Cleveland Cavaliers, Detroit Pistons, Indiana Pacers, and Milwaukee Bucks.

NBA Midwest Division

`http://www.nando.net/sports/`
`bkb/1994/nba/nbamidw.html`

This is the site for Texas basketball fans, as half of the six teams in the Midwest Division are within the Lone Star state. Teams covered here include the Dallas Mavericks (see fig. 5.6), Denver Nuggets, Houston Rockets, Minnesota Timberwolves, San Antonio Spurs, and Utah Jazz.

NBA Pacific Division

`http://www.nando.net/sports/`
`bkb/1994/nba/nbapaci.html`

The aptly named Pacific Division features seven West Coast teams, all covered with links from this site. This includes the Golden State Warriors, Los Angeles Lakers, Los Angeles Clippers, Phoenix Suns, Portland Trail Blazers, Sacramento Kings, and Seattle SuperSonics.

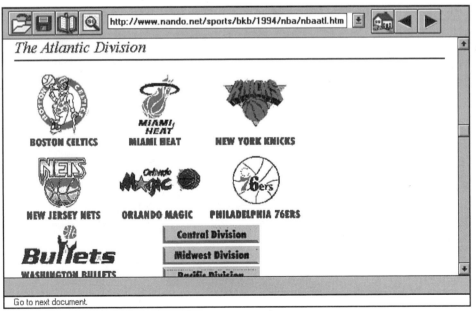

Figure 5.5 `http://www.nando.net/sports/bkb/1994/nba/nbaatl.html`
This site provides a link to information on every team in the NBA's Atlantic Division.

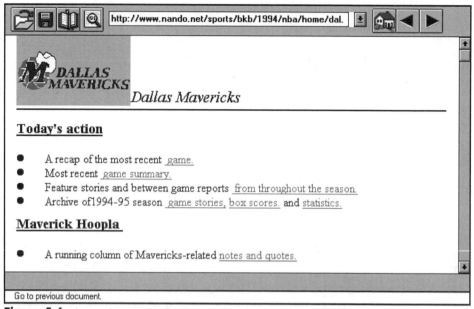

Figure 5.6 `http://www.nando.net/sports/bkb/1994/nba/nbamidw.html`
Once at one of these sites, click a team's logo for more information on that team.

 Satchel Sports NBA Server

`http://www.starwave.com/nba/toc.html`

The Satchel Sports NBA server also offers a home page for every NBA team.

These sites can be accessed from the standings page in the main Satchel NBA server, or by entering the address for a team (the specific addresses appear in the team-by-team list at the end of the chapter).

Each team's home page includes a link to a story on the last game that team played, plus a preview of the next game it will play. Also included are current standings for the division in which that team plays.

Other links are to the following:

- Complete NBA standings
- Team notes
- Team rosters
- Team schedules and results
- Team statistics
- Game-by-game logs of each team's season results

Other Web Sites

These other World Wide Web sites generally aren't linked by a particular home page or server. These are the type of sites that are produced by fans of particular teams; thus the information usually isn't as objective.

In some ways, that makes them more fun because they may contain gossip (such as trade rumors) that you might not find in other home-team sites.

This type of site, often administered by a single individual, can be somewhat elusive. On occasion, you may find that you no longer can reach these sites. Sometimes they reappear, sometimes they don't. We've tried to highlight those that have demonstrated some longevity.

 Orlando Magic

`http://pegasus.cc.ucf.edu/`
`~ec5868/magic.html`

The Orlando Magic is one of America's favorite NBA teams, due in large part to the tremendous exposure given to Shaquille O'Neal. This site includes a great deal of Magic information (see fig. 5.7), including updates on injuries and transactions plus the usual summaries of recent games and the team's outlook for the future.

5

PRO BASKETBALL

Figure 5.7 `http://pegasus.cc.ucf.edu/~ec5868/magic.html`
This Orlando Magic site includes a Picture of the Week.

Houston Rockets

http://www.med.uth.tmc.edu/
misc/rockets.html

Hakeem Olajuwon and the Rockets won the NBA title in 1994, and this site provides the latest news on the Houston franchise.

 ## Seattle SuperSonics

http://www.cs.hmc.edu/people/
byau/sonics.html

This site details all the latest information on one of the NBA's most exciting teams, the Seattle SuperSonics.

 ## Los Angeles Clippers

http://www.primenet.com/~terra/
clip.html

The Los Angeles Clippers began the 1994-95 NBA season with 16 straight losses, one short of an NBA record. As the losing streak grew, this site (see fig. 5.8) played host to a contest asking users to guess the date when the streak would be stopped. Two people—one of them the site administrator—picked the right date, Dec. 7.

Top Newsgroups for NBA Talk

UseNet newsgroups are a great place to meet and exchange information with

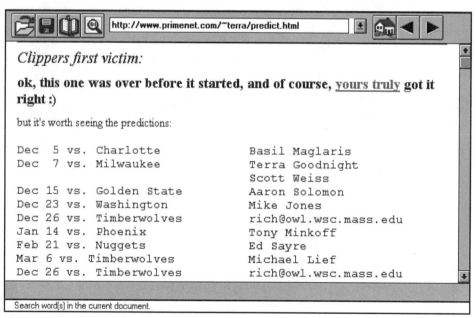

Figure 5.8 http://www.primenet.com~terra/clip.html
These types of sites are not above poking a little fun at the home team.

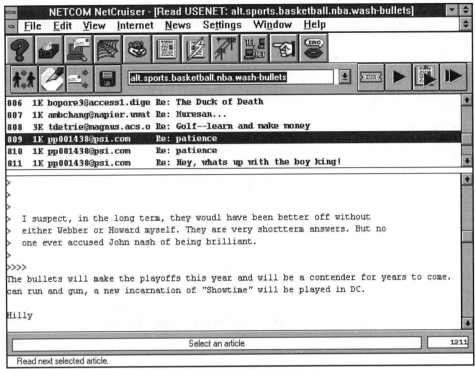

Figure 5.9 `alt.sports.basketball.nba.wash-bullets`
Washington Bullets fans argued on the Internet after the team traded for Chris Webber, the 1994 Rookie of the Year.

other basketball fans. Earlier in this chapter, you learned about the UseNet group `clari.sports.basketball`, which is a news service that contains basketball stories. UseNet also contains newsgroups that operate as bulletin boards for fans to post messages on specific teams and read messages posted by others. At this writing, 19 of the NBA's 27 teams have newsgroups dedicated just to them.

Accessing these groups varies according to the type of Internet connection you have. "Subscribing" to these groups means clicking a mouse in most cases. Consult your Internet service provider's documentation for specific instructions.

Once you've subscribed, you can scroll through a list of headers for UseNet messages posted within a team's newsgroup, pick a topic of your choice, and read that message and the responses of others (see fig. 5.9). You can respond to that message or post your own message on another topic.

TIP

For a list of current UseNet newsgroups, see table 5.1. These addresses are also provided in the team-by-team list at the end of this chapter.

Table 5.1   Current UseNet Newsgroups for NBA Teams

Team	Newsgroup
Atlanta Hawks	`alt.sports.basketball.nba.atlanta-hawks`
Boston Celtics	`alt.sports.basketball.nba.boston-celtics`
Charlotte Hornets	`alt.sports.basketball.nba.char-hornets`
Chicago Bulls	`alt.sports.basketball.nba.chicago-bulls`
Denver Nuggets	`alt.sports.basketball.nba.denver-nuggets`
Detroit Pistons	`alt.sports.basketball.nba.det-pistons`
G. State Warriors	`alt.sports.basketball.nba.gs-warriors`
Houston Rockets	`alt.sports.basketball.nba.hou-rockets`
Los Angeles Lakers	`alt.sports.basketball.nba.la-lakers`
Miami Heat	`alt.sports.basketball.nba.miami-heat`
Minnesota Timberwolves	`alt.sports.basketball.nba.mn-wolves`
New Jersey Nets	`alt.sports.basketball.nba.nj-nets`
New York Knicks	`alt.sports.basketball.nba.ny-knicks`
Orlando Magic	`alt.sports.basketball.nba.orlando-magic`
Phoenix Suns	`alt.sports.basketball.nba.phx-suns`
San Antonio Spurs	`alt.sports.basketball.nba.sa-spurs`
Seattle SuperSonics	`alt.sports.basketball.nba.seattle-sonics`
Utah Jazz	`alt.sports.basketball.nba.utah-jazz`
Washington Bullets	`alt.sports.basketball.nba.wash-bullets`

Other Internet Sources

Mailing lists act as suppliers to parties interested in specific topics. Once you subscribe to a list, you receive (via e-mail) any postings made to the list by other subscribers or the person who administers the list.

Subscribing to a list is as simple as contacting the list's subscription service, or LISTSERV. Then you will receive messages from the list itself, which has a different address to which you can send the messages you would like other subscribers to receive.

Cleveland Sports Mailing List

List address: **aj755@Cleveland.Freenet.Edu**

This list, known as the Cleveland Sports Mailing List, includes postings on the Cleveland Cavaliers, the Cleveland Indians, and the Cleveland Browns.

Boston Celtics Mailing List

List address: **celtics-admin@hillel.com**

This list is dedicated specifically to the Boston Celtics.

Other Interesting Sites

Chances are, you'll find something in this section that's to your liking.

The following sites are found within a variety of tools, including the World Wide Web, FTP, and so on.

Team Schedules

http://www.tns.lcs.mit.edu/cgi-bin/sports/nba/schedule

Does your favorite team have a game tonight? This site will provide you with an answer—it gives you all of tonight's NBA games by showing the teams' logos head-to-head. You also learn where the game is being played and the tip-off time.

If you want to know if your favorite team plays next weekend, this site also gives that option. By pointing to the desired date on a calendar, that day's games are displayed in the same format mentioned before.

Daily Schedules

http://wintermute.unh.edu/cgi-bin/nba-page.pl

When is the next time the Boston Celtics play the Los Angeles Lakers? One way to find out is to pull out an NBA schedule and try to find it yourself. With the page shown in figure 5.10, that's not necessary.

This page does all the work for you, enabling you to sort through the full NBA schedule in the following ways:

- You can pull up a schedule of your favorite team.
- You can pull up a schedule of games played on any chosen date during the entire season.
- You can pull up the full league schedule for the season.
- You can pick out the games played between two specific teams (refer to fig. 5.10) during the season.

5

PRO BASKETBALL

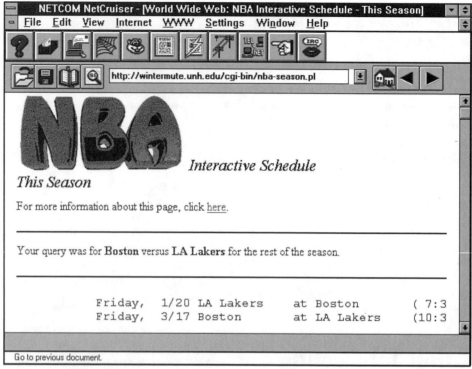

Figure 5.10 `http://wintermute.unh.edu/cgi-bin/nba-page.pl`
This World Wide Web page contains an interactive schedule that enables users to query the games between two specific teams.

 NBA Statistics

`wuarchive.wustl.edu/doc/misc/nbastats/facts`

Numbers, numbers, and more numbers. This site holds all of them. Updated weekly, it serves as a complete statistics database for league leaders and team-by-team statistics, listing every player in the league.

 NBA Fantasy Leagues

`http://www.hal.com/~markg/NBA`

This site is a World Wide Web page that serves as a weekly NBA pool competition, similar to a fantasy league, in which users can participate.

Commercial Online Services

Major commercial online services such as Prodigy, America Online, and CompuServe also provide links to basketball news, scores, statistics, and the like.

Each service has its own link to stories on individual games or other items of league-wide interest.

Part of the beauty of the commercial online service providers is the easy interfaces used to move from place to place. After entering a simple command, these services generally operate on point-and-click interfaces that ease navigating.

> **TIP**
>
> If you're interested in basic information in a slick format, go with Prodigy. America Online provides the most complete offerings, especially in the area of statistics. CompuServe provides a nice mix of the services offered by the other two providers.

Whether you're on the Internet or not, two of the leading commercial online service providers offer enough team-specific information to make a membership worth consideration.

America Online and Prodigy each offer team-by-team breakdowns of statistics and information, but CompuServe doesn't as yet.

 America Online

Keyword: **Basketball**

America Online offers team-by-team notes, which are provided by Sports Ticker—its sports news and information provider. It's a successful partnership because Sports Ticker's offerings are vast. Besides game stories, box-scores, standings, and all the other usual offerings, Sports Ticker gives AOL subscribers a complete list of statistics, updated weekly, for every player in the NBA.

The notes are somewhat difficult to follow because they are all lumped together in a single paragraph. But they contain the typical "extra" information that die-hard fans are looking for (see fig. 5.11).

After entering Keyword: **basketball**, double-click Basketball in the menu provided. Scrolling down the basketball menu leads you to two items, Eastern Conference Notes and Western Conference Notes. Double-click your choice and you'll be able to read briefs on each team in that conference.

 Prodigy

Jump: **ESPNet**

Prodigy has the most complete team-by-team section of any commercial service. Each team's section includes a menu that leads to news and notes, current team statistics, the team's schedule, injury reports, a recap and

5

PRO BASKETBALL

boxscore of the most recent game, and a game-by-game log of the current season.

After entering Jump: **ESPNet**, follow these steps:

1. Click Select a Sport.

2. Click Basketball.

3. Click NBA.

4. Choose Eastern Conference Notes or Western Conference Notes.

5. Click the box next to your team's name.

ESPN's SportsCenter is probably one of your favorite shows. Since the cable network started up in the late 1970s, SportsCenter has been a staple of most sports fans in the U.S.

Prodigy has hooked up with ESPN to provide some of the sports-related information available on the service. It's a truly unique online link; the vast majority of news available on computer comes from a text-based service rather than from television.

The link has proved successful, and ESPNet's basketball offerings are typical of what the network is all about— short and snappy, but full of information and graphics (see fig. 5.12).

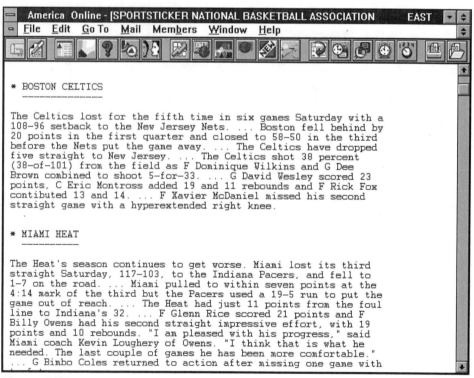

Figure 5.11 Keyword: basketball
America Online's team-by-team notes are lumped together in a single paragraph, but they're informative.

```
┌──────────────────────────────────────────────────────────────────┐
│ ═                    PRODIGY® service - BASKETBALL          ▼ ▲▼   │
│ File  Edit  Jump  Page  Search  Contents  Goodies  Help           │
│ ┌──────────────────────────────────────────────────────────────┐ │
│ │ NBA  SCORES — ESPNET           2/5/95,  9:27 PM ET           │ │
│ │ ┌─┐ SEATTLE      136  FINAL              ┌─────────┐         │ │
│ │ │1│ MIAMI        109                     │Schedules│         │ │
│ │ └─┘                                      └─────────┘         │ │
│ │ ┌─┐ NEW YORK     100  FINAL              ┌─────────┐         │ │
│ │ │2│ ORLANDO      103  IN OT              │Standings│         │ │
│ │ └─┘                                      └─────────┘         │ │
│ │ ┌─┐ WASHINGTON   105  FINAL              ┌──────────┐        │ │
│ │ │3│ CHARLOTTE    111                     │Statistics│        │ │
│ │ └─┘                                      └──────────┘        │ │
│ │ ┌─┐ HOUSTON      124  FINAL    Games of  ┌────┐             │ │
│ │ │4│ PHOENIX      100           Sunday,   │Odds│             │ │
│ │ └─┘                          February 5  └────┘             │ │
│ │ ┌─┐ MINNESOTA     82  FINAL              ┌──────────┐        │ │
│ │ │5│ BOSTON       115                     │East Teams│        │ │
│ │ └─┘                                      └──────────┘        │ │
│ │ ┌─┐ CHICAGO       63  10:07 LEFT         ┌──────────┐        │ │
│ │ │6│ GOLDEN ST     52  3RD QTR            │West Teams│        │ │
│ │ └─┘                                      └──────────┘        │ │
│ │                                          ┌──────┐           │ │
│ │                                          │Awards│           │ │
│ │                                          └──────┘           │ │
│ │                                          ┌─────────┐        │ │
│ │                                          │All-Stars│        │ │
│ │                                          └─────────┘        │ │
│ │                                          ┌──────────┐       │ │
│ │                                          │Prev Games│       │ │
│ │                                          └──────────┘       │ │
│ └──────────────────────────────────────────────────────────────┘ │
└──────────────────────────────────────────────────────────────────┘
```

Figure 5.12 Jump: ESPNet
ESPNet's information is short and snappy, but full of information and graphics.

AP Online—the Associated Press wire service's coverage of NBA action—also is available. This is also available on CompuServe. For more information on the Associated Press (AP), see "What Is the Associated Press?" in Chapter 1.

 **CompuServe**

Go: **APO**

The AP, through Associated Press Online, serves CompuServe's subscribers with basketball and other sports information.

Once you've reached the Associated Press Online menu, simply highlight Basketball and click Select. That immediately brings you to a menu of headers that includes game stories, boxscores, standings, and some statistics.

Chapter Summary

In this chapter, you have learned about several Internet sources for NBA news and statistics, and you have learned some of the top places to go for information on your favorite team.

The List

A complete list of addresses follows, including general basketball sites and a team-by-team list of NBA franchises. If you're not sure how to use an address, see Chapter 12, "Internet Basics."

General Basketball Sites

Servers

Up-to-the-minute scores, statistics, transactions, as well as archived stories:

WWW address: `http://www.starwave.com/nba/toc.html`

Nando X Basketball Server:

WWW address: `http://www.nando.net/sports/bkb/1994/nba/nba.html`

Eric Richards' Professional Basketball Server:

WWW address: `http://www.mit.edu:8001/services/sis/NBA/NBA.html`

The Gate Cybersports NBA Page, including a daily NBA report and links to other NBA information:

WWW address: `http://sfgate.com:80/sports/sports/nba/index.html`

NBA team home pages:

WWW address: `http://tns-www.lcs.mit.edu/cgibin/sports/nba/teams`

Atlantic Division team reports:

WWW address: `http://www.nando.net/sports/bkb/1994/nba/nbaatl.html`

Central Division team reports:

WWW address: `http://www.nando.net/sports/bkb/1994/nba/nbacent.html`

Midwest Division team reports:

WWW address: `http://www.nando.net/sports/bkb/1994/nba/nbamidw.html`

Pacific Division team reports:

WWW address: `http://www.nando.net/sports/bkb/1994/nba/nbapaci.html`

A complete pick-by-pick account of the most recent NBA draft:

WWW address: `http://www.mit.edu:8001/services/sis/NBAdraft_results`

News and Statistics

Who's hot and who's not, previews of upcoming games, and a league-wide tidbits column:

WWW address: `http://www.nando.net/sports/bkb/1994/nba/stat/nbatoday.html`

Daily game stories from the current NBA season:

WWW address: `http://www.nando.net/newsroom/basketball/1994/nba/year/nbaarchive.html`

Daily previews of NBA games:

WWW address: `http://www.nando.net/newsroom/basketball/1994/nba/game/todaysgames.html`

Team-by-Team List

NBA statistics:

> WWW address: `http://www.mit.edu:8001/services/sis/NBA/html/NBAStats.html`

> FTP address: `wuarchive.wustl.edu/doc/misc/nbastats/facts`

Eric Richards' Professional Basketball Server:

> WWW address: `http://www.mit.edu:8001/services/sis/NBA/NBA.html`

Other

A weekly NBA fantasy pool:

> WWW address: `http://www.hal.com/~markg/NBA/`

A basketball simulation game featuring former Golden State coach Don Nelson:

> WWW address: `http://www.nando.net/sports/bkb/1994/shareware/nelly.html`

Schedules

Interactive NBA schedules that enable users to sort the current schedule by team or by matchups:

> WWW address: `http://www.tns.lcs.mit.edu/cgi-bin/sports/nba/schedule`

> WWW address: `http://wintermute.unh.edu/cgi.bin/nba-page.pl`

Atlanta Hawks

Nando X home-team page:

> WWW address: `http://www.nando.net/sports/bkb/1994/nba/home/atl.html`

Satchel Sports home-team page:

> WWW address: `http://www.starwave.com/nba/clb/atl.html`

Newsgroup for discussion on the team:

> UseNet address: `alt.sports.basketball.nba.atlanta-hawks`

Boston Celtics

Nando X home-team page:

> WWW address: `http://www.nando.net/sports/bkb/1994/nba/home/bos.html`

Satchel Sports home-team page:

> WWW address: `http://www.starwave.com/nba/clb/bos.html`

Newsgroup for discussion on the team:

> UseNet address: `alt.sports.basketball.nba.boston-celtics`

Local home page:

> WWW address: `http://www.ics.com/~drisko/celtics.html`

Team-by-Team List

The Celtics mailing list:

To subscribe, send e-mail to :

LISTSERV address: `celtics-admin@hillel.com`

To post messages send e-mail to:

`celtics@HILLEL.com`

Charlotte Hornets

Nando X home-team page:

WWW address: `http://www.nando.net/sports/bkb/1994/nba/home/cha.html`

Satchel Sports home-team page:

WWW address: `http://www.starwave.com/nba/clb/cha.html`

Newsgroup for discussion on the team:

UseNet address: `alt.sports.basketball.nba.char-hornets`

Chicago Bulls

Nando X home-team page:

WWW address: `http://www.nando.net/sports/bkb/1994/nba/home/chi.html`

Satchel Sports home-team page:

WWW address: `http://www.starwave.com/nba/clb/chi.html`

Newsgroup for discussion on the team:

UseNet address: `alt.sports.basketball.nba.chicago-bulls`

Little John's Bulls, a local home page:

WWW address: `http://www.ils.nwu.edu/~richards/bulls.html`

Cleveland Cavaliers

Nando X home-team page:

WWW address: `http://www.nando.net/sports/bkb/1994/nba/home/cle.html`

Satchel Sports home-team page:

WWW address: `http://www.starwave.com/nba/clb/cle.html`

Local home pages:

WWW address: `http://ace.cs.ohiou.edu/personal/kmahoney/Cavs/cavs.html`

WWW address: `http://lady.wariat.org/1/sports/Cavs`

The Cavaliers mailing list:

To subscribe, send e-mail to: LISTSERV address: `aj755@Cleveland.Freenet.Edu`

To post messages, send e-mail to: `@tribe.b15.ingr.com`

Dallas Mavericks

Nando X home-team page:

WWW address: `http://www.nando.net/sports/bkb/1994/nba/home/dal.html`

Satchel Sports home-team page:

WWW address: `http://www.starwave.com/nba/clb/dal.html`

Denver Nuggets

Nando X home-team page:

WWW address: `http://www.nando.net/sports/bkb/1994/nba/home/den.html`

Satchel Sports home-team page:

WWW address: `http://www.starwave.com/nba/clb/den.html`

Newsgroup for discussion on the team:

UseNet address: `alt.sports.basketball.nba.denver-nuggets.`

Detroit Pistons

Nando X home-team page:

WWW address: `http://www.nando.net/sports/bkb/1994/nba/home/det.html`

Satchel Sports home-team page:

WWW address: `http://www.starwave.com/nba/clb/det.html`

Newsgroup for discussion on the team:

UseNet address: `alt.sports.basketball.nba.det-pistons.`

Golden State Warriors

Nando X home-team page:

WWW address: `http://www.nando.net/sports/bkb/1994/nba/home/gld.html`

Satchel Sports home-team page:

WWW address: `http://www.starwave.com/nba/clb/gsw.html`

Newsgroup for discussion on the team:

UseNet address: `alt.sports.basketball.nba.gs-warriors`

Local home page:

WWW address: `http://www.hotwired.com/Staff/michael/gsw/`

Houston Rockets

Nando X home-team page:

WWW address: `http://www.nando.net/sports/bkb/1994/nba/home/hou.html`

Satchel Sports home-team page:

WWW address: `http://www.starwave.com/nba/clb/hou.html`

Team-by-Team List

Newsgroup for discussion on the team:

UseNet address: `alt.sports.basketball.nba.hou-rocket`

Local home page:

WWW address: `http://www.med.uth.tmc.edu/misc/rockets.html`

Indiana Pacers

Nando X home-team page:

WWW address: `http://www.nando.net/sports/bkb/1994/nba/home/ind.html`

Satchel Sports home-team page:

WWW address: `http://www.starwave.com/nba/clb/ind.html`

Los Angeles Clippers

Nando X home-team page:

WWW address: `http://www.nando.net/sports/bkb/1994/nba/home/lac.html`

Satchel Sports home-team page:

WWW address: `http://www.starwave.com/nba/clb/lac.html`

Local home page:

WWW address: `http://www.primenet.com/~terra/clip.html`

Los Angeles Lakers

Nando X home-team page:

WWW address: `http://www.nando.net/sports/bkb/1994/nba/home/lal.html`

Satchel Sports home-team page:

WWW address: `http://www.starwave.com/nba/clb/lal.html`

Newsgroup for discussion on the team:

UseNet address: `alt.sports.basketball.nba.la-lakers`

Local home pages:

WWW address: `http://www.primenet.com/~genzale/lakers.html`

WWW address: `http://www.primenet.com/~terra/laker.html`

WWW address: `http://www.armory.com/~lew/sports/basketball/`

Miami Heat

Nando X home-team page:

WWW address: `http://www.nando.net/sports/bkb/1994/nba/home/mia.html`

Satchel Sports home-team page:

WWW address: `http://www.starwave.com/nba/clb/mia.html`

Newsgroup for discussion on the team:

UseNet address: `alt.sports.basketball.nba.miami-heat`

Milwaukee Bucks

Nando X home-team page:

WWW address: `http://www.nando.net/sports/bkb/1994/nba/home/mil.html`

Satchel Sports home-team page:

WWW address: `http://www.starwave.com/nba/clb/mil.html`

Minnesota Timberwolves

Nando X home-team page:

WWW address: `http://www.nando.net/sports/bkb/1994/nba/home/min.html`

Satchel Sports home-team page:

WWW address: `http://www.starwave.com/nba/clb/min.html`

Newsgroup for discussion on the team:

UseNet address: `alt.sports.basketball.nba.mn-wolves`

New Jersey Nets

Nando X home-team page:

WWW address: `http://www.nando.net/sports/bkb/1994/nba/home/njn.html`

Satchel Sports home-team page:

WWW address: `http://www.starwave.com/nba/clb/njn.html`

Newsgroup for discussion on the team:

UseNet address: `alt.sports.basketball.nba.nj-nets`

New York Knicks

Nando X home-team page:

WWW address: `http://www.nando.net/sports/bkb/1994/nba/home/nyk.html`

Satchel Sports home-team page:

WWW address: `http://www.starwave.com/nba/clb/nyk.html`

Newsgroup for discussion on the team:

UseNet address: `alt.sports.basketball.nba.ny-knicks`

Team-by-Team List

Local home page:

WWW address: `http://
www.mit.edu:8001/afs/
athena.mit.edu
/user/e/f/efgilmou/WWW/
knicks.html`

Orlando Magic

Nando X home-team page:

WWW address: `http://
www.nando.net/sports/bkb/
1994/nba/home/orl.html`

Satchel Sports home-team page:

WWW address: `http://
www.starwave.com/nba/clb/
orl.html`

Newsgroup for discussion on the team:

UseNet address: `alt.sports.
basketball.nba.orlando-magic`

Local home pages:

WWW address: `http://
pegasus.cc.ucf.edu/
~ec5868/magic.html`

WWW address: `http://
www.primenet.com/
~genzale.magic.html`

Philadelphia 76ers

Nando X home-team page:

WWW address: `http://
www.nando.net/sports/bkb/
1994/nba/home/phi.html`

Satchel Sports home-team page:

WWW address: `http://
www.starwave.com/nba/clb/
phi.html`

Phoenix Suns

Nando X home-team page:

WWW address: `http://
www.nando.net/sports/bkb/
1994/nba/home/pho.html`

Satchel Sports home-team page:

WWW address: `http://
www.starwave.com/nba/clb/
pho.html`

Newsgroup for discussion on the team:

UseNet address: `alt.sports.
basketball.nba.phx-suns`

Local home pages:

WWW address: `http://
www.primenet.com/
~shannon/index.html`

WWW address: `http://
www.nd.edu/StudentLinks/
mecheves/suns/suns.html`

Portland Trail Blazers

Nando X home-team page:

WWW address: `http://
www.nando.net/sports/bkb/
1994/nba/home/por.html`

Satchel Sports home-team page:

WWW address: `http://www.starwave.com/nba/clb/por.html`

Sacramento Kings

Nando X home-team page:

WWW address: `http://www.nando.net/sports/bkb/1994/nba/home/sac.html`

Satchel Sports home-team page:

WWW address: `http://www.starwave.com/nba/clb/sac.html`

San Antonio Spurs

Nando X home-team page:

WWW address: `http://www.nando.net/sports/bkb/1994/nba/home/san.html`

Satchel Sports home-team page:

WWW address: `http://www.starwave.com/nba/clb/sas.html`

Newsgroup for discussion on the team:

UseNet address: `alt.sports.basketball.nba.sa-spurs`

Seattle SuperSonics

Nando X home-team page:

WWW address: `http://www.nando.net/sports/bkb/1994/nba/home/sea.html`

Satchel Sports home-team page:

WWW address: `http://www.starwave.com/nba/clb/sea.html`

Newsgroup for discussion on the team:

UseNet address: `alt.sports.basketball.nba.seattle-sonics`

Local home page:

WWW address: `http://www.cs.hmc.edu/people/byau/sonics.html`

Utah Jazz

Nando X home-team page:

WWW address: `http://www.nando.net/sports/bkb/1994/nba/home/uta.html`

Satchel Sports home-team page:

WWW address: `http://www.starwave.com/nba/clb/uth.html`

Newsgroup for discussion on the team:

UseNet address: `alt.sports.basketball.nba.utah-jazz`

Team-by-Team List

Vancouver Grizzlies

Local home page:

WWW address: `http://www.uniserve.com/swbbs/grizzlie.html`

Washington Bullets

Nando X home-team page:

WWW address: `http://www.nando.net/sports/bkb/1994/nba/home/was.html`

Satchel Sports home-team page:

WWW address: `http://www.starwave.com/nba/clb/was.html`

Newsgroup for discussion on the team:

UseNet address: `alt.sports.basketball.nba.wash-bullets`

Chapter 6
Pro Hockey

With the recent strike, hockey fans could have finally grown weary of the arrogance of professional athletes and management. They didn't.

Pro hockey fans, much like their pro baseball counterparts, were held hostage at the end of 1994. Just before a new season was about to begin in October, National Hockey League owners locked out their players.

The NHL was fresh off the wave of publicity created by improved television exposure and the New York Rangers' first Stanley Cup title in more than half a century.

The 1994-95 season could have marked the turning point for a league that has long been considered fourth among the four major professional sports leagues. Instead, it was put on hold for more than three months.

In January, however, a settlement was reached and play resumed. Although the fans could have finally grown weary of the arrogance of professional athletes and management, they didn't. The players were greeted with sellout crowds upon their return.

During the lockout, much of the Internet activity surrounding the NHL went dormant. Home pages devoted to teams were put on hold because there were no teams to talk (or write) about. Newsgroups carried few messages; those that did appear generally dealt with team information specific to start off the new regular season.

Only news Internet sources were active, carrying wire service and newspaper accounts of the negotiations.

Once they reached a settlement, Internet traffic immediately picked up. Was the traffic directed by fans proclaiming that they would never return to the rinks?

No.

Instead, it involved fans searching for revised schedules (see fig. 6.1), talking about roster spots, and their favorite team's chances, and arguing about which team would win the '95 Stanley Cup.

It's part of the nature of being a fan—when the games are on, we pay attention, regardless of what has occurred in the past. Some cynics turn away for a time, then find themselves being pulled back into the action. Only the most jaded fans turn away for good.

Hockey still has its chance. A true sign of the fans' dedication to the sport is that all of the team home pages that were on the Internet at the time of the Rangers' championship returned to activity after the strike—with the addition of some new ones.

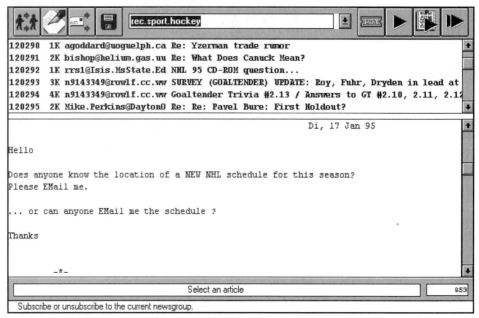

Figure 6.1   rec.sport.hockey
The NHL strike settlement sent hockey fans to this site looking for information about the league's revised schedule.

This chapter is for the hockey fan—the one who will stick with it through thick and thin, the one who isn't quite sure and, yes, even the one that promises never to go back.

Getting the News and Statistics

Now that there is hockey again—for a few years at least—hockey fans are looking for news and statistics sources on a nightly basis.

Hockey is still the least-covered, least-watched sport among the four major pro sports. At times, fans struggle to find coverage of the NHL. This is especially true in areas of the United States that don't have a nearby NHL franchise.

For news coverage of the NHL, check out UseNet's Clarinet and the World Wide Web. The Web and FTP servers are great places to check for statistics sources.

Because the NHL is not yet as popular in the United States as the NBA, NFL, and Major League Baseball, NHL coverage on the Internet is vastly different. In each of the other three sports, news sources on the Internet are plentiful—even though some are unreliable.

With hockey, it's difficult to find a strong Internet source for news—that is, game stories, features, and breaking news stories like trades, injuries, contract disputes, and so on.

Those hockey fans who are on the Internet and aren't willing—or can't afford—to pay the monthly fee of a commercial service provider aren't completely out of luck, however.

 Satchel Sports

```
http://www.starwave.com/nhl/
toc.html
```

6

PRO HOCKEY

Like all of Satchel Sports' home pages, the NHL pages includes one link that few others offer—the up-to-the-minute scoreboard of games in progress.

It gives you the feel of being in the newsroom at ESPN (see fig. 6.2), with the primary exception that you won't be able to actually *watch* the games in progress. But the scores are updated constantly, so stopping off at this site at any time of night gives you a picture of what's going on in the NHL at that moment.

Shortly after each game concludes, a written recap of the action is available, along with a boxscore so you can check who got all the goals and assists.

This site is the best source for news stories that keep you informed on all the happenings around the NHL. Other NHL links include the following:

- Reports on each team
- Daily schedules and team schedules
- An updated list of transactions
- Previews of certain games
- Rosters for every team
- A running column called "Inside the NHL"

Figure 6.2 `http://www.starwave.com/nhl/toc.html`
Satchel Sports operates one of only a few NHL news sources on the Internet.

Wayne Gretzky

What's left to be said about Wayne Gretzky?

The Great One, as he is known, has broken just about every offensive record in the NHL record book. Included are all the biggies: most career goals, most career assists, most career points—plus all the single-season records in these categories.

Most importantly, he's a winner, having won four Stanley Cups with the Edmonton Oilers.

During his greatest seasons, which came in the 1980s, Gretzky was more dominant in his sport than any other athlete in any other sport at any time in history.

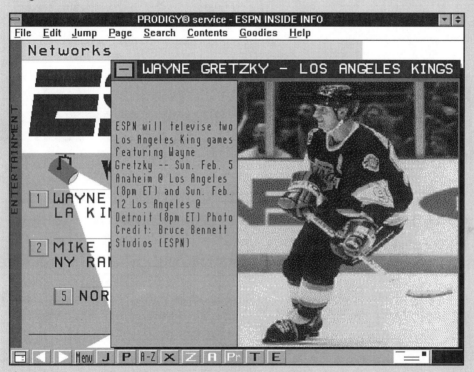

Figure 6.3 Jump: ESPNet
No player has scored more NHL goals than Wayne Gretzky.

 **UseNet's Clarinet**

clari.sports.hockey

The Clarinet portion of the UseNet network contains the newsgroups dedicated to news gathering. This hockey newsgroup is full of Associated Press and Canadian Press stories on NHL games (see fig. 6.4), plus the boxscores that accompany them.

These items don't appear online as quickly as those on the aforementioned Satchel Sports site, but they offer complete game coverage.

> **NOTE**
>
> Some service providers charge extra for the use of Clarinet newsgroups. Also, access to Clarinet is subject to whether your Internet provider actually carries it.

The stories are written by professional sportswriters and often include quotes from the players and coaches. The package includes a boxscore on each game, league standings, and league leaders (updated nightly). For more information on the Associated Press, see "What Is the Associated Press?" in Chapter 1, "Sports News."

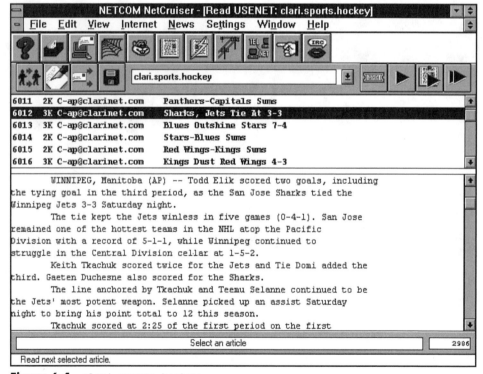

Figure 6.4 `clari.sports.hockey`
An Associated Press story on an NHL game from the 1994-95 season.

NHL Statserver

`http://terrapin.umd.edu/`
`nhl.html`

Numbers, numbers, and more numbers! If you're an NHL fan, this site (see fig. 6.5) provides you with an incredible list of resources. If you're a history buff, the offerings are even more amazing.

Let's start with the schedule. You can use the current season's schedule as a complete day-by-day listing, or you can call up a specific team's slate of games. Even better, you can pull up a month-at-a-glance schedule that looks like a

page off your desk calendar, with each square containing a list of that day's games.

So you want to find out where to pick up a game on the radio? This site links you to a listing, by team, of radio stations that carry the games. It also includes team addresses and phone numbers and a complete payroll for each NHL squad.

TIP

If you're a history buff, look no further than the NHL Statserver for the best site to find all the historical information you'll likely ever need.

Locker Rooms Can Be Confusing Places

I was involved in the Associated Press' coverage of the Stanley Cup finals between the Pittsburgh Penguins and the Minnesota North Stars in the spring of 1991.

For major events like this, media outlets often send extra reporters, some of whom have been covering extra beats and aren't familiar with the players. That—combined with the North Stars' unexpected run to the finals and the lack of exposure NHL players received at the time—led to one of the funniest locker room scenes I've witnessed.

I approached a North Stars player who was being interviewed by a television

reporter. The reporter was asking about what it meant to Neal Broten to be a Minnesota native representing his state's hockey team in the Stanley Cup finals.

The problem was, the player he was interviewing was Dave Gagner. Even better, Gagner answered all the reporters' questions with a straight face, giving well-thought-out, seemingly heartfelt responses.

Later, I asked Gagner if he had set the reporter up. Ganger confided, "He came up to me and said, 'Neal, can I talk to you for a minute?' and I just didn't have the heart to embarrass the guy."

TIME OUT

6

PRO HOCKEY

The new schedule has been installed. Thanks George!
The NHL Page contains links to NHL and other hockey resources, stats, historical information, and schedule information for the current NHL season. The schedule is updated daily. If you have a comment, a suggestion or a new link, please send it to knox@monster.umd.edu.

Documents compiled by: Glenn Chin, Lydia Mancini, Tom Wilson and Garry Knox.

Last Updated: January 15, 1995

NHL 94-95 (after lockout) schedule for Friday, 1/20...

Figure 6.5 `http://terrapin.umd.edu/nhl.html`
The NHL Statserver offers more than a plateful of information.

On the statistics front, this site links you to team-by-team stats, standings, and a schedule that includes the results of completed games. Also available is a link to team-vs.-team records, so you can find out how the Rangers have done against, say, the Devils thus far this season.

But perhaps the most impressive part of this site is the link to an archive of historical information that takes you as far back into NHL lore as you desire.

The offerings include the following:

- All-time team records
- Stanley Cup champions (including their records in the season immediately following their title year)
- A yearly list of regular-season champions and playoff results

- Records from the 1980s
- Playoff records for current NHL teams
- An archive of NHL dynasties and teams that nearly became dynasties
- A list of all-time Stanley Cup finalists
- A chart that documents the history of expansion in the NHL
- A complete list of every uniform number that has been retired by each NHL team
- A list of each NHL postseason award and the players who have won them

If that isn't enough to satisfy your appetite, then you're a stat-aholic of the highest order.

Hawaii's NHL Home Page

`http://maxwell.uhh.hawaii.edu/`
`hockey/hockey.html`

The words "Hawaii" and "hockey" seldom appear in the same sentence, unless that sentence is, "There is no hockey in Hawaii."

That may be true, but Hawaii's NHL Home Page (see fig. 6.6) is an excellent statistics server based in Honolulu. While the NHL Statserver is clearly the best site for historical information, this is the best place to go for statistics on the current season or even the most recent season.

This site links you to team-by-team results, offensive and defensive rankings, complete statistics (including league leaders), streaks, and home/road records for each NHL team.

It also contains some history, including a Stanley Cup playoffs archive and a list of all-time winners of each NHL award.

This home page has a section called "Other NHL Information on WWW," which links to other hockey-related areas on the World Wide Web.

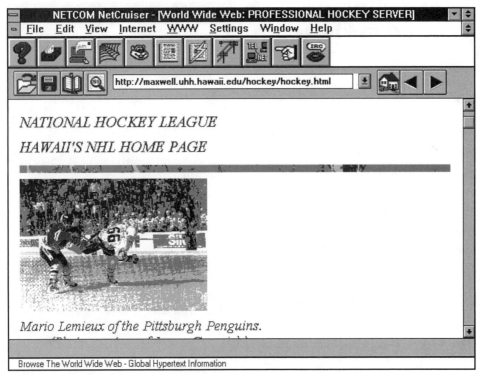

Figure 6.6 `http://maxwell.uhh.hawaii.edu/hockey/hockey.html`
Hawaii's NHL Home Page is the best source for statistical information on the current season.

Gate Sports NHL Page

`http://sfgate.com/sports/`
`sports/nhl/index.html`

This site is news-based; it originates from the *San Francisco Examiner* newspaper. While it concentrates on the local team, the San Jose Sharks, it includes league-wide feature stories and a column on the league called "Tony Cooper on the NHL."

A newspaper strike forced this site to fall behind, but under normal circumstances, it's a strong hockey site.

Information on Your Favorite Team

The NHL has been somewhat difficult for the casual fan to follow during the early 1990s. Five teams joined the league, another (the Minnesota North Stars) moved to Dallas, the divisions were renamed, a new commissioner was appointed, and there already have been two battles between the players and the owners.

Somehow, out of all that, the league has become stronger, gaining popularity in markets such as Florida, California, and Texas—markets that before had barely even noticed the league existed.

The league's renewed emphasis on marketing itself as a North American sport—not just the northern part of America—has brought about a great deal of success.

The new teams, as well as changes in logos and color schemes of some existing ones, have resulted in some rare sights in shopping malls around the country—youngsters walking around wearing the colors of their favorite *hockey* team.

Those of us who have grown up with the sport know that hockey had a life long before the Disney movie "The Mighty Ducks" helped spawn a franchise that now bears its name.

Like fans of any sport, just about everybody who pays close attention to the NHL has a favorite team (or two).

> **NOTE**
>
> A complete team-by-team listing of Internet sites appears at the end of this chapter.

The vast majority of NHL teams are represented on the Internet by some type of home-team site, be it a World Wide Web page or a UseNet newsgroup.

World Wide Web

The World Wide Web (WWW) is the fastest-growing area on the Internet, so it seems only fitting that it would provide a home to several sites for teams in the fastest-growing pro sports league.

Unlike the all-encompassing Nando X server for the National Basketball Association, there isn't an NHL source that has created home pages on all of the teams in the league. There are some NHL pages that offer links to home-team pages, but there isn't one large source that has created home-team pages on every team.

In some ways, that makes the NHL home pages more interesting. While they are all similar in some ways, each adds its own personal twist. They don't fit into a specific formula.

Although some lack credibility, they're interesting nonetheless.

The following example home-team pages are scattered all over the World Wide Web. A few of the servers discussed in this section offer links to some of these home-team pages.

> **NOTE**
>
> In this section, we will highlight a couple of the more interesting home-team pages available. Check the list at the end of the chapter for information on other home-team sites.

New York Rangers' Champions Page

`http://tardis.union.edu/`
`~haravayj/rangers.html`

For years, chants of "1940! 1940!" rang out at New York Rangers playoff games. On the road, fans used that chant to taunt the Rangers, one of the original six NHL teams and a team that had not won the Stanley Cup since—you guessed it—1940.

Late in the spring of 1994, Rangers captain Mark Messier hoisted the Stanley Cup above his head on the ice

of Madison Square Garden as fans in the arena chanted, "1994! 1994!"

The Rangers' first Stanley Cup title in 54 years brought out the best in New Yorkers and spawned a site on the Internet (see fig. 6.7).

Throughout the offseason and the lockout, this Rangers home page was devoted to the Rangers' championship. It carried a round-by-round description of the Rangers' fight through the playoffs, including a game-by-game account of the thrilling Stanley Cup finals against the Vancouver Canucks.

It includes pictures of some of the Rangers players in action and carries complete regular-season and playoff statistics for the team.

It's unclear whether the site will eventually convert to a current-season format or remain as a tribute to the champions. But even after the NHL resumed action, it has remained a tribute to the Rangers.

San Jose Shark Bytes

`http://www.armory.com/~lew/`
`sports/hockey/sharks.html`

As if the name isn't enough to get your attention, this site (see fig. 6.9) is also a top-notch resource for Sharks fans.

San Jose, the first of the expansion teams of the 1990s, has quickly become one of the league's most popular teams. Their surprising playoff berth and upset win over the Detroit Red Wings in the first round of the 1994 playoffs only helped them grow.

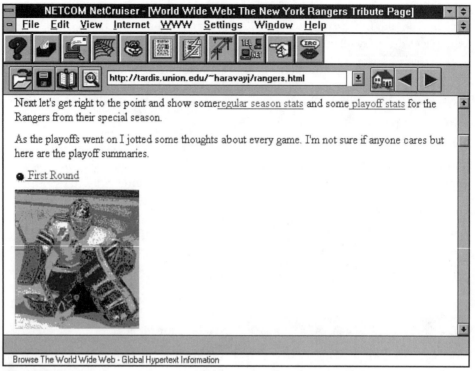

Figure 6.7 `http://tardis.union.edu/~haravayj/rangers.html`
A site that exists solely as a tribute to the 1994 Stanley Cup Champions.

This page is a good example of the possibilities of home-team pages. It includes recaps of all games, a team (and league) schedule, notes, outlook, pictures, and more.

Sports Talk Sites

UseNet newsgroups are a great place for hockey fans to share opinions and information on their favorite (or least-favorite) NHL teams. These team-specific sites were generally dormant during the lockout at the beginning of the 1994-95 season, but quickly moved back into an active mode once the players ratified a new collective bargaining agreement.

At this writing, 18 of the NHL's 26 teams had a UseNet newsgroup devoted just to them.

Once you've subscribed to one of these groups, you can post messages, read those left by others, and respond if you wish.

Subscribing to UseNet newsgroups is usually as easy as the click of a mouse, depending on what type of service provider you have. Consult your service provider's documentation for specific information on how to subscribe.

Mike Richter

Mark Messier was brought to the New York Rangers to give their die-hard fans what they had gone without for too long: a Stanley Cup.

While Messier's grit, desire, and influence on his teammates were major factors in the team finally delivering the treasured Cup to New York in 1994, the team couldn't have done it without goalie Mike Richter.

In the early 1990s, Richter and John Vanbiesbrouck were perhaps the best one-two goalie combination in the NHL. When the NHL expansion draft allowed teams to protect only one goalie, the Rangers had a tough decision to make.

They chose Richter, allowing Vanbiesbrouck to depart. Richter proved the Rangers right in the spring of 1994, when his outstanding goaltending won a few games singlehandedly and gave the Rangers' offense a chance to win the rest.

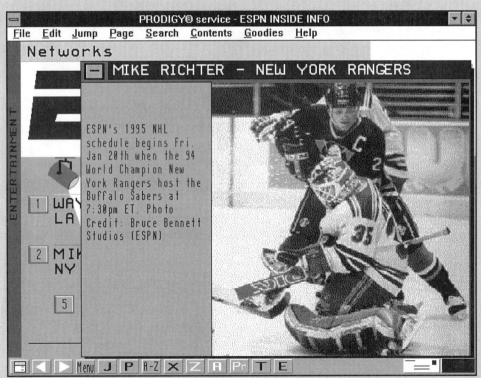

Figure 6.8 Jump: ESPNet
New York Ranger goalie Mike Richter played a strong role in bringing the Stanley Cup home to Rangers' fans.

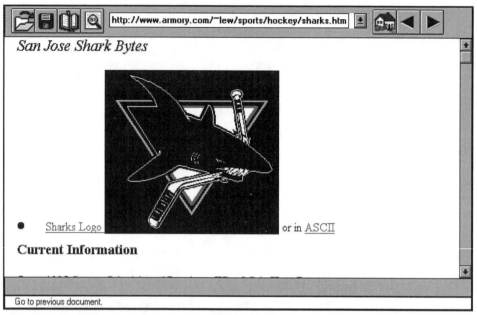

Figure 6.9 `http://www.armory.com/~lew/sports/hockey/sharks.html`
A home page devoted to the San Jose Sharks.

UseNet newsgroups currently exist for the teams listed in Table 6.1.

Other Internet Sites of Interest

This section includes some interesting sites that don't quite fit into any of the

Table 6.1 Current UseNet Newsgroups and Addresses	
Team	**Address**
Boston Bruins	`alt.sports.hockey.nhl.boston-bruins`
Buffalo Sabres	`alt.sports.hockey.nhl.buffalo-sabres`
Chicago Blackhawks	`alt.sports.hockey.nhl.chi-blackhawks`
Dallas Stars	`alt.sports.hockey.nhl.dallas-stars`
Hartford Whalers	`alt.sports.hockey.nhl.hford-whalers`
Los Angeles Kings	`alt.sports.hockey.nhl.la-kings`
Montreal Canadiens	`alt.sports.hockey.nhl.mtl-canadiens`

Team	Address
New Jersey Devils	`alt.sports.hockey.nhl.nj-devils`
New York Islanders	`alt.sports.hockey.nhl.ny-islanders`
New York Rangers	`alt.sports.hockey.nhl.ny-rangers`
Philadelphia Flyers	`alt.sports.hockey.nhl.phila-flyers`
Pittsburgh Penguins	`alt.sports.hockey.nhl.pitt-penguins`
Quebec Nordiques	`alt.sports.hockey.nhl.que-nordiques`
San Jose Sharks	`alt.sports.hockey.nhl.sj-sharks`
Toronto Maple Leafs	`alt.sports.hockey.nhl.tor-mapleleafs`
Vancouver Canucks	`alt.sports.hockey.nhl.vanc-canucks`
Washington Capitals	`alt.sports.hockey.nhl.wash-capitals`
Winnipeg Jets	`alt.sports.hockey.nhl.winnipeg-jets`

categories previously mentioned. These sites are out-of-the-ordinary in content, but not necessarily hidden in out-of-the-way places.

 ### NHL Goaltender Home Page

`http://www.wwu.edu/~n9143349/goalie.html`

If the thought of a goalie mask brings to mind hockey players, not Jason from Friday the 13th, this is the page for you (see fig. 6.10).

It is topped by this statement: "This Web page is dedicated to the goaltenders who have helped to make the sport of hockey one of the most exciting on this Earth."

Goalies are to the NHL what kickers are to the NFL and what relief pitchers are to baseball—they tend to be odd, quirky, colorful figures laden with superstitions brought on by the fact that the outcomes of many games rest squarely on their shoulders.

> **TIP**
>
> The NHL Goaltender Page contains some links to information about the guys who shoot the puck as well. In fact, it links to many of the other top NHL sites on the Internet.

This page brings all that out and more, featuring biographies of current NHL goalies, a goalie trivia contest, goalie statistics and roster information, awards and honors won by goalies, and a link to "quotes, passages, miscellany"—all about goalies.

If you're a fan of netminders, well, the puck stops here.

 NHL Images and Movies

`http://deathstar.rutgers.edu/`
`people/jimg/nhl/nhlhome.html`

Among other offerings, this site includes pictures and movies from NHL games—perfect for the multimedia enthusiast who also loves the sport of hockey (see fig. 6.11).

There is a link to dozens of still photographs of current players and those from years gone by (including hall-of-famers like Phil Esposito).

A second link is to a much smaller index of movies of current players. This site also links to other NHL servers that are included in this chapter.

 NHL Logos

`http://web.cps.msu.edu/`
`~vergolin/wings/logo.html`

Want to download the logo of an NHL team to spice up your stationery or start your own home page? This is the site for you (see fig. 6.12).

The home page lists every NHL team and includes a mini-logo. Clicking on the name of any team leads you to a large logo of the team.

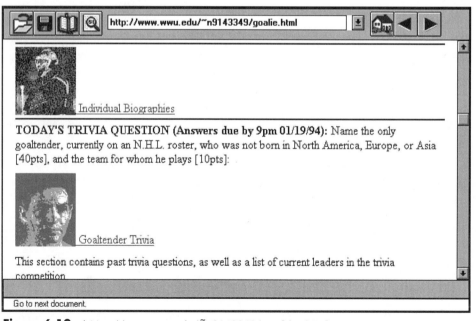

Figure 6.10 `http://www.wwu.edu/~n9143349/goalie.html`
At this site, learn more about the men behind the masks.

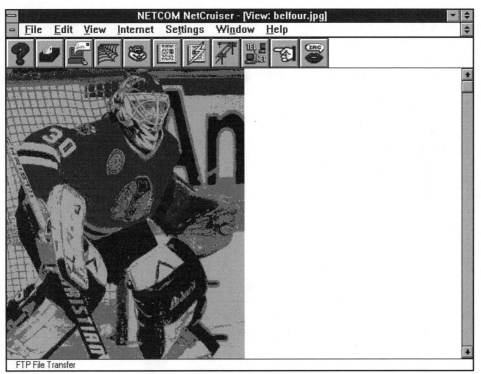

Figure 6.11 `http://deathstar.rutgers.edu/people/jimg/nhl/nhlhome.html`
An image of Ed Belfour, Chicago Blackhawks goalie.

Commercial Online Services

When it comes to the daily online coverage of the sport, the major commercial online service providers (Prodigy, America Online, and CompuServe) do an outstanding job. In some ways, they outperform their Internet counterparts because commercial online services offer a complete integrated package; on the Internet, you have to search for the various parts you want.

The major commercial online services are often the best links for news stories (especially game stories and boxscores) because of their tight associations with the Associated Press and Sports Ticker news wires. But they offer more than just news; they provide message areas similar to UseNet newsgroups for sports talk, sports pools, and sports files.

> **TIP**
>
> Prodigy and America Online provide the most complete team-oriented package for fans.

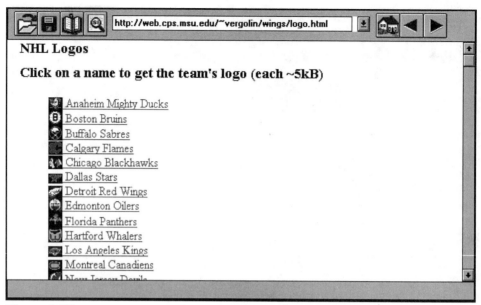

Figure 6.12 `http://web.cps.msu.edu/~vergolin/wings/logo.html`
The logos of every NHL team are available at this site.

 Prodigy

Jump: **hockey**

Prodigy has a strong hockey package based on its connection with the Associated Press.

Beyond the usual game stories and boxscores, Prodigy includes a complete schedule, standings, and statistics. Prodigy also offers team-by-team reports and an archive of NHL award-winners.

The main hockey menu (accessed directly from Jump: **hockey**), also links you to information on minor league hockey. For NHL information, simply click NHL and then click the selection of your choice.

For game stories and/or boxscores, click AP Online.

Prodigy's team reports offer commercial online service users the most complete coverage of the NHL. Included are team-by-team scores, division standings, team-by-team statistics and schedules, and even a summary of each conference's all-star teams.

From Prodigy's main hockey menu, simply click the conference in which your teams plays (either East Team Reports or West Team Reports). That brings up the menu of all the conference teams, as shown in figure 6.13.

The team reports consist of information such as injuries, notes from recent games, statistical streaks, and more. It's a great tool to use when you're out of town and want to check in on your team's progress, or when you're checking on teams outside of the city in which you reside.

America Online

Keyword: **hockey**

America Online also offers a strong NHL package that includes notes, statistics, and rosters (see fig. 6.14).

Keyword: **hockey** actually brings you to the main sports menu, from which you need to double-click Hockey. The next menu consists of a list of stories and statistics files, such as a game-by-game results log for each team.

All three of the major commercial online services offer NHL coverage to some degree, but America Online and Prodigy have the most complete list of resources.

America Online's news and statistics are provided by Sports Ticker. Game stories and boxscores appear shortly after the end of each game, giving fans an opportunity to find out what took place without waiting for the morning newspaper.

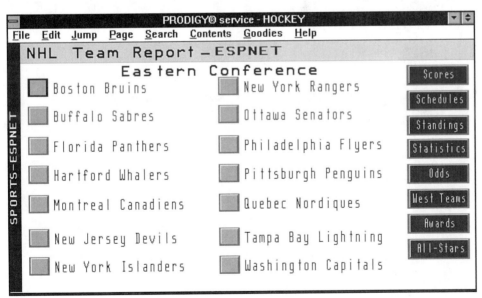

Figure 6.13 Jump: hockey
Prodigy users can call up complete team reports on any NHL team.

Also included are complete standings and statistics (updated daily), rosters for each NHL team (see fig. 6.15), and a notes package to keep you updated on items that might never find space in the newspaper or time in the sports-cast.

 **CompuServe**

Go: **APO**

CompuServe's news and statistics hockey coverage is sound, but it lacks some of the other areas offered by America Online and Prodigy.

CompuServe also uses the Associated Press for its league coverage, which includes game stories, features, boxscores and standings, and hockey news updates.

From the main Associated Press Online menu (Go: **APO**), click Sports. Then click Hockey and choose any headline from the menu provided.

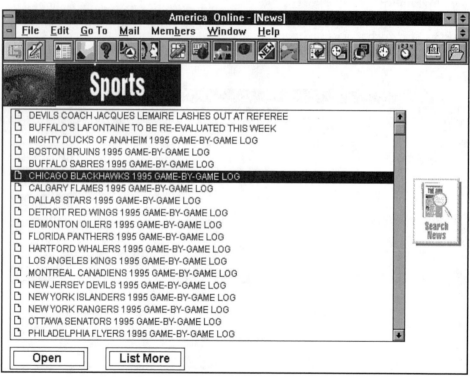

Figure 6.14 Keyword: hockey
America Online's hockey menu offers a strong all-around package.

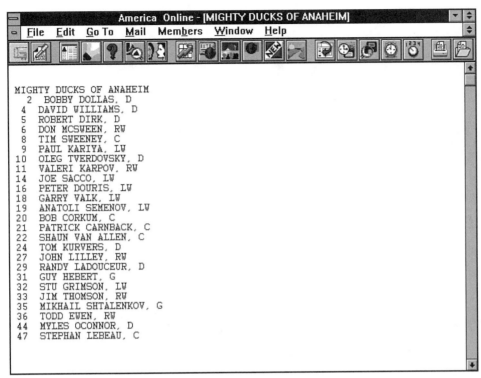

```
America Online - [MIGHTY DUCKS OF ANAHEIM]
 File   Edit   Go To   Mail   Members   Window   Help

MIGHTY DUCKS OF ANAHEIM
  2   BOBBY DOLLAS, D
  4   DAVID WILLIAMS, D
  5   ROBERT DIRK, D
  6   DON MCSWEEN, RW
  8   TIM SWEENEY, C
  9   PAUL KARIYA, LW
 10   OLEG TVERDOVSKY, D
 11   VALERI KARPOV, RW
 14   JOE SACCO, LW
 16   PETER DOURIS, LW
 18   GARRY VALK, LW
 19   ANATOLI SEMENOV, LW
 20   BOB CORKUM, C
 21   PATRICK CARNBACK, C
 22   SHAUN VAN ALLEN, C
 24   TOM KURVERS, D
 27   JOHN LILLEY, RW
 29   RANDY LADOUCEUR, D
 31   GUY HEBERT, G
 32   STU GRIMSON, LW
 33   JIM THOMSON, RW
 35   MIKHAIL SHTALENKOV, G
 36   TODD EWEN, RW
 44   MYLES OCONNOR, D
 47   STEPHAN LEBEAU, C
```

Figure 6.15 Keyword: hockey
Shortly after the NHL lockout was settled, America Online provided complete team rosters in its hockey package.

Chapter Summary

In this chapter, we have summarized the Internet sources for information on the NHL and its teams. Other hockey sites are covered in Chapter 9, "Olympic and International Sports." Collegiate hockey is covered in Chapter 10, "College Sports."

The List

A complete list of addresses follows, including general hockey sites and a team-by-team list of NHL franchises. If you're not sure how to use an address, see Chapter 12, "Internet Basics."

6

PRO HOCKEY

General Hockey Sites

Servers

Dan's Hockey Page:

WWW address: `http://www.pitt.edu/~dtgst1/hockey.html`

Hawaii's NHL home page:

WWW address: `http://maxwell.uhh.hawaii.edu/hockey/hockey.html`

Index to hockey links:

WWW address: `http://www.wwu.edu/~n9143349/links.html`

International Hockey League news:

Gopher address: `xavier.xu.edu:79/0074345`

Klootzak's Internet Hockey Archive:

FTP address: `ftp.u.washington.edu/public/hockey/`

NHL FTP archive:

FTP address: `wuarchive.wustl.edu/doc/misc/sports/nhl`

Satchel Sports NHL Home Page:

WWW address: `http://www.starwave.com/nhl/toc.html`

Schedules

NHL schedule by team:

WWW address: `http://www.cs.ubc.ca/nhl`

Schedules, records, and tidbits:

WWW address: `http://terrapin.umd.edu/nhl.html`

News and Statistics

Game summaries, statistics, and news:

CompuServe address:
Go: `APO`

News, features, and columns:

WWW address: `http://sfgate.com/sports/sports/nhl/index.html`

Rosters, news, and game summaries:

America Online address:
Keyword: `hockey`

Scores, schedules, team reports, and awards archive:

Prodigy address:
Jump: `hockey`

SportsWorld Statistics Service:

WWW address: `http://www.uniserve.com/swbbs/swbbs.html`

Other

DIVE IN—The Hockey Pool Report:

WWW address: `http://www.liii.com/~richr/home.html`

The Goaltender Page:

WWW address: `http://www.wwu.edu/~n9143349/goalie.html`

NHL images and movies:

WWW address: `http://`
`deathstar.rutgers.edu/`
`people/jimg/nhl/nhlhome.html`

NHL logos:

WWW address: `http://`
`web.cps.msu.edu/`
`~vergolin/wings/logo.html`

Team-by-Team List

Boston Bruins

Local home page:

WWW address: `http://`
`terrapin.umd.edu/bruins.html`

Newsgroup on the team:

UseNet address: `alt.sports.`
`hockey.nhl.boston-bruins`

Buffalo Sabres

Local home page:

WWW address: `http://`
`gretzky.vphsc.sunysb.edu/`
`sabres.html`

Newsgroup on the team:

UseNet address: `alt.sports.`
`hockey.nhl.buffalo-sabres`

Calgary Flames

Local home page:

WWW address: `http://`
`gwis2.circ.gwu.edu:80/`
`~farben/flames`

Chicago Blackhawks

Local home page:

WWW address: `http://`
`www.iia.org/~zabolots/`
`blkhawks.htm`

Newsgroup on the team:

UseNet address: `alt.sports.`
`hockey.nhl.chi-blackhawks`

Dallas Stars

Local home page:

WWW address: `http://`
`www.lan.unt.edu/`
`cc1/home/price/www/stars.htm`

Newsgroup on the team:

UseNet address: `alt.sports.`
`hockey.nhl.dallas-stars`

Detroit Red Wings

Local home page:

WWW address: `http://`
`web.cps.msu.edu/`
`~vergolin/wings.html`

Hartford Whalers

Local home page:

WWW address: `http://`
`access.digex.net/`
`~kayleigh/whalers.html`

Newsgroup on the team:

UseNet address: `alt.sports.`
`hockey.nhl.hford-whalers`

Team-by-Team List

Los Angeles Kings

Newsgroup on the team:

UseNet address: `alt.sports.hockey.nhl.la-kings`

Montreal Canadiens

Local home page:

WWW address: `http://www.pipeline.com/~amir/habs/`

Newsgroup on the team:

UseNet address: `alt.sports.hockey.nhl.mtl-canadiens`

New Jersey Devils

Local home page:

WWW address: `http://gwis2.circ.gwu.edu/~jaxon/devils.html`

Newsgroup on the team:

UseNet address: `alt.sports.hockey.nhl.nj-devils`

New York Islanders

Local home pages:

WWW address: `http://www.liii.com/~richr/isles.html`

WWW address: `http://poe.acc.virginia.edu/~dss2k/isles.html`

Newsgroup on the team:

UseNet address: `alt.sports.hockey.nhl.ny-islanders`

New York Rangers

Local home page:

WWW address: `http://www.csh.rit.edu/memb/homep/kenny/rangers.html`

Tribute to the Rangers' run to the 1994 Stanley Cup:

WWW address: `http://tardis.union.edu/~haravayj/rangers.html`

Newsgroup on the team:

UseNet address: `alt.sports.hockey.nhl.ny-rangers`

Ottawa Senators

Local home page:

WWW address: `http://magi.com/~joe/senators.html`

Philadelphia Flyers

Local home page:

WWW address: `http://www.islandnet.com/~mkp/flyers.html`

Newsgroup on the team:

UseNet address: `alt.sports.hockey.nhl.phila-flyers`

Pittsburgh Penguins

Local home page:

WWW address: `http://honus.pc.cc.cmu.edu/PenguinsHome.html`

Newsgroup on the team:

UseNet address: `alt.sports.hockey.nhl.pitt-penguins`

Quebec Nordiques

Newsgroup on the team:

UseNet address: `alt.sports.hockey.nhl.que-nordiques`

San Jose Sharks

Sharks information page:

WWW address: `http://www.armory.com/~lew/sports/hockey/sharks.html`

Sharks mailing list archive:

FTP address: `ftp.apple.com/pub/lsefton`

Newsgroup on the team:

UseNet address: `alt.sports.hockey.nhl.sj-sharks`

St. Louis Blues

Local home page:

WWW address: `http://atg1.wustl.edu/~ashkar/`

Tampa Bay Lightning

Local home pages:

WWW address: `http://nyx10.cs.du.edu:8001/~anon0aa7/Lightning.html`

WWW address: `http://www.med.usf.edu/PUBAFF/tbl/tbl1.html`

Toronto Maple Leafs

Local home page:

WWW address: `http://www.undergrad.math.uwaterloo.ca/~gahudson/maple.html`

Newsgroup on the team:

UseNet address: `alt.sports.hockey.nhl.tor-mapleleafs`

Vancouver Canucks

Local home pages:

WWW address: `http://imagineer.com.PuckHead`

WWW address: `http://www.ugrad.cs.ubc.ca/spider/s3g192/canuck.html`

Newsgroup on the team:

UseNet address: `alt.sports.hockey.nhl.vanc-canucks`

Team-by-Team List

Washington Capitals

Newsgroup on the team:

UseNet address: `alt.sports.hockey.nhl.wash-capitals`

Winnipeg Jets

Local home page:

WWW address: `http://www.ee.umanitoba.ca/~ddueck/jets/jets.html`

Newsgroup on the team:

UseNet address: `alt.sports.hockey.nhl.winnipeg-jets`

Chapter 7
Other Pro Sports

This chapter is designed to meet the needs of fans of motor sports, pro golf, pro tennis, horse racing, and boxing.

In this chapter
- *Where to find information about motor sports*
- *Where to find information about pro golf*
- *Where to find information about pro tennis*
- *Where to find information about horse racing*

In other chapters
→ *The recreational aspects of sports such as golf and tennis are covered in Chapter 11*

→ *If you're not sure how to use the addresses in this chapter, see Chapter 12*

First, I'd like to apologize to fans of the pro sports included within this chapter.

Some of you will likely ask, "Why does hockey get its own chapter and golf doesn't?" Or you may point out that worldwide, there are more people interested in motor sports than in hockey or even American football.

That may be the case. But the chapters in this book were organized solely on the basis of Internet activity.

The fact is that each sport included in this chapter is hugely popular and followed by a group of fans that is just as devoted as those of the so-called major sports.

In the body of this chapter, we will highlight some of the top sites on the Internet for each sport. The chapter concludes with a more complete list of sites for each sport.

Motor Sports

In certain parts of the United States and most of Europe, motor sports are followed like the Dallas Cowboys in Texas.

Motor sports are also developing a following on the Internet; racing fans say they often find better information online than they can get from any other source.

The reason is that many of the most prestigious events—especially Formula One races—occur overseas, and American television and newspapers don't give them the kind of time and space they devote to sports such as golf.

Even races in the U.S.—excluding the Indianapolis 500 and the Daytona 500, of course—are overlooked by newspapers in non-racing cities.

Part of the beauty of the Internet is that there are no editors or news directors to worry about the amount of time or space provided to a given event. For example, all auto racing sites are set up for auto racing fans *worldwide*. If they want the information, they can get it; if they don't, they can pass on by.

Many of these sites—especially those covering Formula One racing—are hosted in Europe, but most of the accompanying material is written in English.

We've uncovered several sites that motor sports fans won't want to miss.

Internet Sites

 NASCAR News

http://www.acpub.duke.edu/
~jwcarp/nascarhome.html

Auto racing is split between Formula One, NASCAR, and IndyCar. Some Internet sites are devoted only to one of them. Others, however, are dedicated to racing in general.

This site (see fig. 7.2), called NASCAR News, is a home page that can be broken out to links covering even more specific areas within the NASCAR circuit.

Primary links are to Winston Cup News, Busch Grand National News, Winston Racing Series News, and 1994 Cup points standings. Each page includes updated racing information, such as a 1995 racing schedule, race results, points standings, and news from around the track.

Pete Fenelow's Motor Racing Page

**http://
dcpu1.cs.york.ac.uk:6666/pete/
racing/index.html**

Pete Fenelow's Motor Racing Page, which originates in the United Kingdom, is a home page full of motor racing information and links. However, it's atypical of most racing pages in that it isn't oriented toward results and schedules.

Instead, it includes a link with information on various manufacturers, links to other Internet resources, and the Murray Walker Quotes Page.

Ayrton Senna

WHO'S HOT

Brazilian Ayrton Senna was one of the world's foremost drivers, yet he went largely unnoticed in the United States. Senna dominated the Formula One circuit, but because that mostly European sport fails to attract serious attention in America, Senna was known only to the most ardent auto racing fans.

Senna joined the Grand Prix circuit in 1984 at age 24. Throughout the ensuing 10 years, he won three Grand Prix world championships and amassed 41 Grand Prix victories.

He was at the peak of his career when he was killed in a crash during a Grand Prix race in Italy in 1994.

Figure 7.1 `http://dcpu1.cs.york.ac.uk:6666/pete/racing/index.html`
Ayrton Senna, killed in a 1994 Grand Prix crash, was a dominant force on the Formula One circuit.

The R.A.S. Racer Archive

http://www.eng.hawaii.edu/
Contribs/carina/
ra.home.page.html

The R.A.S. Racer Archive covers Formula One, NASCAR, and IndyCar racing. It includes results, schedules, points standings, plus a lot more.

 The Motorsport News International Index

http://www.metrics.com/MNI/
index.html

The Motorsport News International Index covers just about every aspect of motor racing and includes a very

impressive and lengthy list of documents that can be examined.

Online Services

 Prodigy

Jump: **auto racing**

Prodigy offers the best auto racing package of the three major commercial online services (see fig. 7.3).

It includes all of the latest statistics from the NASCAR, Formula One, and IndyCar circuits—plus Prodigy adds NHRA information. The package includes race winners and lists of leading money-winners, plus a complete racing calendar.

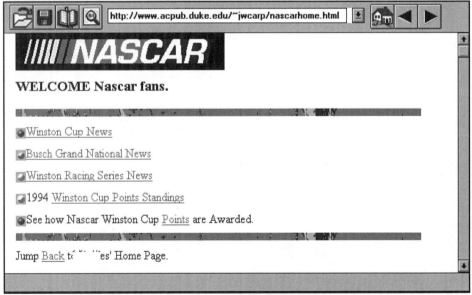

Figure 7.2 http://www.acpub.duke.edu/~jwcarp/nascarhome.html
At this NASCAR site, you can find information about upcoming races, point standings, and more.

Figure 7.3 Jump: auto racing
Prodigy's auto racing coverage is best among the three major commercial online services.

 America Online

Keyword: **sports**

America Online's auto racing package includes coverage of the NASCAR, Formula One, and IndyCar circuits (see fig. 7.4).

From America Online's main sports menu, double-click More Sports, and then double-click Auto Racing. You'll find the latest news stories from all three circuits combined into one menu.

 CompuServe

Go: **sports**

CompuServe's auto racing news is accessed from the main sports menu. It includes stories on the latest races and previews of upcoming events (see fig. 7.5).

Choose Olympics and Other Sports from the main sports menu, and then choose Auto Racing.

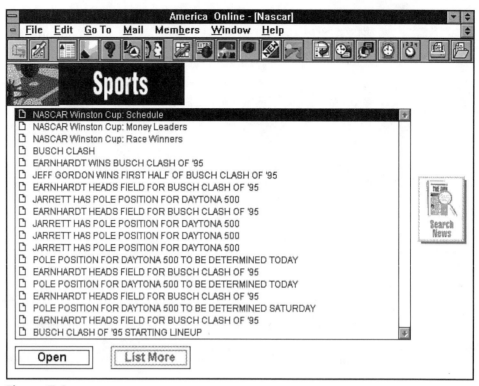

Figure 7.4 Keyword: sports
America Online offers news on the NASCAR, IndyCar, and Formula One circuits.

Golf

In the late 1980s and the first half of the 1990s, golf grew in popularity more than any other recreational sport in the U.S.

The popularity of both the PGA Tour and LPGA Tour also has grown, and so has the money pro golfers can win in such tournaments. The addition of the Senior Tour—for male golfers age 50 or older—has only added to pro golf's phenomenal success story.

While hotshot long-hitters such as John Daly carry the load on the PGA Tour, recognizable names and personalities such as Chi Chi Rodriguez, Lee

Trevino, and Jack Nicklaus help the Senior Tour thrive.

> **TIP**
>
> As previously stated, golf remains a burgeoning recreational sport, as well as a pro sport. This chapter is devoted to the pro end of the game. Recreational golf—including a great deal of information on how to find good courses for that next golf vacation—is included in Chapter 11, "Hobbies and Recreational Sports."

Golf's increase in popularity has brought about more coverage of the sport, both on television and in newspapers across the country and around the globe.

Coverage of pro golf on the Internet appears to still be in its infancy; most online sites devoted to golf focus on the recreational aspect of the game. But there are some good places to go for information on the pro game.

Internet Sites

At present, there are only a handful of good Internet sites devoted to pro golf, but, most likely, that will change in the coming months.

A few sites are devoted solely to the pro game, while others cover both pro and recreational golf.

 The 19th Hole

`http://zodiac.tr-riscs.`
`panam.edu/golf/19thhole.html`

When it comes to covering all aspects of pro golf on the Internet, this site (see fig. 7.7), called The 19th Hole, rests easily at the top of the leaderboard.

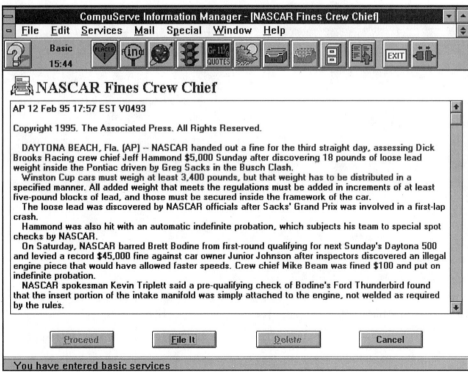

Figure 7.5 `Go: sports`
Stories such as this are part of CompuServe's auto racing package.

Jack Nicklaus

Since turning professional after a stellar amateur career in 1961, Jack Nicklaus' name has been synonymous with golf in the United States.

There isn't much any writer can say to sum up Nicklaus' career, so here are some stats:

> Nicklaus has won more majors (20) than any other golfer.
>
> He won the U.S. Amateur twice.
>
> He won six Masters, five PGAs, and four U.S. Opens.

In 1986, he became the oldest man to win the Masters.

He has been named PGA Player of the Year five times.

He has been the tour's leading money winner eight times.

He has since embarked on a career on the Senior Tour and is an accomplished golf-course designer. Thanks to the Senior Tour and made-for-TV events such as the Skins Game, Nicklaus remains a major player on the golf landscape.

Figure 7.6 `http://zodiac.tr-riscs. panam.edu/golf/ 19thhole.html`
Jack Nicklaus, downloaded from The 19th Hole, is perhaps the finest golfer in the history of the game.

The best part is that unlike some others, this home page offers information on all pro tours—even the so-called minor leagues of golf, such as the Nike Tour.

Information includes schedules of upcoming tournaments and results of past tournaments from all of the tours. It also links you to the following:

- A page that includes the complete rules of golf
- The Golf Digest record book (provided by Golf Digest magazine)
- Frequently asked questions
- A listing of golf associations
- Recommendations of other good golf pages you might like to check out

The Golf Data On-Line Home Page

`http://www.gdol.com/`

The Golf Data On-Line home page links you to several golf publications and contains information on the PGA, LPGA, and Senior tours. It also contains information for the recreational golfer.

Online Services

 America Online

Keyword: `golf`

If you're looking for an online host for information on the three major pro golf tours, America Online is the place to be. The service, which leads the major commercial online services in providing statistics on just about every sport, offers a full line of golf information (see fig. 7.8).

Along with America Online's typical event coverage, provided by Sports Ticker, the service also has a strong statistics package that includes the following:

- Leading money-winners
- Schedules of upcoming tournaments
- Statistical leaders (such as putts-per-round average, driving accuracy, driving distance, and greens-in-regulation).

America Online's golf menu offers clear choices to get you to these spots.

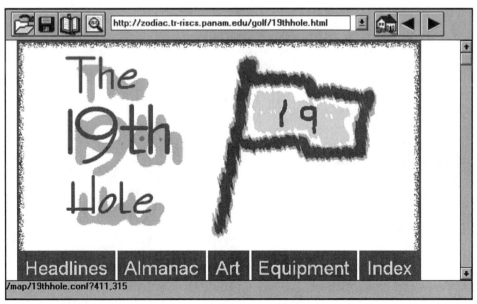

Figure 7.7 `http://zodiac.tr-riscs.panam.edu/golf/19thhole.html`
Of the sites on the Internet that cover pro golf, The 19th Hole is by far the best.

Coverage of pro golf on the Internet appears to still be in its infancy...

 Prodigy

Jump: **golf**

Prodigy also includes the latest tour news (provided by Associated Press), plus current results, money leaders, and tournament results from the three major tours.

 CompuServe

Go: **sports**

CompuServe's coverage of the PGA, Senior, and LPGA tours is provided by the Associated Press (see fig. 7.9).

It includes preview stories on upcoming tournaments, plus round-by-round coverages of the events as they unfold. Also available are statistical leaders and leading money-winners.

From the main sports menu, choose Tennis/Golf. The menu of headlines that is provided is a combination of new stories from the two sports.

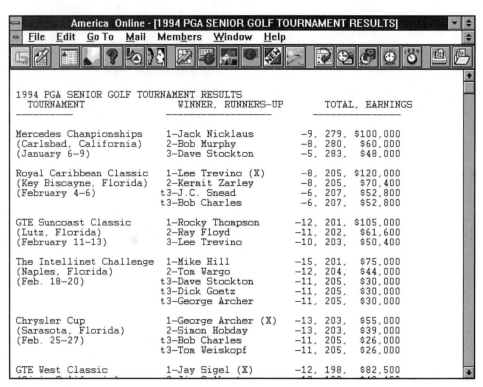

Figure 7.8 Keyword: golf
News and statistics from all three major tours are available in America Online's golf package.

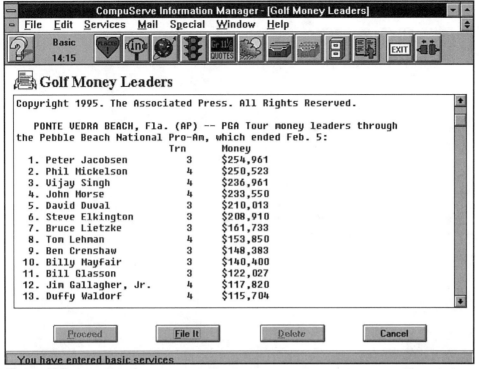

Figure 7.9 `Go: sports`
The PGA Tour's leading money-winners are available on CompuServe.

Tennis

Tennis' popularity as a spectator sport peaked in the late 1970s and early 1980s, when Jimmy Connors, Bjorn Borg, and John McEnroe dominated the men's circuit and Chris Evert and Martina Navratilova controlled the women's game.

As those players gradually moved out of the limelight and were replaced by others who failed to grab the attention of the average sports fan, the interest in tennis slipped slightly.

In 1994, *Sports Illustrated* ran a cover with the question "Is Tennis Dead?" The answer to that question is "No, of course not." That story concentrated on the perceived lack of true superstars in the pro ranks today and an apparent lack of talent coming up in the future.

Then Andre Agassi kept America on the edge of its collective seat during his run to his first U.S. Open championship. On the women's circuit, a tearful farewell was bid to Navratilova just as teenager Venus Williams played her first pro tournament and Jennifer Capriati returned to action.

Now, much like in golf, senior tours are in the works and the tennis world is hoping it will catch the country's imagination the way the Senior PGA tour has—by giving spectators a chance to see the big-name players compete again.

Gabriella Sabatini

Gabriella Sabatini carries a heavy load these days.

Martina Navratilova and Chris Evert, whose rivalry fueled women's tennis for years, have both retired. Monica Seles hasn't returned to competition since she was stabbed by a crazed fan during a match. Steffi Graf has battled injuries.

That leaves Sabatini in a position to take control of the women's tennis circuit. She's not alone, of course.

But no other women's tennis player is as popular worldwide as Sabatini. And no one is in a better position to return the sport to the forefront than she is.

Figure 7.10
Gabriella Sabatini is the most popular female tennis player in the world.

The Internet is home to a few excellent sites for the die-hard tennis fan.

Internet Sites

As with golf, some the best sites for tennis news are in the major commercial online services. But the larger Internet is also a good place to go for tennis information.

 The Tennis Server Home Page

```
http://arganet.tenagra.com/
Racquet_Workshop/Tennis.html
```

Along with a catchy slogan—"Encouraging tennis players everywhere to go to the 'NET for tennis information and equipment"—this site, called the Tennis Server Home Page, is jam-packed with tennis.

It includes the ATP Tour Weekly Electronic Newsletter (see fig. 7.11) and links to other tennis news sources.

The newsletter is lively and packed with information. This site also includes previews of upcoming tour tournaments, player rankings, and an archive of past newsletter issues.

In another format, that of Daily News Postings, this site also includes a link to a second magazine-style newsletter on both the men's and women's tours. These postings cover basic news and notes, plus information on the state of the sport (with a positive slant).

Outside of the pro ranks, this site also links you to information about tennis games for the SEGA® home entertainment system and tennis merchandise—this site claims to be the first tennis store to open on the World Wide Web.

> *...the larger Internet is also a good place to go for tennis information.*

 General

`http://www.cdf.toronto.edu/DCS/FUN/tennis.html`

This site (see fig. 7.12) isn't as flashy—it's more newsy and more direct.

It includes ATP Rankings, WTA Rankings, ATP/WTA Doubles Rankings, Rules of Tennis, and The Code of Tennis (etiquette).

It also covers frequently asked questions about both individual players and pro tennis in general.

Figure 7.11 `http://arganet.tenagra.com/Racquet_Workshop/Tennis.html`
The ATP Tour Weekly Electronic Newsletter updates tennis fans on the latest action.

Online Services

 Prodigy

Jump: `tennis`

Prodigy's tennis coverage (see fig. 7.13) which includes the latest tournament results and news provided by the AP, leads the commercial online service providers. The remainder of the Prodigy tennis package includes charts of the rankings and earnings of ATP and WTA players.

 America Online

Keyword: `tennis`

America Online's tennis package isn't exactly breathtaking, but it covers the basics well.

It includes news stories provided by Sports Ticker, tournament results from both the men's and women's tours, and schedules of upcoming tournaments and other events.

 CompuServe

Go: `sports`

CompuServe's tennis coverage consists of news of upcoming tournaments, stories on the tournaments as they progress, and general tennis news stories.

From the main sports menu, choose Tennis/Golf. The menu of headlines

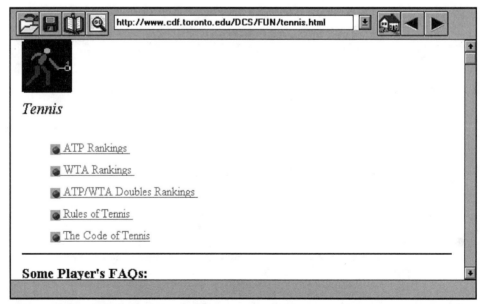

Figure 7.12 `http://www.cdf.toronto.edu/DCS/FUN/tennis.html`
Player rankings, tournament results, and more can be found here.

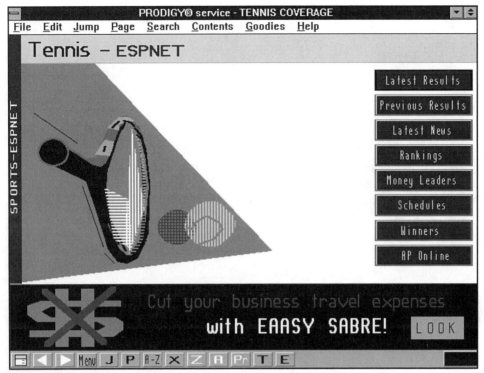

Figure 7.13 Jump: tennis
Prodigy's main tennis menu is the best among the three major commercial online services.

that appears is a combination of Associated Press' tennis and golf packages.

Horse Racing

Horse racing has long been dominated by its thoroughbred division. And while the sport has seen its share of scandals and other controversies in recent years, it remains a thriving sport—home to a thriving industry as well—in the U.S. and abroad.

Internet Sites

If you're on the Internet and you're looking for horse racing information, there is really only one site you need to find.

General Horse Racing Site

http://www.inslab.uky.edu/
~stevem/horses/

It should surprise absolutely no one that the most complete home for horse racing information on the Internet is found at the University of Kentucky.

Horse racing has always been defined by its premier event—the Kentucky Derby. This site includes a link to Kentucky Derby information, past and present. Among the attractions are results of previous runnings of the "greatest two minutes in sports" and a listing of contenders for the next running of the race.

Figure 7.14 Jump: horse racing
Prodigy's horse racing coverage includes both thoroughbred and harness racing.

For the serious fan, there is also a link to ticket information at Churchill Downs, home to the race every year.

This site also links you to a similar site covering the Breeders' Cup, with locations of future Breeders' Cups, results of the 1994 Cup races, and an archive of previous years' results.

This site also includes links to race information at Keeneland and a Horse Racing Photo Gallery.

Online Services

 Prodigy

Jump: **horse racing**

If you're trying to decide between the commercial online services and you're a fan of thoroughbred or harness racing, Prodigy should be your choice (see fig. 7.14).

All of the commericial services cover the big events—like the aforementioned Kentucky Derby and Breeders' Cup—but Prodigy goes above and beyond the call by including, on a regular basis, the results of the National Thoroughbred Poll.

The Prodigy service also includes—for the serious handicapper—lists of the leading money-winning horses, jockeys, and trainers.

 **CompuServe**

Go: `sports`

CompuServe uses its connection with the Associated Press to cover horse racing in the U.S. From the main sports menu, choose Olympic and Other Sports, and then choose Horse Racing.

You'll find a menu of stories on upcoming and completed races (see fig. 7.15).

 America Online

Keyword: `sports`

America Online's horse racing package includes news stories, thoroughbred rankings, and the National Thoroughbred Poll (see fig. 7.16).

From the main sports menu, double-click More Sports, and then double-click Horse Racing. The menu of stories is thorough enough to please even avid horse racing fans.

Chapter Summary

In this chapter, we have covered the best Internet spots for golf, tennis, motor sports, and horse racing—four of the most popular "other" pro sports.

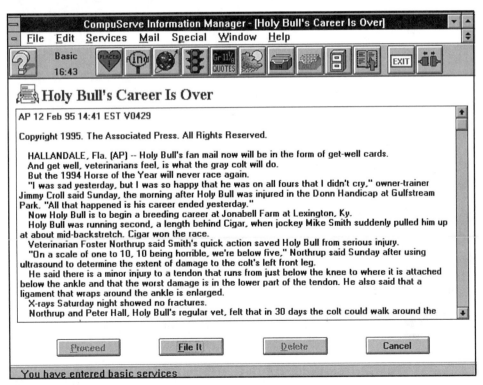

Figure 7.15 Go: `sports`
Associated Press news stories make up CompuServe's horse racing coverage.

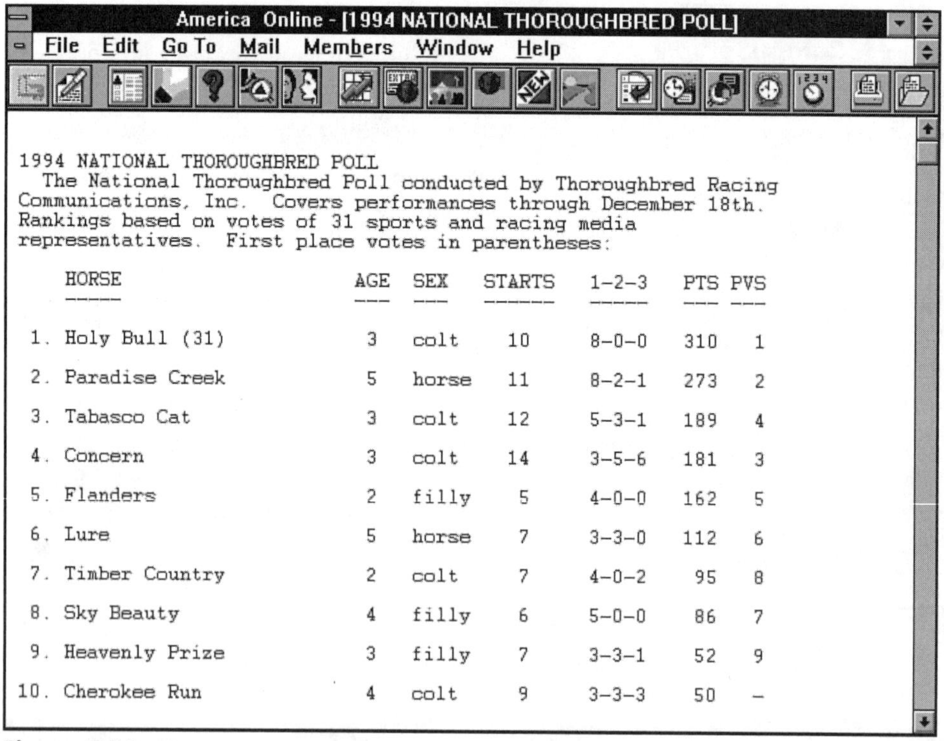

```
America Online - [1994 NATIONAL THOROUGHBRED POLL]
 File  Edit  Go To  Mail  Members  Window  Help
```

```
1994 NATIONAL THOROUGHBRED POLL
  The National Thoroughbred Poll conducted by Thoroughbred Racing
Communications, Inc.  Covers performances through December 18th.
Rankings based on votes of 31 sports and racing media
representatives.  First place votes in parentheses:
```

HORSE	AGE	SEX	STARTS	1-2-3	PTS	PVS
1. Holy Bull (31)	3	colt	10	8-0-0	310	1
2. Paradise Creek	5	horse	11	8-2-1	273	2
3. Tabasco Cat	3	colt	12	5-3-1	189	4
4. Concern	3	colt	14	3-5-6	181	3
5. Flanders	2	filly	5	4-0-0	162	5
6. Lure	5	horse	7	3-3-0	112	6
7. Timber Country	2	colt	7	4-0-2	95	8
8. Sky Beauty	4	filly	6	5-0-0	86	7
9. Heavenly Prize	3	filly	7	3-3-1	52	9
10. Cherokee Run	4	colt	9	3-3-3	50	–

Figure 7.16 Keyword: sports
The National Thoroughbred Poll is available on America Online.

Remember, the recreational aspects of sports such as golf and tennis are covered in Chapter 11, "Hobbies and Recreational Sports."

The List

The following list includes more sites for the sports mentioned in this chapter. Each of the four major pro sports—baseball, football, basketball, and hockey—has its own chapter.

If you're not sure how to use the addresses in this chapter, see Chapter 12, "Internet Basics."

Auto Racing

Fantasy

The Formula One Pick 6—a fantasy sports challenge:

> WWW address: `http://essi.cerisi.fr/Pick6/pick6.html`

News and Statistics

Formula One racing news and information:

> WWW address: `http://www.abekrd.co.uk/Formula1/`

Motorsport News International Index:

WWW address: `http://www.metrics.com/MNI/index.html`

News stories:

UseNet address: `clari.sports.motor`

Speedway news:

WWW address: `http://www.amg.gda.pl/speedway/speedway.html`

Newsgroups

Newsgroups:

UseNet address: `rec.sport.autos`

UseNet address: `rec.sport.f1`

UseNet address: `rec.sport.indy`

UseNet address: `rec.sport.info`

UseNet address: `rec.sport.nascar`

UseNet address: `rec.sport.tech`

Servers

Formula SAE racing:

WWW address: `http://www.me.mtu.edu/~loew/`

NASCAR News home page:

WWW address: `http://www.acpub.duke.edu/~jwcarp/nascarhome.html`

Pete Fenelow's Motor Racing page:

WWW address: `http://dcpu1.cs.york.ac.uk:6666/pete/racing/index.html`

R.A.S. Racer Archive:

WWW address: `http://www.eng.hawaii.edu/Contribs/carina/ra.home.page.html`

Time-speed-distance road rallying information:

WWW address: `http://www.contrib.andrew.cmu.edu/usr/ef1c/plug.html`

Boxing

Newsgroup:

UseNet address: `rec.sport.boxing`

Golf

Fantasy

Fantasy golf challenge:

WWW address: `http://caligari.dartmouth.edu/~ryde/ryde.html`

News

Fore Play golf newsletter:

WWW address: `http://www.deltanet.com/4play/newsltr.html`

The List

Online Services

America Online address:

Keyword: `golf`

Prodigy address:

Jump: `golf`

Servers

The Golf Data On-Line home page:

WWW address: `http://www.gdol.com/`

Golf home page:

WWW address: `http://ausg.dartmouth.edu/~pete/golf/`

The 19th Hole covers all pro tours:

WWW address: `http://zodiac.tr-riscs.panam.edu/golf/19thhole.html`

Skins Game information:

WWW address: `http://www.cyberplex.com/CyberPlex/Fun/Skins/skinmenu.html`

Horse Racing

Derby and Breeders' Cup information, photos:

WWW address: `http://www.inslab.uky.edu/~stevem/horses/`

Prodigy address:

Jump: `horse racing`

Tennis

News and Statistics

News stories:

UseNet address: `clari.sports.tennis`

Player rankings:

WWW address: `http://www.cdf.toronto.edu/DCS/FUN/tennis.html`

Newsgroups

Newsgroup:

UseNet address: `rec.sport.tennis`

Online Services

America Online address:
Keyword: `tennis`

Prodigy address:
Jump: `tennis`

Servers

Goddard Tennis Club home page:

WWW address: `http://epims1.gsfc.nasa.gov/tennis/GTC_homepage.html`

The Tennis Server home page:

WWW address: `http://arganet.tenagra.com/Racquet_Workshop/Tennis.html`

Chapter 8

Fantasy Sports

Interest in fantasy sports has exploded in recent years, and this chapter shows you where you can satisfy your needs on the Internet.

In this chapter

- *Fantasy sports basics*
- *How fantasy leagues work*
- *Fantasy sports go online*
- *Places to go for fantasy talk*
- *Using the Internet to get an edge in your league*
- *Playing in leagues organized within online services*

In other chapters

→ *For information on other sports-related hobbies, see Chapter 11*

→ *If you're not sure how to use an address in this chapter, see Chapter 12*

I n recent years, sports fans have been taking a more active interest in the games—and for a different reason. Fantasy (or rotisserie) sports have become one of the fastest-growing sports hobbies in the world.

Years ago, fans who wanted to take on the role of a team owner, general manager, or coach would purchase and use a board game—Strat-O-Matic games were the most popular—and draft their own teams and set up leagues with their friends.

Somewhere along the line, however, someone decided that it would be more fun (or, perhaps, *just as much fun*) if you used the actual performance of real players from real teams (see the next section, "How Fantasy Sports Leagues Work," for more information).

Today, fantasy sports leagues exist in all sports—not just football and baseball (although those leagues are prevalent).

Whether it all started with a fantasy football league or a fantasy baseball circuit (baseball leagues are usually called rotisserie leagues) is widely debated. Also hotly debated is the best kind of league: football or baseball.

Leagues now exist in all four of the major pro sports—football, baseball, basketball, and hockey—as well as golf, tennis, auto racing, horse racing, and more.

How Fantasy Sports Leagues Work

Here's a quick look at how fantasy sports leagues work.

In all leagues organized around the four major professional sports, leagues are typically started among a group of friends, each of whom owns a "franchise." A draft is held, in which each team selects professional players to use during the fantasy season.

The draft order is usually determined in random fashion—such as picking the owner's names out of a hat—for the odd-numbered rounds, and teams draft in reverse order in the following round. In other words, the team that drafts first in the first round drafts last in the second round. A new random draw is held for the third round, it reverses for the fourth round, and so on.

These players earn points based on their actual game performances. A schedule for the fantasy league is set up, and they compete against each other—with league winners earning money, prizes, or simply bragging rights.

In football, offensive players get points for scoring touchdowns or field goals, and many leagues give additional points for yardage gained. Some leagues include defenses, which earn points for sacks, shutouts, or points scored.

In basketball, players typically earn points for points scored, rebounds, and assists.

In hockey, players usually earn points for goals and assists, and goalies earn points for shutouts or some other graded system based on goals allowed.

Baseball leagues usually have the most complex scoring system. Hitters generally earn points for batting averages, runs batted in, home runs, and stolen bases; pitchers generally earn points for earned run averages, saves, wins and runners allowed per nine innings.

In individual sports such as golf, tennis, or auto racing, fantasy players draft the individuals and earn points based on their finishes in tournaments or races. Some are set up based on the money earned by the real-life players. In horse racing, players typically draft jockeys from one or more track(s) and earn points based on races won.

There are some computer programs that help track statistics for fantasy leagues on the market. On the Internet, there are some home pages that advertise a statistics service (for a fee).

Fantasy Sports Go Online

Computers entered the fantasy fray early on, when league commissioners began to publish their periodic league reports through word-processing or desktop-publishing packages.

Now, more and more leagues are using the Internet in some manner. Many fantasy franchise owners conduct their league business through e-mail because it allows complete and instantaneous transfer of information from one site to another.

Some Fantasy Sports Nuts Need Therapy

Are fantasy leagues getting out of control?

In Minneapolis-St. Paul (where I live), the local all-sports radio stations spend an average of four hours per week during the fall talking about fantasy football. Some professional athletes have complained in recent years that fantasy sports have clouded the fans' view of the games—that fans would rather see their fantasy players do well than have the home team win. Some pro athletes say that even after a big victory for the team, they have been confronted by angry fans because their individual performance didn't contribute enough to that fan's fantasy team.

My feeling is that the leagues are fun—as long as you don't have so much money invested in them that it becomes *important* that you win. When you start taking it too seriously, it's time to find something else to do with your time... like therapy.

TIME OUT

Fantasy sports leagues are often set up by co-workers. In fact, several leagues have been run entirely through a company's e-mail system.

Commercial online services were quick to capitalize on the fantasy sports boom, setting up forums or bulletin boards expressly for fantasy nuts to use as a means to exchange information. Accurate information is the cornerstone of successful fantasy team ownership because an injury that goes unnoticed or a slump that goes unexplained can cost a franchise points and, thus, victories—maybe even money.

Some Internet service providers have even set up leagues within the service in which people from all over the country compete for prizes—which can be anything from free online time to travel packages.

The Internet also helps fantasy sports fanatics by providing timely news and statistics through one of many services, such as Associated Press Online, Sports Ticker, or some other news service.

The statistics help league commissioners compile league summary sheets and help owners learn about emerging or slumping players without waiting for the following day's newspapers.

Fantasy Talk

Fantasy sports aren't any fun without talk. Whether it's attempting to make a trade with a fellow owner or merely discussing the success or failure of a particular player, talk is the centerpiece of an enjoyable fantasy season.

The Internet has become an active home for such talk. In leagues conducted either completely or in part on the Internet, talk is plentiful through such channels as e-mail, newsgroups, and other discussion groups.

Just about everyone who is online through a service provider has access to some type of fantasy talk format.

TIME OUT

No Work And All Play Means Trouble

Here's an example of a dangerous use of modern technology. I have omitted the names in an effort to prevent pink slips.

I know of a fantasy football league that consists of 10 people who work for a certain company. This league held its entire draft—which took nearly three hours—over e-mail *during working hours*.

Try to remember that technology helps us use our brains to their fullest; it doesn't allow us to get along without them.

Many companies where fantasy leagues generate a little too much conversation have established specific rules as to when, if at all, such talk can take place.

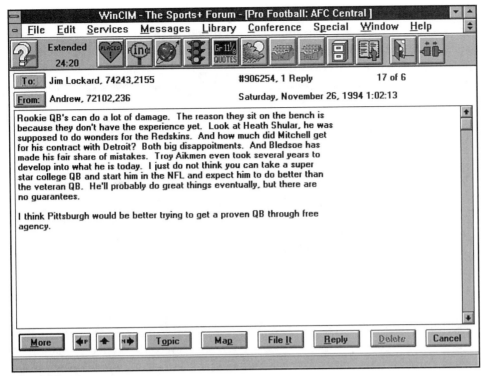

Figure 8.1 Go: `fans`
Once inside the CompuServe Sports Forum, fantasy sports information is just a click or two away.

People use these services for a variety of reasons. Some use them as a means to get information from others around the country. Some use them to get the latest scuttlebutt on professional players. Some use them to chat with others about their problems or concerns. Some use them to get advice from others. Topics can often take a sharp turn off the track, but there is a great deal of useful information to be gathered in these groups.

The forums/discussion groups organized by commercial online services such as America Online, CompuServe, and Prodigy are an excellent place to get started in this type of communication.

These forums give you the opportunity to share your opinions through posting messages (see fig. 8.1) for the entire group to read or by moving into private or semi-private conversation "rooms." For those who want to keep their messages private, some services allow them to move away from the large group into private conferences, or they can step away from the discussion quickly and send a message through e-mail.

But the vast majority of forum group discussions are held for the benefit of the entire group.

These discussions can be held "live" with two or more people conversing directly with each other. But, more often than not, someone posts a message for anyone to read and others who sign on read it and respond.

These off-the-shelf online services typically offer point-and-click technology that makes responding to a message as simple as clicking a Respond button, typing a note, then clicking Send.

> **NOTE**
>
> If you're a beginning user or if you're unfamiliar with these types of services, don't worry. They are covered in Chapter 13, "Commercial Online Services."

If you're on the full Internet, or have access to it, UseNet newsgroups are an excellent place to meet and share information with other fantasy sports participants. UseNet has a vast list of newsgroups, including several fantasy-related areas.

UseNet newsgroups operate as bulletin boards, where you can post messages for others to read. If you like, you can respond.

 ## UseNet Newsgroups

`rec.sport.baseball.fantasy`

`rec.sport.football.fantasy`

The `rec.sport.baseball.fantasy` site is everything the name implies. It's a great source for fantasy baseball information. If fantasy football is on your mind, check out `rec.sport.football.fantasy`.

Both newsgroups are full of general conversation among fantasy fans from around the country. Every fantasy fan knows it can be difficult, especially in football, to find out if an injured player is going to play before fantasy lineups are due for the week. These newsgroups are littered with requests from Joe Fantasy, asking, "Is so-and-so going to play this week? We can't get any information on him up here." Conscientious fans who live in the city in which that injured player plays respond with the best information they have, usually citing a source (for example, "I read in the *Miami Herald* today that…")

An Information Overload

I love `rec.sport.football.fantasy`, but at times getting all of the "inside information" can be as frustrating as knowing nothing at all. One time during the football season, I scoured the newsgroup for information on a specific player on my team and found no fewer than 22 messages on his condition. Unfortunately, about half said he would play, and the other half said he wouldn't.

We help out others in the newsgroup because others have returned the favor for us.

The best information comes from those in the know. Certain newsgroup users in some cities have taken it upon themselves to post weekly reports in `rec.sport.football.fantasy` (see fig. 8.2) on various NFL teams. They can be very detailed, including perceived game plans and the tendencies of both teams in a given game. Or they can merely list, in paragraph form, injured players and their chances of seeing action in the coming week.

During the season-ending baseball strike in 1994, `rec.sport. baseball.fantasy` became a clearing-house for frustrated baseball fans, with many of them complaining (much like Cleveland Indians fans) that their team was having a great season and got

burned when the season was cut short. League commissioners used the newsgroup to discuss with each other and get ideas on how to wrap up the loose ends of a ruined season. If you were merely a casual baseball fan, `rec.sport.baseball.fantasy` was not the place to be in September and October of 1994; it was pretty depressing reading.

UseNet has thousands of newsgroups, many of them with sports themes. While these are the only two I've seen lately that are dedicated solely to fantasy sports, most of the other newsgroups that fall under the `rec.sport` area include some fantasy chatter. After all, the name of the newsgroup doesn't necessarily determine the topics. It's really up to the users.

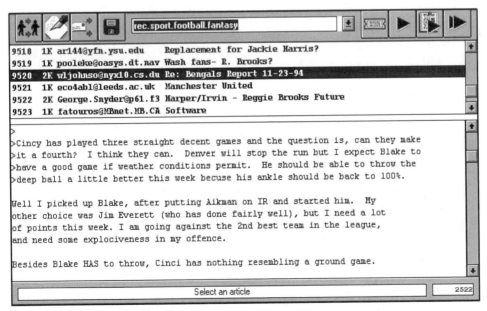

Figure 8.2 `rec.sport.football.fantasy`
Fantasy football is the sole topic of discussion here.

If it's fantasy basketball you're into, try `rec.sport.basketball.misc`. I've seen some fantasy hockey talk on `rec.sport.hockey`.

UseNet also has newsgroups devoted to just about every professional team in the four major sports. These newsgroups are another good place to go for information on specific players. For example, if you wanted to know the status of Barry Bonds, you'd consult `alt.sports.baseball.sf-giants`, where you would post a message and check back later for a response.

> **NOTE**
>
> Complete lists of team-specific UseNet newsgroups are included at the end of each chapter devoted to a pro sport in Part II. For example, if you want information on a player on a specific hockey team, check the end of Chapter 6, "Pro Hockey."

World Wide Web

On the World Wide Web, there are a number of fantasy sports-related addresses that provide a variety of services. Yahoo Sports is an Internet host that provides a wide variety of sports information and includes home pages for fantasy baseball, basketball, and football. A true fantasy sports fan will find something to their liking at one of the following:

> `http://`
> `akebono.stanford.edu/yahoo/`
> `Entertainment/`

`Sports/Baseball/Fantasy` is a fantasy baseball home page.

> `http://`
> `akebono.stanford.edu/yahoo/`
> `Entertainment/`
> `Sports/Basketball/Fantasy` is a fantasy basketball home page.

> `http://`
> `akebono.stanford.edu/yahoo/`
> `Entertainment/`
> `Sports/Football_American/`
> `Fantasy` is a fantasy football home page.

Getting an Edge in Your League

Have you ever been involved in a league in which one or two owners had easy access to inside information that no one else did? That can be an unpleasant experience—unless you're the one with the inside information.

Getting that type of information online is easy. You don't have to be an insider to access all sorts of information that can give you that advantage. And that's what success in fantasy sports is all about: getting an edge and using it to your advantage.

What if you had access to the league boxscores a full 12 hours or more earlier than your competitors? What if you had easy access to information such as injuries or benchings that no one else had? What if you could find out how much one of your key players was going to play—just before your lineups for the week were due?

Any of those would give you a head-start toward a win.

Getting and Giving Advice

The Internet—specifically UseNet newsgroups—is a great source of information for fantasy players around the country. There are thousands of UseNet groups and those virtually guarantee that there is an avenue for you to find the information for which you're looking.

Even the most advanced fantasy sports players need an occasional piece of advice from a friend. UseNet groups are full of "friends"—that is, people who are interested and knowledgeable enough about fantasy games that they're willing to respond to a question.

All it takes is the simple posting of a message through any of a number of services. Because thousands—maybe even millions—of people are in touch with these services, a response is virtually guaranteed.

Let's say you've been offered a trade by another owner. It sounds intriguing to you, but you'd feel a lot better about it if a neutral third party would give it his or her blessing (see fig. 8.3).

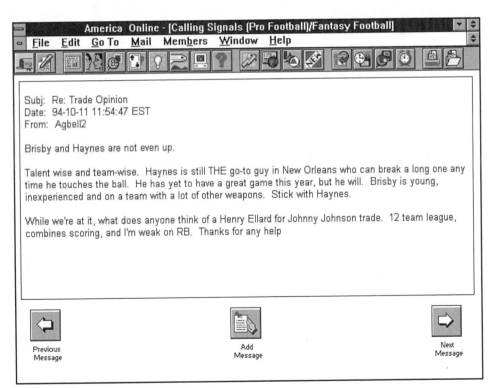

Figure 8.3 Keyword: grandstand
When an America Online user posted a message about a trade offer he had received, several others responded with their advice.

Injuries are the bane of fantasy sports. How many times have you included a player in your starting lineup for a fantasy game, only to find out his *real* coach decided to hold him out because of an injury? You're left wondering what could have been—how your game might have turned out if only you had known.

This problem is especially acute in fantasy football. While most major daily newspapers publish full injury reports early enough in the week to help fantasy players, they can be confusing. When a player is listed as "doubtful" or "probable," we generally know what it means. But what about "questionable?"

UseNet newsgroups provide a forum for clearing up these issues (see fig. 8.4).

Statistics

Fantasy owners spend a lot of time scouring professional rosters for players that might improve their teams. Because few media outlets provide complete statistics, more and more fans are going online and getting that information quickly and completely.

On the Internet, FTP servers are generally the best place to access up-to-date statistics on the major professional sports. These are typically archives of statistics that generally are free.

Here's a quick list of a few of the best places to get stats on the Internet.

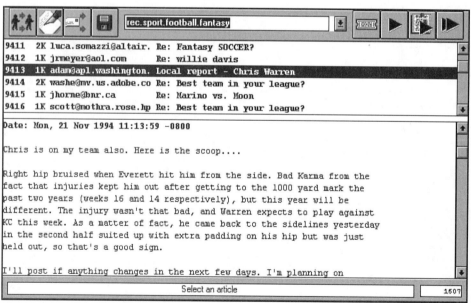

Figure 8.4 `rec.sport.football.fantasy`
When Chris Warren of the Seattle Seahawks suddenly turned up on the injury report, a local fan provided information for fantasy players around the country.

```
─  NETCOM NetCruiser - [World Wide Web: /pub/Sports/Baseball/Majors/Stats/94/MLB.  ▼ ▲
─  File   Edit   View   Internet   WWW   Settings   Window   Help                    ▲
```

	NAME	W	L	IP	HIT	RUN	ER	BB	SO	ERA	SA
1	Howe	3	0	39.1	28	8	8	7	18	1.83	15
2	Wickman	5	4	70.2	54	26	24	27	56	3.06	6
3	Key	17	4	168.0	177	68	61	52	97	3.27	0
4	Pall	1	2	35.0	43	18	14	9	21	3.60	0
5	Kamieniecki	8	6	117.1	115	53	49	59	71	3.76	0
6	MPerez	9	4	151.1	134	74	69	58	109	4.10	0
7	Hitchcock	4	1	49.1	48	24	23	29	37	4.20	2
8	JAbbott	9	8	160.1	167	88	81	64	90	4.55	0
9	Hutton	0	0	3.2	4	3	2	0	1	4.91	0
10	PGibson	1	1	29.0	26	17	16	17	21	4.97	0
11	Ausanio	2	1	15.2	16	9	9	6	15	5.17	0
12	Harris	0	1	5.0	4	5	3	3	4	5.40	0
13	XHernandez	4	4	40.0	48	27	26	21	37	5.85	6
14	Mulholland	6	7	120.2	150	94	87	37	72	6.49	0
15	Reardon	1	0	9.2	17	9	9	3	4	8.38	2
16	Murphy	0	0	1.2	3	3	3	0	0	16.20	0
17	Ojeda	0	0	3.0	11	8	8	6	3	24.00	0

```
Go to next document.
```

Figure 8.5 etext.archive.umich.edu/pub/Sports/Baseball/Majors/Stats
A Major League baseball statistics server is located at this FTP site.

 FTP Baseball Site

**etext.archive.umich.edu/pub/
Sports/Baseball/Majors/Stats**

This site provides league standings and leaders in a variety of statistical categories, plus complete statistics for every Major League player that are updated weekly (see fig. 8.5).

 FTP Basketball Site

**wuarchive.wustl.edu/doc/misc/
nbastats/facts/stats**

This site is updated weekly with complete NBA stats.

 FTP Football Site

**ftp.vnet.net/pub/football/
PRO/STATS**

This is a very thorough source of NFL stats.

 FTP Hockey Site

terrapin.umd.edu/nhl.html

This is a solid source for NHL stats.

Web Site

http://debussy.media.mit.edu/
dbecker/docs/swbbs.html

This site provides statistics on a variety of sports, including baseball and football.

 America Online

Keyword: **sports**

Among commercial online service providers, America Online has by far the best statistics service available (see

fig. 8.6). Updated on a regular basis, these statistics are available on every player in all of the four major professional sports.

Help for the Commissioner

Acting as commissioner of a fantasy league is generally a thankless job, unless you happen to run a league in which the commissioner is compensated in some form.

One of the commissioner's primary functions is keeping track of scores for each of his or her league's games. Anyone who has ever served as a league commissioner knows how frustrating it

```
America Online - [NBA TEAM-BY-TEAM STATISTICS    PACIFIC DIVISION THROUGH F
  File   Edit   Go To   Mail   Members   Window   Help

NBA TEAM-BY-TEAM STATISTICS
     PACIFIC DIVISION
THROUGH FRIDAY, NOVEMBER 25 GOLDEN STATE WARRIORS
-------------------------------------------------------------

                                         REBOUNDS
                  G    PPG    RPG   APG   OFF-DEF --TOT  STL  BLK   TO   PF

Latrell Sprewell  10   26.4   5.1   3.8   13-  38-   51   17    8   39   14
Tim Hardaway      10   23.3   3.2   7.9    4-  28-   32   10    4   39   24
Ricky Pierce       9   17.9   3.1   1.4    4-  24-   28    9    0    5   10
Tom Gugliotta       9   13.0   7.8   2.7   27-  43-   70   21   13   21   28
Chris Gatling     10    9.8   7.9   0.9   22-  57-   79    4   13   14   35
Keith Jennings    10    9.1   2.1   5.9    3-  18-   21   14    0   18   22
Rony Seikaly      10    8.0   7.8   1.0   29-  49-   78    5   16   24   36
Carlos Rogers      6    8.0   4.2   0.5   13-  12-   25    4    2    7   14
Clifford Rozier    2    6.0   5.0   0.0    5-   5-   10    0    3    1    4
Victor Alexander   8    5.4   3.0   0.6    4-  20-   24    4    2    9   32
David Wood         9    4.8   2.8   0.4    6-  19-   25    2    1    6   20
Manute Bol         5    3.0   2.4   0.0    1-  11-   12    0    9    1   10
Rod Higgins        5    2.0   1.4   0.6    4-   3-    7    1    1    1    7


                  FG            3PT          FT
                  M-A    PCT    M-A    PCT    M-A    PCT   PTS   HI

Sprewell        84-195   .431   18-55   .327   78-94   .830   264   39
Hardaway        77-167   .461   27-74   .365   52-62   .839   233   30
Pierce          50-99    .505   16-33   .485   45-53   .849   161   27
Gugliotta       38-106   .358   5-17    .294   36-48   .750   117   24
Gatling         43-62    .694   0-0     .000   12-33   .364    98   16
```

Figure 8.6 Keyword: basketball
Professional basketball statistics from America Online are updated regularly and can be a valuable resource for fantasy basketball players.

can be to have to wait for the morning newspaper for statistics. For those who don't live on the West Coast, it can be especially frustrating because box-scores from games played on the West Coast often don't make it into newspapers in other parts of the country.

Getting online can take away that frustration.

For baseball—where fantasy league statistics are often cumulative over the course of a season and an individual Major League boxscore isn't as vital as in, say, football—the statistics sources covered in the previous section are a great place to start.

But in other sports, which generally rely on results from individual professional games, quickly getting a box-score on each game is essential.

UseNet's Clarinet operates like a clearinghouse of wire service stories, standings and statistics. Professional box-scores are generally posted to these addresses within an hour of the conclusion of each game.

> **NOTE**
>
> Some service providers charge extra for the use of Clarinet newsgroups. Also, access to Clarinet is subject to whether your Internet provider actually carries it.

The following is a list of Clarinet addresses that are self-explanatory:

```
clari.sports.baseball
clari.sports.baseball.games
clari.sports.basketball
clari.sports.football
clari.sports.football.games
```

These sites include Associated Press boxscores (see fig. 8.7), which come in handy when it comes time to track how your fantasy players are doing.

If you are—or if you plan to be—connected to a commercial online service, you can often find game statistics there.

CompuServe offers Associated Press Online as a basic service, and box-scores (see fig. 8.8) are posted to these files generally within an hour of the end of each game (although sometimes it takes longer for football).

CompuServe's Go: **APO** brings you to the main Associated Press Online screen. Choose sports, then choose the sport of your choice for a menu of options within that sport.

America Online offers a similar service through its Sports News area. This includes Sports Ticker, which is an information service that provides—among other things—scoring updates for broadcasters to pass on to viewers (or listeners) during games. Once the games are complete, Sports Ticker issues a complete boxscore that is available on America Online.

Use Keyword: **sports**, then double-click the sport of your choice. You are presented with a menu of files, including boxscore files.

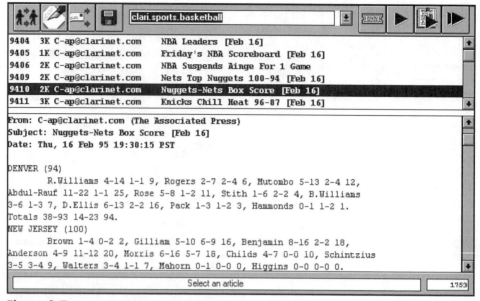

Figure 8.7 `clari.sports.basketball`
Associated Press boxscores are available on UseNet's Clarinet.

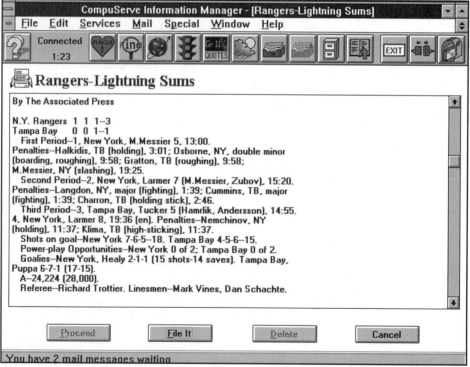

Figure 8.8 Go: APO
CompuServe's Associated Press game boxscores usually are posted within an hour of the end of games.

Playing Online

Most fantasy players got started in leagues set up in neighborhoods, workplaces, dorms, and so on. As the hobby grew, mail leagues began springing up around the country. They were set up by companies that, for a fee, would establish a league and run it for you.

The problem with this type of league was that you didn't know any of the other players, so it was difficult to really enjoy the league to its fullest. Trades were costly because they usually involved a long-distance phone call.

Playing online provides the enjoyment you get from a league of friends and eases the problems involved with play-by-mail leagues.

Leagues within Online Services

America Online and CompuServe offer online fantasy leagues in all four major professional sports.

America Online's leagues are run out of The Grandstand (Keyword: **grandstand**). CompuServe's leagues are accessed from its sports forum (Go: **fans**).

These leagues carry an additional fee over the cost of the service. Because online time is consumed participating in league business, charges accrue.

However, these leagues are run very professionally—their rules are clearly

defined and they're very popular (see fig. 8.9).

In America Online, all of the fantasy leagues are accessed through The Grandstand. Once you've mailed your registration fee for playing in the league, you're ready to go. A large number of leagues are run for each sport and America Online does its best to place you in a league that holds its draft and league meetings at dates and times that fit your schedule.

> **NOTE**
>
> Among the commercial online service providers, I prefer America Online's fantasy leagues. The rules, league notes, updates, sign-up procedures—*everything!*—is easily accessible at any time during the season. But you can't go wrong with any of them.

In CompuServe, fantasy leagues are run through the Sports+ Forum, which is an "extended" service—meaning you're charged for the time you spend in it. Because basic online usage is unlimited with CompuServe (while America Online allows five free hours per month), the actual cost of the online time is probably the same playing fantasy sports on either service.

Once you're in a CompuServe league, you get league updates, post your transactions, and so on in the Sports+ Forum.

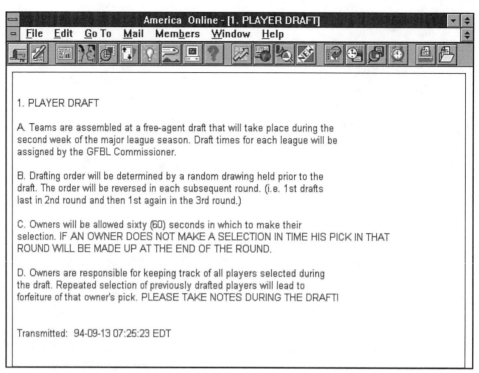

Figure 8.9 Keyword: grandstand
The America Online fantasy baseball league's rules for the draft and other aspects are available throughout the season for league participants.

Finding a League to Join

If you'd like to be in a league but you don't want to join one run by an online service, the various commercial online forums and UseNet newsgroups, etc., are a great place to begin. All you need to do is post a message to one or more of these sites (making sure to leave your e-mail address) and wait for the responses to come rolling in.

Sometimes, you can even find a league looking for a new owner (see fig. 8.10).

(see fig. 8.10).

> **TIP**
>
> Be wary of any league that offers you a spot and asks you to send an entry fee to a post-office box. Post-office boxes can easily be closed, and you don't want your hard-earned cash to walk away from you. I recommend asking for the names of other franchise owners in the league and calling them for a reference.

Starting a League

Starting a league is also easy on the Internet. Using the same sources

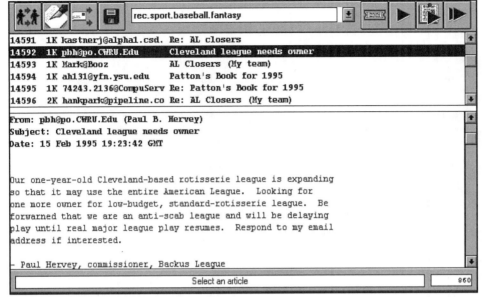

Figure 8.10 `rec.sport.baseball.fantasy`
Finding a fantasy league to join can be as easy as scanning the messages in UseNet's fantasy newsgroups.

mentioned previously, post a short message in one of the forums asking interested parties to respond to you if they have an interest in joining a league.

Once you have enough responses, send each person an e-mail detailing how your league will be run, and you're off.

Chapter Summary

In this chapter, you've learned where to find information and services useful in furthering your interest in fantasy sports.

For information on how to use the various Internet tools described in this chapter, see Chapter 12, "Internet Basics" and Chapter 13, "Commercial Online Services."

The List

A complete list of addresses follows, including general sites for fantasy talk, servers, and statistics. If you're not sure how to use an address, see Chapter 12, "Internet Basics."

Fantasy Talk

Newsgroups:

    rec.sport.baseball.fantasy
    rec.sport.football.fantasy

America Online address:

    Keyword: grandstand

CompuServe address:

    Go: fans

The List

Prodigy address:

Jump: `sports bb`

Servers

Fantasy Baseball home page:

WWW address: `http:// www.cm.cf.uk/Gwyn.Price/ fantasy_baseball.html`

Fantasy Basketball home page:

WWW address: `http:// akebono.stanford.edu/yahoo/ Entertainment/Sports/ Basketball/Fantasy`

Fantasy Football home page:

WWW address: `http:// akebono.stanford.edu/yahoo/ Entertainment/Sports/ Football_American/Fantasy`

Statistics

All sports:

WWW address: `http:// debussy.media.mit.edu/ dbecker/docs/swbbs.html`

America Online address:

Keyword: `sports`

CompuServe address:

Go: `APO`

Major League Baseball Statistics:

FTP address: `etext.archive. umich.edu/pub/Sports/ Baseball/Majors/Stats`

NBA Statistics:

FTP address: `wuarchive. wustl.edu/doc/ misc/nbastats/facts/stats`

Newsgroups:

`clari.sports.baseball`

`clari.sports.baseball.games`

`clari.sports.football`

`clari.sports.football.games`

`clari.sports.basketball`

NFL Statistics:

FTP address: `ftp.vnet.net/pub/ football/PRO/STATS`

NHL Statistics:

WWW address: `http:// terrapin.umd.edu/nhl.html`

Prodigy address:

Jump: `espnet`

Chapter 9
Olympic and International Sports

International sports competitions have always been able to capture the fancy of the American sporting public.

In this chapter

- *The Olymics and other international competitions*
- *The 1996 Summer Olympics (Atlanta)*
- *The 1998 Winter Olympics (Nagano, Japan)*
- *The World Cup and European League soccer*
- *The Tour de France*
- *Figure skating and speed skating*

In other chapters

← *Although golf and tennis could be considered international sports, refer to Chapter 7 for specific information on these sports*

← *If you don't find what you're looking for in the list at the end of this chapter, it's probably covered in another chapter. For example, Formula One auto racing is covered in Chapter 7*

→ *If you're not sure how to use the addresses in this chapter, see Chapter 12*

The greatest of the international competitions—the Olympic Games—have such a profound impact on sports fans that they tend to make fans out of those who otherwise wouldn't classify themselves as such.

Even before Nancy Kerrigan and Tonya Harding lit up the tabloid television shows with their bizarre story that began well before the Olympics and continued well past the Games' conclusion, figure skating competitions in the Olympics brought to the television set millions of people who couldn't give a rip about the Super Bowl.

This chapter is for you, the sports fan who would just as soon watch Bonnie Blair skate to a gold medal as Wayne Gretzky dash around a defenseman; the fan who would just as soon see Tony Meola facing a penalty kick as Shaquille O'Neal pounding down another monster dunk.

Perhaps more than for any other type of sports competition, the Internet is the perfect place for information on international competitions. After all, the Internet is an international network of networks.

This chapter includes coverage of the Olympics and other international competitions, like the Goodwill Games.

But it also covers other sports that have major championships on the line in an international venue, such as soccer (the World Cup) and cycling (the Tour de France).

Like the other chapters in Part II of this book, there's a list of sites at the end of this chapter. The list includes even more places to go for information on the major topics—plus some strong Internet sites on other international or European sports (such as cricket,

Bonnie Blair

Besides being one of the most likable athletes in American sports, Bonnie Blair has also carved herself a place in Olympic history.

Blair is the only American woman to win five gold medals in Olympic competition—she did it in three Olympic Games.

Blair comes from a family of speed skaters, and she became its most famous member when she won the 500-meter race at the 1988 Winter Games.

In 1992, Blair repeated in the 500-meter race and backed it up with a gold medal in the 1,000-meter competition. She repeated as champ in both races during the 1994 Games in Albertville.

Figure 9.1 Go: newspix
Bonnie Blair (downloaded from CompuServe) is the only American woman to win five gold medals in Olympic competition.

rugby, swimming and diving, and more).

So dig in, and enjoy.

TIP

Here's a tip for the chapter-jumpers. While golf and tennis, for example, have major competitions on an international basis (such as the British Open and Wimbledon), those are professional sports with tours based in the U.S. Therefore those sports are covered in Chapter 7, "Other Pro Sports."

Past Olympic Games and Other International Competitions

The Olympics have been a source of American pride for more than a century, and it's easy to see why. This isn't Lakers vs. Celtics, Yankees vs. Dodgers, Steelers vs. Cowboys. It's the one sporting event in which Americans, as a nation of people, can throw their collective support behind one team.

The end of the cold war and the inclusion of professional athletes has taken some of the fervor out of the events, but the primary focus is still there.

It's us against them. There are still enough sports where strong rivalries exist between nations (for information

on which ones, check out *Politics on the Net*, also published by Que) and enough American heroes, like Dan Jansen and Bonnie Blair, for us to identify with.

Although the next Summer Games won't arrive until 1996 in Atlanta, and there won't be another Winter Games until 1998 in Nagano, Japan, sites for these Games already exist on the Internet (for more information, see the sections, "1996 Summer Olympics" and "1998 Winter Olympics," later in this chapter).

And while the most recent Olympics—the Winter Games in Lillehammer, Norway—are a year behind us, sites on the Internet remain active.

Unlike many of the sites you can find for American professional sports, Olympic sites are often commissioned by the government (or the Olympic Organizing Committee) of their country of origin. They are typically very professionally organized and they include just about every tidbit of information available—for people who are watching on television and those who can attend the Games.

Attending Olympic events in foreign countries is often out of reach of the average sports fan, but with the next Games coming up in Atlanta, there's a decent chance you might attend.

For the history buff, there are several archives of Olympic results and more—including an effective database within Prodigy.

Olympic History

 The 1994 Olympics

`http://www.sun.com/OL/`
`OL94-mirror.html`

This site includes complete summary information on the 1994 Winter Olympics in Lillehammer. It is a mirror of a Norwegian site that operated during the Games, and no timeline is available for when this site might vanish.

It includes lists of events, medal standings, point standings, a big-image archive, a few audio clips, and more.

 Prodigy

Jump: **olympics**

Of the major commercial online services, Prodigy has, by far, the best archive of Olympic information (see fig. 9.3). During any Olympics, any of these services can keep fans updated on information, such as event results and medal standings, through their various news service agencies. Prodigy maintains an archive of Olympic history for its subscribers.

TIME OUT

America³ Sails Into Online Waters

The major commercial online services do an excellent job of providing special areas during special events. A perfect example of that is the America's Cup package offered by America Online.

Linda Linquist, left, leads a tacking maneuver for the America 3.

America Online added a special area to its sports package during the qualifying races leading up to the Cup. It provided general news on the events and special coverage of America³, the first all-female team to compete for the Cup.

The area, which was accessible from America Online's main sports menu, included a special news section devoted to only the America³ team—crew member biographies and photos, a photo gallery of the crew in action, and crew merchandise.

Figure 9.2
The America³ team in action— downloaded from America Online.

On the two most recent Games—the 1994 Winter Olympics and the 1992 Summer Olympics—Prodigy offers the following information:

- News and results
- Medal standings
- Medal winners from the United States
- A photo gallery
- An Olympic sites map
- Rules of various events

Summary information, including lists of medal-winners, is available on all past winter and summer Olympics.

From Prodigy's Olympics menu, simply choose the menu item you want to access. The historical information can be searched by Olympic year, Olympic sport, or by the gender of the athletes.

Other International Competition History

 The 1994 Goodwill Games

`http://www.com/goodwill/index.html`

This site covers the 1994 Goodwill Games. Since these games have finished, some of the available links here are no longer needed—such as the television schedule for the games and ticket information.

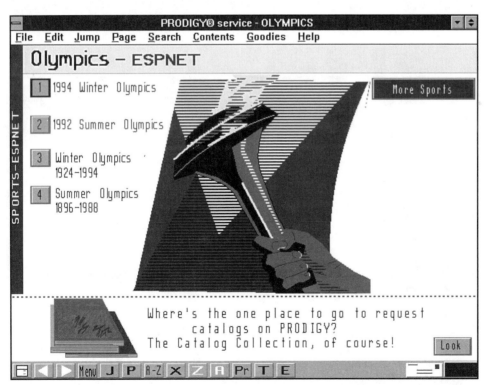

Figure 9.3 Jump: olympics
Prodigy's Olympics archive is, by far, the best of the major commercial online services.

The site remains intact, however, and contains a link to historical information on previous Goodwill Games—plus a list of world records that have been set during Goodwill Games competitions.

This site is likely to be converted soon to provide information on the next Goodwill Games, scheduled for 1998.

As of this writing, however, it includes results of the 1994 games.

1996 Summer Olympics

 The Atlanta Games

`http://`
`www.mindspring.com/`
`~royal/olympic.html`

The next Olympics are within the boundaries of the United States (Atlanta), which creates an opportunity for diehard Olympic fans to attend the Games. If that is something you've been thinking about, or if you're simply interested in how Atlanta is going about staging the Games, this is the site for you (see fig. 9.4).

It includes everything from maps of the Olympic venues to some hot night spots to hit in the city after a busy day of attending events.

This site includes the following information:

- Ticket information
- Hotel accommodations
- Sightseeing
- Public transportation
- Merchandise

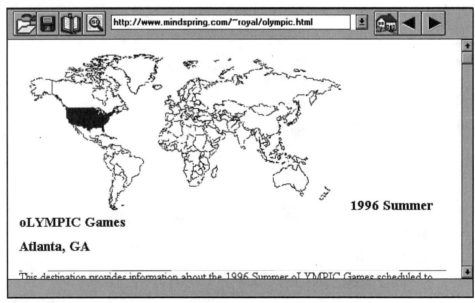

Figure 9.4 `http://www.mindspring.com/~royal/olympic.html`
For those who might want to attend the 1996 Summer Games in Atlanta, this site is the place to go.

The site contains a message cautioning you that the links are in graphical formats—and some are large. Your patience, however, will be rewarded; this is a thorough, well-managed site.

Housing information is divided into sections based on distance from the Olympic Village, with special sections for housing near other Olympic venues and campgrounds.

There are also links that include maps of Atlanta, lists of things to do (including night life, family attractions, and golf courses), and transportation options.

For visitors from outside the U.S., there are links that contain information on currency exchange centers, translation services, and a list of consulates and honorary consulates.

 Olympics Information Project

`http://www.gatech.edu/`
`olympics/intro.html`

This site is actually a class project undertaken by Georgia Tech University. But don't immediately assume this is just a bunch of college kids playing on the Internet.

It's an excellent site that contains a link to event results—an element the previous site doesn't yet have. While that link won't actually come into play until the Games begin, it should be a valuable addition.

This site includes links to information similar to that found at the previous site:

- Event locations
- Ticket information
- Travel information (directions to Atlanta and getting around once you're there).

It also links you to information on the countries that will be competing in the Games, as well as a link for comments and complaints about this site itself.

1998 Winter Olympics

 The Nagano Games

`http://www.linc.or.jp/`
`Nagano/index.html`

Attending the Olympics in the U.S. is too boring and you want to go to Japan, you say? It's never too early to start planning, and this is a great place to begin (see fig. 9.5).

This site, operated out of Japan, is written in English—although there's a link to a similar site written in Japanese (we're assuming at this point that you'll stick to the English version).

There is a link to an Announcements page, which exists mainly because these games are a fair distance off in the future, so notices of changes in plans or new plans are coming out all the time.

This site also links you to an outline for the Games, including the two themes: "From round the world to flower as one" and "I want to make winter my friend and meet people from all over the world. My dream will come true in Nagano."

The XVIII Olympic Winter Games

NAGANO
1 9 9 8

Home page in Japanese is _here_ .

Vision for the 1998 Nagano Olympic Winter Games

Figure 9.5 `http://www.linc.or.jp/Nagano/index.html`
This Japanese site is available in both Japanese and English.

Also, there are links to information on event venues and access to Nagano (including maps and information about airports, railways, and highways).

There is even a link to information on the Games' official mascots, "Snowlets," which are cartoon-style owls depicting the owls found in the forests of Nagano (see fig. 9.6).

The World Cup and International Soccer Leagues

The World Cup is regarded as the most watched sports championship on the planet. That was never more true than in 1994, when the World Cup came to America for the first time.

Much of the nation's press ridiculed the event in its early stages, but when the U.S. team suddenly became a threat and the Cup ended in a shoot-out victory for Brazil, most people changed their tune.

Soccer in the United States has never compared—either in talent or in spectator interest—to that in other parts of the world. But interest and participation continue to grow here.

On the Internet, there is a great deal of information available on the World Cup during Cup years. Throughout the years, there is strong coverage of the often-maniacal European soccer leagues.

World Cup

 World Cup '94

`http://`
`mirach.cs.buffalo.edu/`
`~khoub-s/WC94.html`

This World Cup '94 site (see fig. 9.7) was a great place to go during the event, and it remains active even though the event came to a dramatic conclusion.

It includes information on the history of the World Cup and other links to qualifying tournament information, groups, players, sites of the games, results of the "friendly" matches, news, and pictures.

 Prodigy

Jump: **espnet**

Prodigy was a leader among the commercial online services in its coverage of the World Cup in the United States, and the information was available well after the event concluded (see fig. 9.8).

World Cup fans could find news, scores and schedules, team standings and statistics, historical information on the Cup, and more.

At this writing, the site was still active. From the main ESPNet menu, click Select a Sport. Then click Soccer and, finally, click World Cup.

Figure 9.6 `http://www.linc.or.jp/Nagano/snowlets/html`
These "Snowlets" are the official mascots of the 1998 Winter Olympics.

Figure 9.7 `http://mirach.cs.buffalo.edu/~khoub-s/WC94.html`
This World Cup site continues to operate months after the event concluded.

International Soccer Leagues

 Web Sites

`http://iamwww.unibe.ch/`
`~ftiwww/Sonstiges/`
`Tabellen/Eindex.html`

If you're a fan of international soccer in general—not just the World Cup—this is your home. Not only does it offer excellent information on the latest action, it includes a huge archive of past results.

It also includes a link to the latest league standings in 18 countries, including the United States. Most of these sites, however, are in the language of the country in which the league exists.

There are also links to World Cup '94 sites from six countries, including the United States (these are in English). However, as the Cup gradually becomes another part of history, these sites are vanishing.

The archive link is the largest. It includes the following historical information:

- World Cups from 1930-94
- European Championships from 1960-92
- The 1993-94 European Cup
- The Continental Cup from 1960-94
- The Champion's Cup from 1958-93
- National championships in six countries
- Worldwide soccer mailing list archive
- List of main pages from various European countries

Tour de France

In 1994, Greg LeMond announced his retirement from competitive racing. It was a sad day for him, and a sad day for American fans of the Tour de France.

It was LeMond, after all, who turned an event that previously earned a five-minute network highlight recap into a media event that is covered stage-by-stage nightly by networks and local affiliates alike.

LeMond won the event three times and, in the process, gave Americans another international event worthy of holding their interest. Although Miguel Indurain of Spain has dominated the race over the past few years, its test of strategy, strength, and endurance makes it an event worth watching.

 VeloNews

`http://cob.fsu.edu/`
`velonews/`

VeloNet, the Global Cycling Network, has a wide variety of resources available for everyone from Tour de France fans to weekend mountain bikers.

This site (see fig. 9.9) is dedicated solely to the Tour de France. It's a useful site year-round, and it promises to be a dynamite location during the event.

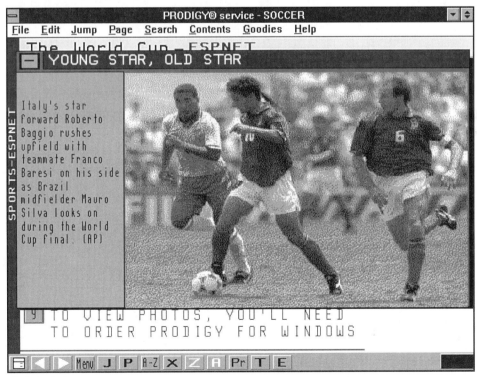

Figure 9.8 Jump: espnet
Prodigy offers a World Cup area full of valuable information.

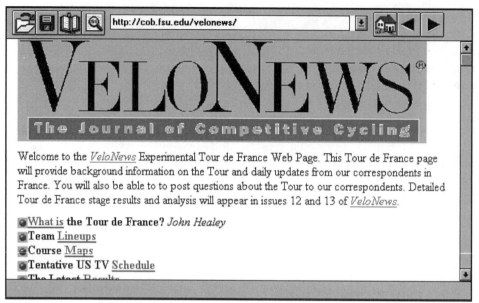

Figure 9.9 http://cob.fsu.edu/velonews/
VeloNews' Tour de France site provides daily updates during the event.

VeloNet's resources include correspondents in France who provide the coverage of the event when it's in progress. You'll be able to post messages or questions to these correspondents during the race.

Background information on the event is already available, and background on the competitors will be added as that information becomes available.

This site includes links to the following information:

- What is the Tour de France?
- Team lineups
- Course maps
- Schedule of U.S. television coverage (subject to change)
- Daily results

The VeloNews Tour de France site is currently labeled "experimental," but it's likely it will become a strong

addition to VeloNet—especially if another American fills LeMond's shoes as a strong annual challenger.

 1994 Tour de France

**http://
wwwhep.phys.soton.ac.uk/
tdf/**

This site recaps the 1994 Tour de France, including overall results, lists of leaders by stage, and other valuable information on the race.

 America Online

Keyword: **sports**

America Online's cycling coverage includes the Tour de France, as well as other major cycling races around the world.

The Reuter news service, an international wire service, provides the bulk of the news that's available on America Online.

From the main sports menu, double-click More Sports, and then double-click Cycling. The next menu will be a list of headlines of cycling stories from which you can choose.

Figure Skating and Speed Skating

Long before figure skating became the twisted Nancy vs. Tonya sideshow that included tabloid newspapers and television shows, there were skaters who made headlines *on* the ice.

Figure skating, both in the Olympics and in other international competitions, has long been one of the most popular Olympic events. It has also become an immensely popular sport during non-Olympic years, with its world championships and professional championship earning extensive network coverage in the United States.

While speed skating has yet to reach those heights, skaters such as Eric Heiden, Bonnie Blair, and Dan Jansen have helped that sport grow with each passing Olympic Games.

Figure Skating

Figure Skating Home Page

`http://www.cs.yale.edu/`
`HTML/YALE/CS/HyPlans/`
`loosemore-sandra/`
`skate.html`

VeloNews Provides Glimpse Into The Future

News editors are involved in a constant search to provide readers/viewers with the news and information they want. Sometimes, however, they have a difficult time determining exactly what that is.

The Internet has helped to solve that problem for editors in all mediums, including those who manage Internet sites. More and more media outlets are offering the opportunity to correspond with editors via e-mail. That opens a line of communication that wasn't avail-

able before (many editors don't take direct phone calls from their readers/viewers).

The VeloNews Tour de France site discussed in this chapter is covering the event in 1995 through the use of on-site correspondents. Users of the site will be able to post messages to those correspondents through the site.

That type of interaction between news gatherers and news consumers is the wave of the future.

This site (see fig. 9.10), generated out of Yale University, ranges from detailed, insightful, and thought-provoking to downright tacky and weird.

On the tacky side is the Tonya Harding Fan Club Page, which isn't for Tonya fans at all. Instead, it includes the latest Tonya jokes and invites users to send their own scanned images and jokes for inclusion in the page.

On the weird side are the links to two pages of images of frogs figure skating. That one cannot be explained.

Fortunately, there's some real information here as well. There are links to two pages covering the figure skating competition in the 1994 Olympics, plus a page covering the upcoming 1998 Games.

There are links to information on various tours and competitions, pictures of various skaters, articles, an index of figure skating periodicals, a Nancy Kerrigan MPEG movie, and frequently asked questions.

Speed Skating

 Speed Skating Home Page

http://
www.twi.tudelft.nl/Local/
sports/skating.html

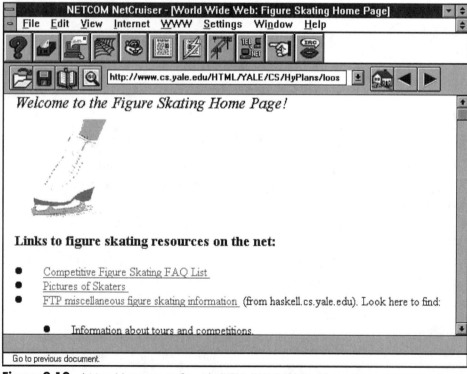

Figure 9.10 http://www.cs.yale.edu/HTML/YALE/CS/HyPlans/loosemore-sandra/skate.html

A well-rounded figure skating home page.

This speed skating home page is based on information—not entertainment—and it succeeds in that manner.

The site includes links to the following information:

- Men's and women's personal records (per distance)
- Men's and women's world records
- A list of all world champions
- Results from the 1992 Olympics
- Results from the 1994 Olympics
- Coverage of the 1994 World Championships
- Coverage of the 1995 World Championships

Chapter Summary

In this chapter, we have covered the major international competitions—centering primarily on the Olympics. There are, of course, many more sports with international tournaments and events. Much of that information is included in the next section, "The List."

This list also includes sports based primarily overseas, such as cricket and rugby.

If you don't find what you're looking for in the list, it's probably covered in another chapter in this book. For example, Formula One auto racing is covered in Chapter 7, "Other Pro Sports."

The List

A complete list of addresses for international tournaments and events follows, including sports based primarily overseas (such as cricket and rugby). Again, if you don't find what you're looking for in this list, it's probably covered elsewhere in this book.

If you're not sure how to use one of the following addresses, see Chapter 12, "Internet Basics."

Olympics

Archive of Olympic results from all years:

> Prodigy address:
> Jump: `olympics`

1994 Winter Olympics in Lillehammer, Norway:

> WWW address: `http://www.sun.com/OL/OL94-mirror.html`

1996 Summer Olympics in Atlanta, Georgia:

> WWW address: `http://www.mindspring.com/~royal/olympic.html`

> WWW address: `http://www.gatech.edu/3020/olympics/olym-proj/intro.html`

1998 Winter Olympics in Nagano, Japan:

> WWW address: `http://www.linc.or.jp/Nagano/index.html`

The List

Other International Competitions

1994 European Championships in Athletics:

WWW address: `http://helsinki94.eunet.fi/`

1994 Goodwill Games:

WWW address: `http://www.com/goodwill/index.html`

Basketball

Olympiakos basketball:

WWW address: `http://www.engin.umich.edu/~etentz/basket.html`

Panathinaikos Basketball Club:

WWW address: `http://www-server.bcc.ac.uk/~ucess8k/basket/basket.html`

Cricket

Australian cricket:

WWW address: `http://www.physics.su.oz.au/~mar/cricket.html`

CricInfo Cricket Database:

Gopher address: `cricinfo.cse.ogi.edu:7070/11/link_to_database`

The Cricket Page:

WWW address: `http://cuda3.me.mtu.edu:8023/home/maxwell-a.ee/kmushtaq/.mosaic/cricket.html`

General information:

WWW address: `http://pipkin.lut.ac.uk/~ben/Cricket/`

WWW address: `http://cuda3.me.mtu.edu:8023/home/maxwell-a.ee/kmushtaq/.mosaic/cricket.html`

Cycling

Professional cycling:

WWW address: `http://www.informatik.uni-tuebingen.de:8080/sport/rad/rad.html`

Tour de France, 1994:

WWW address: `http://wwwhep.phys.soton.ac.uk/tdf/`

VeloNet Tour de France page:

WWW address: `http://cob.fsu.edu/velonews/`

Rugby

Rugby League Web page:

WWW address: `http://www.brad.ac.uk/~cgrussel/`

Rugby Union Home Page:

WWW address: `http://rugby.phys.uidaho.edu/rugby/`

Rugby World Cup:

> WWW address: `http://rugby.phys.uidaho.edu/rugby/games/World_Cup/wc.html`

Rugby WWW server:

> WWW address: `http://rugby.phys.uidaho.edu/rugby.html`

Skating

Figure skating home page:

> WWW address: `http://www.cs.yale.edu/HTML/YALE/CS/HyPlans/loosemore-sandra/skate.html`

Rec.skate, the Web page:

> WWW address: `http://www.cs.fsu.edu/misc/skate/rec.skate.html`

Speed skating home page:

> WWW address: `http://www.twi.tudelft.nl/Local/sports/skating.html`

Soccer

Facts:

> WWW address: `http://www.di.unipi.it/fos/fos.html`

Football Club Nantes Atlantique:

> WWW address: `http://www.unantes.univ-nantes.fr/~boulange/Soccer/football.html`

French Soccer Web Server:

> WWW address: `http://www.cc.columbia.edu/~yn25/soccer.html`

Games:

> WWW address: `http://www.atm.ch.cam.ac.uk/sports/games.html`

German Bundesliga results:

> WWW address: `http://ls2www.informatik.uni-dortmund.de/Buli/Buli.html`

Hammarby IF:

> WWW address: `http://www.nada.kth.se/~nv92-tek/Hammarby.html`

International soccer results and archive:

> WWW address: `http://iamwww.unibe.ch/~ftiwww/Sonstiges/Tabellen/Eindex.html`

International Soccer Results:

> WWW address: `http://www.pitt.edu/~rlpst/international.html`

International Soccer Server:

> WWW address: `http://sotka.cs.tut.fi/riku/soccer.html`

The List

Italian soccer:

WWW address: `http://www.cedar.buffalo.edu/~khoubs/WC94.nations/Italy.html`

Laws of Soccer:

WWW address: `http://mirach.cs.buffalo.edu/~khoub-s/FIFA_rules.html`

Mailing lists:

WWW address: `http://www.atm.ch.cam.ac.uk/sports/lists/`

Manchester United Football Club:

WWW address: `http://dallas.ucd.ie/~rmeade/index.html`

Newcastle United Football Club:

WWW address: `http://bonnard.lif.icnet.uk/nufc.html`

Northern European Rec.Sport.Soccer Statisticians Foundation:

WWW address: `http://info.risc.uni-linz.ac.at:70/1/misc-info/rsssf/nersssf.html`

Nottingham Forest Football Club:

WWW address: `http://unicorn.nott.ac.uk/~ccznffc/NFFC.html`

Norwich City Football Club:

WWW address: `http://www.sys.uea.ac.uk/Recreation/Sport/ncfc/ncfc.html`

Olympiakos soccer:

WWW address: `http://www.engin.umich.edu/~etentz/soccer.html`

Panathinaikos Soccer Club:

WWW address: `http://www-server.bcc.ac.uk/~ucess8k/football/football.html`

Queens Park Rangers Football Club:

WWW address: `http://akebono.stanford.Edu/yahoo/Entertainment/Sports/Soccer/Clubs/Queens_Park_Rangers_Football_Club/`

Sheffield Wednesday Football Club:

WWW address: `http://www.crg.cs.nott.ac.uk/Users/anb/Football/index.html`

Swindon Town Football Club:

WWW address: `http://www.bath.ac.uk/~ee3cmk/stfc.html`

Tottenham Hotspur Football Club:

WWW address: `http://www2.sys.uea.ac.uk/recreation/sport/thfc/thfc.html`

U.S. soccer:

WWW address: `http://www.cs.cmu.edu:8001/afs/cs/usr/mdwheel/www/soccer/us-soccer.html`

Web page `rec.sports.soccer`:

WWW address: `http://www.atm.ch.cam.ac.uk/sports/`

West Bromwich Albion:

WWW address: `http://www.esu.edu/~andrews/westbrom.html`

World Cup 1994 information:

WWW address: `http://mirach.cs.buffalo.edu/~khoubs/WC94.html`

Chapter 10

College Sports

As more and more fans become disgruntled with pro sports, interest in college sports skyrockets to new levels—and the Internet meets those needs.

In this chapter

- *Where to find information on men's basketball*
- *Where to find information on women's basketball*
- *Where to find information on football*
- *Where to find information on other college sports*

In other chapters

→ *If you don't know how to use an address in this chapter, see Chapter 12*

→ *If you would like more information on the commercial online services listed in this chapter, see Chapter 13*

When you think of Michael Jordan, do you think of the 19-year-old who hit the game-winning shot in the NCAA championship game? When you think of the classic Magic Johnson-Larry Bird matchups, do you think of an NCAA Final between Michigan State and Indiana State?

When you think of Joe Montana's fourth-quarter heroics, do you think of Notre Dame football?

If so, then this is the chapter for you. Of course, you don't have to close your eyes to the professional ranks to be a true college sports fan. But college sports generate more heartfelt feelings of joy and anguish in their fans than any pro sport ever could.

With two professional leagues shutting down in 1994 due to labor strife, numerous teams threatening to leave their home cities in favor of better deals elsewhere, and hundreds of players planning to do the same, the "big four" professional sports leagues are at a crossroads.

College sports, always a staple in the American sports fan's diet, are growing in popularity and only stand to gain from their big brothers' problems.

Every day, new sites are opening on the Internet for fans of college sports—especially for football and men's basketball (although women's basketball is one of the fastest-growing segments of college sports on the Internet).

On the Internet, you can find everything from Utah State's men's basketball schedule to information on UCLA's water polo team. Part of what makes college sports on the Internet fun is that in most cases, the sites are operated out of the universities they cover and often are produced by college students.

That makes them enjoyable to read. For example, the game recaps are usually one-sided. You'll discover that when the alma mater loses, these sites provide some choice words about the game officials.

College basketball is all over the Internet. On the World Wide Web, there are several excellent home pages that serve as catch-alls for college basketball news, statistics, and other information.

Men's Basketball

If someone held a gun to your head and said you could only watch sports one day each year, which day would you pick? Many American sports fans would pick the NCAA men's basketball national semifinals, otherwise known as the Final Four.

It doesn't really matter whether you agree or not. If you're a college basketball fan at any level, the Internet has tons of possibilities for you.

You can find pages on the World Wide Web on many of the top teams in the country, and you can find some kind of home page for most of the top conferences. The sites covered below are home pages that cover college basketball in general. Some of them link to specific conferences or even specific teams. Those addresses can be found in the list at the end of this chapter.

Scott Reilly's College Basketball Page

`http://www.cs.cmu.edu:8001/afs/`
`cs.cmu.edu/user/wsr/Web/bball/`
`bball.html`

Scott Reilly's College Basketball Page (see fig. 10.1) is a top-notch clearing-house for men's college basketball information. It features several links, including some that link you to information that's generally not available from other home pages.

A couple of examples of this are the links to the ESPN schedule of televised games and a general television schedule of games—essential information for the true college hoops fan.

The site tends to place its loyalty in the Atlantic Coast Conference, but if you're going to lean to a conference, that's not a bad place to start. It includes links to the ACC schedule and a special site for the ACC postseason tournament.

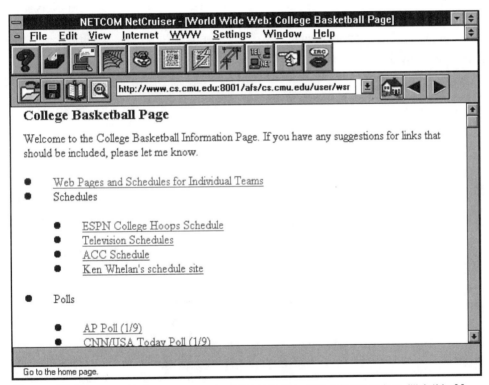

Figure 10.1 `http://www.cs.cmu.edu:8001/afs/cs.cmu.edu/user/wsr/Web/bball`
`bball.html`
This is one of the top college basketball home pages.

Otherwise, its links are to more general pages, including the following:

- Team schedules
- AP, CNN/USA Today, UPI, and Division III polls
- Top college basketball news stories from other services
- Game summaries and boxscores from games involving Top 25 teams
- Satchel Sports' Top 25 scoreboard, which includes games in progress
- A list of team nicknames
- A complete statistics server
- An FTP site
- Last year's NCAA tournament results
- Standings, schedules, and statistics from select conferences
- The 1995 Final Four weekend schedule of events
- A link to other top college basketball sites

 Satchel Sports College Basketball Page

`http://www.starwave.com/ncb/`
`toc.html`

The Satchel Sports college basketball page does what all the Satchel pages do—an excellent job of covering the basics. There aren't many frills in this home page, but there probably isn't a better place to go for the staples.

As with all the Satchel pages, it links you to a scoreboard that includes games in progress—just about every Division I-A game. There's a Top 25 scoreboard, but there are also links to regional scoreboards.

There are other links to game recaps and boxscores, national rankings, standings, and statistics.

Bobby Knight

If Bobby Knight's basketball teams weren't so successful, he might not be coaching at all.

Knight, the head coach of the Indiana Hoosiers, has gained as much attention for his sideline antics and handling of his players as he has for his coaching ability.

Knight has won three national championships at Indiana, more than 600 games in his coaching career, and more than 500 with the Hoosiers.

Although he has hoisted the national championship trophy three times, perhaps he'll be best remembered for the chair he heaved across a basketball floor.

He is also known for belittling his players, badgering officials, and beating up a courtside telephone. He is a rare combination—both famous and notorious.

Nando X College Basketball

`http://www.nando.net/sports/`
`bkb/1994/col/college.html`

The Nando X Sports Server's college basketball home page is not as complete as most of Nando's offerings, but it does a good job of covering the action.

The college basketball coverage includes stories from the Associated Press (AP), plus AP's weekly poll and "How The Top 25 Fared" graphic. It also provides links to standings, weekly schedules, feature stories, and daily game previews.

 Yahoo Sports Server

`http://akebono.stanford.edu/`
`yahoo/Entertainment/Sports/`
`Basketball/College/Men/`

At the main home page in the Yahoo Sports Server (see fig. 10.2), you'll find links to the top basketball conferences in the country. Once you jump to one of the conferences, you'll find links to all kinds of specific information on teams within those conferences.

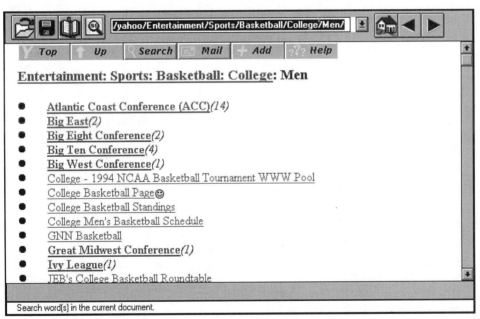

Figure 10.2 `http://akebono.stanford.edu/yahoo/Entertainment/Sports/`
`Basketball/College/Men/`
Yahoo's college basketball server offers links to all major conferences.

For example, the Atlantic Coast Conference site includes team schedules, weekly schedules of conference games, team rosters, standings, results of the most recent conference tournament, and information on the upcoming conference tournament.

There are also some outstanding sites on individual teams. Some are part of a group of sites on several teams (in one conference, for example), while others are generated from within the university they cover and are operated by students or members of that university's sports information department. These and other sites can be found in the list at the end of the chapter.

Women's Basketball

NCAA women's basketball has grown by leaps and bounds in recent years, but it's far from being an overnight sensation.

This has been a hard-fought battle, with initial inroads paved primarily out West and in the Southeast. Now, women's basketball is moving closer to being a major player (and perhaps a major money-maker) within the world of college athletics.

TIME OUT

Women's Basketball Comes Of Age

Whatever the reason, women's basketball is blossoming all over the country. In Minnesota, it was barely covered—if at all—by the major media outlets in the Twin Cities.

But in 1993, when the University of Minnesota's women's team made its first trip to the NCAA tournament, things began to change. Suddenly, both newspapers assigned beat writers to the team, the local all-sports radio station carried the games live, and the team's games were previewed and covered on nightly television news shows.

Now, two years later, more and more of the team's games are covered by newspaper staff writers, and the local

television stations have highlights of the games on the newscasts.

It's great to see, albeit a little late. As the father of a little girl (and two boys) and a big-time sports fan, I worry sometimes that my daughter doesn't see sports figures to whom she can relate—unless it's an Olympic year or a major event like the women's Final Four.

I don't know if my daughter will ever have an interest in sports. But it's refreshing to me that when she sees me reading the newspaper and wants to look at the pictures, I can show her photos of girls' (or women's) basketball, soccer, gymnastics, or whatever.

Players such as Ann Meyers and Cheryl Miller helped women's hoops gain popularity. Meyers was the first woman to earn a tryout with a professional (men's) team and Miller is a former USC standout who now is the Trojans' coach—her brother, Reggie, stars for the Indiana Pacers.

Their heroics—and the national media coverage that accompanied it—provided young girls with strong role models. In turn, more girls began to play the game, which increased the competition and improved the level of play—thereby increasing fan and media interest.

Today, you may hear comments such as, "I like women's basketball because it's basketball the way the game was meant to be played. The focus is more on the fundamentals—like strong ballhandling and sound passing—than on high-flying acrobatics." Still, when a North Carolina women's player dunked during a game earlier this season, it received national media coverage.

On the Internet, women's basketball is still in its infancy, but it's improving in both quality and quantity. New sites for individual teams are popping up all the time, but overall there are still only a few good home pages on women's basketball.

 GNN Women's Basketball Site

`http://gnn.com/gnn/meta/sports/basketball/women/index.html`

The Global Network Navigator women's basketball site (see fig. 10.3) continues to grow into an excellent site for fans of the sport.

Its home page indicates the site is "working to give a BIG voice to women's hoops," and it's doing just that. Plans for the site include adding Sports Ticker's game recaps and boxscores, which would nicely round out this site. That service should be in place by the time you read this.

There is also a link to the GNN Top 25 Poll, in which Internet users (called "Netizens" on this page) can cast their own ballots.

It doesn't yet include information on all major conferences, but it does include links to Atlantic Coast Conference standings and statistics and a Southwest Conference Report.

Other features include the following:

- NCAA Statistics
- The Roundup—The Scoop in Women's Hoops
- Team Schedules
- Game Writeups

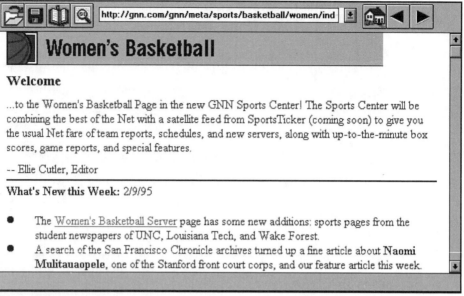

Figure 10.3 http://gnn.com/gnn/meta/sports/basketball/women/index.html
The GNN women's basketball site is the deepest women's basketball site on the Internet.

Many of the Game Writeups are supplied by Internet users, and the site invites users to provide e-mail on their favorite team's games.

 Satchel Sports Women's Hoops Server

`http://www.starwave.com/ncw/`
`toc.html`

Satchel Sports women's basketball home page does a solid job of providing women's basketball information.

It includes a link to a notes section entitled "Inside Women's College Basketball," which keeps fans up to date on the latest happenings and tidbits from around the country.

The remainder of the links are general in nature, but—as is always the case

with Satchel—they are professionally done.

Links include the following:

- A Top 25 scoreboard (including games in progress)
- News stories
- Game recaps
- Boxscores
- Rankings
- Statistics

College Football

So who was number one, Nebraska or Penn State?

The polls said it was Nebraska, but there are thousands of football fanatics in Pennsylvania who disagree.

Division I-A college football is unique in the sports world in that it's the only sport whose champion is determined by a vote. That fact alone makes it one of the most discussed—make that most *debated*—sport in the land.

Despite the frustration expressed by fans all over the country, college football remains one of the country's most treasured sports.

Internet activity reflects that interest. There are college football sites on specific conferences, specific teams, even specific bowl games.

There are perhaps more outstanding college football sites on the Internet than for any other sport—pro or college. The one you pick depends on your personal tastes. Of the following sites, at least one should fill your needs.

 Web Site

`http://www.math.ufl.edu/`
`~mitgardt/rsfc.html`

At the risk of getting a little carried away, the World Wide Web's college football site is one of the most complete sites on any subject on the Internet (see fig. 10.4). If there is a college football angle that isn't covered here, we're not aware of it.

Not only does it go beyond the ordinary in the information it supplies, it also offers college football fans across the country the opportunity to chip in and provide some inside information themselves.

It includes a link to notes on all conferences—updated on a daily basis—and the notes include such things as injuries, game previews, and so on.

It covers the basics (AP game summaries, polls, and Top 25 results), but also goes in-depth with a link to recruiting information so you can catch up on how your alma mater might fare down the road.

As the summer winds down, check this site for preseason prognostications and

Some College Sites Are All-Inclusive

When you look into some of the team-specific sites that are included in this chapter, you'll find that many of them include links to other sports at that school.

For example, if you enter a site that this book lists as devoted to North Carolina men's basketball, you will probably find links to the women's basketball team and other sports at North Carolina.

The point is that while your alma mater's swimming teams may not have sites devoted solely to them, there may be information on those teams within a link from another site.

Part of the fun of surfing the net is digging around, trying to find the information for which you're looking.

TIME OUT

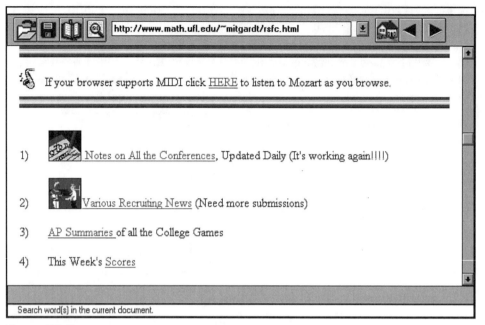

Figure 10.4 `http://www.math.ufl.edu/~mitgardt/rsfc.html`
This is one of the most complete sites on any subject on the Internet.

recaps of the previous season's statistics. It also includes a complete schedule for the current (or upcoming) season.

Unlike most college football sites, this one isn't limited to just Division I-A schools. There are also links to fairly complete coverage of Division I-AA and Division III schools.

 Nando X College Football Page

`http://www.nando.net/football/`
`1994/college/college.html`

Nando's college football page doesn't go as in-depth into the sports as some of their other pages, but it's a solid source of college football information.

With its link to the AP, Nando offers conference-by-conference rundowns of each Saturday's action, plus further coverage in the form of news, notes, and profiles.

Perhaps the most unique link is to "Images of Game Day," (see fig. 10.5) which includes pictures from some of the top games across the country each week.

Other links include the following:

- Associated Press, CNN/*USA Today* weekly polls
- Conference standings
- Weekly roundups (capsules that preview each Saturday's games)
- Scoreboards
- Top 25 game summaries

- AP's "How the Top 25 Fared"
- Statistics

 Darryl E. Marsee's Football Page

`http://erau.db.erau.edu/`
`~marseed/fb_page.html`

A good, basic site for college football information, this page offers the following (see fig. 10.6):

- Weekly power ratings and polls
- Predictions on the upcoming weekend's action
- Scores, schedules, and predictions for the entire season for each team

- Scores of each team's games during the current season.

This site's power rankings helped fuel the Nebraska-Penn State debate; it ranked Penn State No. 1 and Nebraska way down at No. 4—behind Florida State and Florida.

Every Division I-A football team is listed in the power rankings.

Other College Football Sites

There are a lot of college football sites on the Internet, especially on the World Wide Web. The following sites

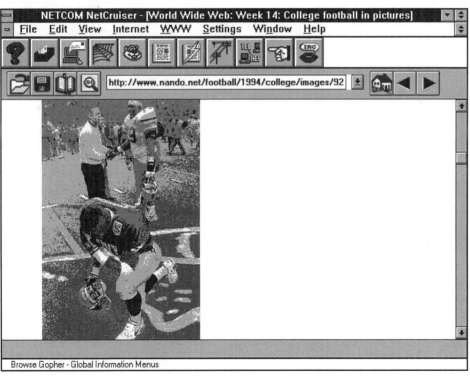

Figure 10.5 `http://www.nando.net/football/1994/college/college.html`
Nando's "Images of Game Day" is an example of the information provided by this site.

```
http://erau.db.erau.edu/~marseed/fb_rnk.txt

MARSEE FINAL DIV I-A COLLEGE FOOTBALL COMPUTER RANKINGS FO
                    (Power ratings in parenthesis)
 1.  Penn State      (967)    37.  Air Force        (629)    73.  O
 2.  Florida State   (921)    38.  Baylor           (628)    74.  C
 3.  Florida         (910)    39.  Mississippi      (622)    75.  M
 4.  Nebraska        (893)    40.  Purdue           (619)    76.  H
 5.  Miami           (853)    41.  N Carolina St    (617)    77.  N
 6.  Illinois        (829)    42.  East Carolina    (615)    78.  I
 7.  Colorado        (822)    43.  South Carolina   (611)    79.  M
 8.  Ohio State      (811)    44.  Louisiana St     (601)    80.  G
 9.  Michigan        (804)    45.  Bowling Green    (597)    81.  S
10.  Tennessee       (787)    46.  Oklahoma         (592)    82.  T
11.  Alabama         (782)    47.  Oregon State     (588)    83.  T
12.  Southern Cal    (768)    48.  Kansas           (587)    84.  T
13.  Wisconsin       (765)    49.  Minnesota        (583)    85.  W
14.  Auburn          (757)    50.  West Virginia    (582)    86.  P
15.  Oregon          (754)    51.  TX Christian     (576)    87.  C
```

Figure 10.6 `http://erau.db.erau.edu/~marseed/fb_page.html`
This site's power rankings listed Penn State as the nation's No. 1 team.

are particularly interesting because of the unique features they offer.

Traveller NCAA Football

`http://www.traveller.com/`
`sports/ncaa_fb/`

Are you tired of letting a group of sportswriters or coaches (or both) determine the national champion in Division I-A college football? Then check out this site (see fig. 10.7).

This site isn't noted for its coverage of the sport itself; it's known for its unique "People's Choice Poll." Internet users can cast their own ballot through this site, and the result is an interesting poll—even if it's somewhat unscientific.

NCAA I-AA Home Page

`http://www.vt.edu:10021/bev/`
`Users/gunner/1-aahome.html`

Although Division I-AA football is a step below Division I-A and it has an ardent following, there aren't a lot of Division I-AA sites out there on the Internet yet. However, this site (see fig. 10.8) is a solid home page for Division I-AA fans.

Its links include the following:

- A Top 25 list for Division I-AA
- Scores of the previous week's games
- Conference standings
- A schedule of games for the coming week

- News, notes, and other information
- Previews of upcoming games
- Links to other college football sites

Other College Sports

Naturally, there are a lot of other college sports, including some—like hockey, volleyball, and baseball—that have huge, loyal followings in certain regions of the United States.

But these sports are largely absent from the Internet (except for the occasional team-specific site).

Most college sports have UseNet newsgroups devoted to them. Some of these newgroups, which are set up as a means for fans to discuss specific sports, are dedicated solely to one sport at the collegiate level.

Others are more general in nature, but can be used to exchange information with other fans about the collegiate sport. For example, **rec.sport. volleyball** might contain messages on international volleyball, but most of the discussion is about men's and women's college volleyball.

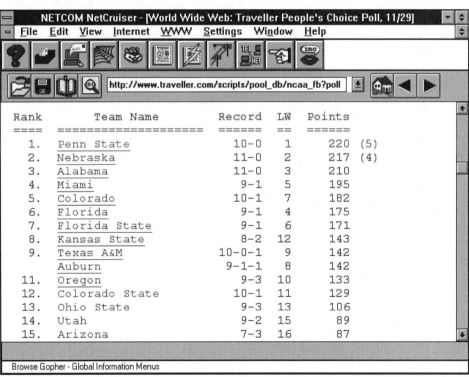

Figure 10.7 `http://www.traveller.com/scripts/pool_db/ncaa_fb?poll`
The People's Choice Poll enables Internet users to cast their votes for college football's national champion.

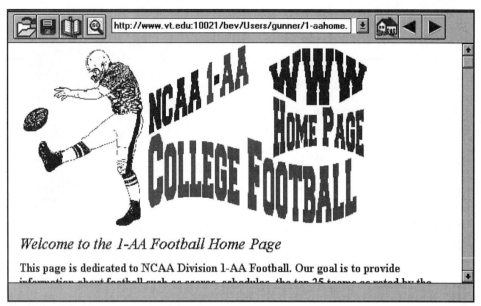

Figure 10.8 `http://www.vt.edu:10021/bev/Users/gunner/1-aahome.html`
This is the top Division I-AA site on the Internet.

The following is a list of UseNet newsgroups that include discussions of collegiate sports:

Baseball: **`rec.sport.baseball.college`**

Basketball: **`rec.sport.basketball.college`**

Field Hockey: **`rec.sport.hockey-field`**

Football: **`rec.sport.football.college`**

Rowing: **`rec.sport.rowing`**

Rugby: **`rec.sport.rugby`**

Soccer: **`rec.sport.soccer`**

Swimming: **`rec.sport.swimming`**

Tennis: **`rec.sport.tennis`**

Volleyball: **`rec.sport.volleyball`**

Water polo: **`rec.sport.water-polo`**

Chapter Summary

In this chapter, we have covered some of the top sites for three of the top collegiate sports—men's basketball, women's basketball, and football.

These sites are general in nature—that is, they don't cover specific conferences or teams, just the sports in general. Often they link you to information from specific conferences or teams.

The List

The following list includes all of the sites covered in the body of this chapter. It also includes more specific listings of sites that deal with specific conferences, schools, or teams.

The list is really two lists. First, there is a general list of sites devoted to specific colleges or universities. For example, if you wanted a site that covered sports at UCLA—not just the UCLA women's basketball team—this first list is the place to look.

The second portion of the list is divided by sport. This is where you would look for a site devoted solely to the University of Michigan football team, for example.

If you're not sure how to use an address in this chapter, see Chapter 12, "Internet Basics."

TIP

Just because there isn't a site listed for a specific team in the second list doesn't mean there is no information on that team on the Internet. Say, for example, you want information on the University of Florida's swimming and diving teams and you don't see a site listed under "Swimming and Diving." You'll probably find what you want in the general sites for the University of Florida.

School-Based General Sites

Arkansas Razorbacks (men's schedules):

WWW address: `http://www.sibylline.com/nwa/uark/sports/mens/schedule.html`

Arkansas Razorbacks (women's schedules):

WWW address: `http://www.sibylline.com/nwa/uark/sports/womens/schedule.html`

Big 10 Conference schools:

WWW address: `http://meteor.atms.purdue.edu/sports`

Brigham Young Cougars:

WWW address: `http://www.cs.byu.edu/sports/sports.html`

Cal-Berkeley Bears:

WWW address: `http://www.cs.cmu.edu:8001/afs/cs.cmu.edu/user/landay/pub/www/sports/cal/cal.html`

Cincinnati Bearcats—The Global Bearcat:

WWW address: `http://ucunix.san.uc.edu/~zureick/bearcat.html`

Florida Gators:

WWW address: `http://www.library.health.ufl.edu/~bill/ufsports.html`

Florida Gators—*Gator Bait* magazine:

WWW address: `http://www.interactive.line.com/gator/.cover_gator.html`

Georgia Bulldogs—*The Georgia Bulldog*:

WWW address: `http://www.interactive.line.com/bull/table.html`

The List

Purdue Boilermakers:

WWW address: `http://`
`meteor.atms.purdue.edu/sports`

Tennessee Volunteers:

WWW address: `http://`
`loki.ur.utk.edu/sports/`
`sports.html`

Texas Longhorns

WWW address: `http://`
`ftp.netcom.com/pub/dl/`
`dlcrow/ut.sports/index.html`

UCLA Bruins

WWW address: `http://`
`avicenna.icsl.ucla.edu:8001/`
`UCLA_Sports/general.html`

USC Trojans:

WWW address: `http://`
`cwis.usc.edu/users/`
`rbaily/uscsports/`

Sport-Specific Sites

Baseball

Florida Gators:

WWW address: `http://`
`www.library.health.ufl.edu/`
`~bill/BB/index.html`

Newsgroup:

UseNet address:
`rec.sport.baseball.college`

Basketball—Men

General Sites

Conference, Atlantic Coast
Conference:

WWW address: `http://`
`www.cs.fsu.edu/~smiths/`
`acc.html`

Conference, Big 12 (records):

WWW address: `http://`
`penguin.cc.ukans.edu/`
`Big12_hoops.html`

Home page, college basketball:

WWW address: `http://`
`www.cs.cmu.edu:8001/afs/`
`cs.cmu.edu/user/wsr/Web/`
`bball/bball.html`

Home page, Global Network Navigator
(GNN):

WWW address: `http://`
`www.digital.com/gnn/news/`
`sports/basketball/ncaa/`
`index.html`

Home page, Nando X's NCAA
basketball:

WWW address: `http://`
`www.nando.net/sports/`
`bkb/1994/col/college.html`

Home page, NCAA basketball:

WWW address: `http://`
`www.traveller.com/`
`scripts/pool_db/`
`ncaa_bb?menu=main`

Polls, CNN/USA Today:

WWW address: `http://`
`www.nando.net/newsroom/`
`basketball/1994/col/feat/`
`usat25.html`

Polls, current:

WWW address: `http://`
`www.traveller.com/scripts/`
`pool_db/ncaa_bb?list=polls`

Polls, Dick Vitale's:

WWW address: `http://`
`www.cs.cmu.edu:8001/afs/`
`cs.cmu.edu/user/wsr/Web/`
`bball/dv-poll.html`

Polls, *Sporting News* preseason:

WWW address: `http://`
`www.cs.cmu.edu:8001/afs/`
`cs.cmu.edu/user/wsr/Web/`
`bball/sn-poll.html`

Polls, *Street & Smith's* preseason:

WWW address: `http://`
`www.cs.cmu.edu:8001/afs/`
`cs.cmu.edu/user/wsr/Web/`
`bball/ss-poll.html`

Pools, NCAA men's tournament:

WWW address: `http://`
`hoohoo.ncsa.uiuc.edu/`
`NCAApool/NCAApool.html`

Schedules:

WWW address: `http://`
`www.nando.net/newsroom/`
`basketball/1994/col/feat/bkc/`
`msked.html`

Standings:

WWW address: `http://`
`www.nando.net/newsroom/`
`basketball/1994/col/stat/`
`standings.html`

Team-Specific Sites

Arkansas Razorbacks:

WWW address: `http://`
`law.uark.edu/bball/razor.html`

Cal-Berkeley Bears:

WWW address: `http://`
`www.cs.cmu.edu:8001/afs/`
`cs.cmu.edu/user/landay/pub/`
`www/sports/cal/basketball/`
`basketball.html`

Cal-Berkeley Bears (boxscores):

WWW address: `http://`
`uxa.cso.uiuc.edu/`
`~mattb/cal_bb/bbindex.html`

Clemson Tigers:

WWW address: `http://`
`www.cs.fsu.edu/~smiths/`
`cu.html`

Duke Blue Devils:

WWW address: `http://`
`www.cs.fsu.edu/~smiths/`
`duke.html`

WWW address: `http://`
`www.cs.cmu.edu:8001/afs/`
`cs.cmu.edu/user/wsr/Web/`
`bball.duke.html`

The List

Florida Gators:

WWW address: `http://`
`www.library.health.ufl.edu/`
`~bill/MBB/basketball.html`

Florida State Seminoles:

WWW address: `http://`
`www.cs.fsu.edu/~smiths/`
`fsu.html`

Georgia Tech Yellowjackets:

WWW address: `http://`
`www.cs.fsu.edu/~smiths/`
`gt.html`

Indiana Hoosiers:

WWW address: `http://`
`silver.ucs.indiana.edu/`
`~fulton/sports.html`

Kansas Jayhawks:

WWW address: `http://`
`falcon.cc.ukans.edu/`
`~mcmillan/bball.html`

Kentucky Wildcats:

WWW address: `http://`
`www.digimark.net/flattop/`
`uk.html`

Kentucky Wildcat, The Unofficial:

WWW address: `http://`
`www.ewl.uky.edu/~etw/bball/`
`wildcats.html`

Louisville Cardinals (schedule):

WWW address: `http://`
`www.comm.louisville.edu/`
`schedule.html`

Maryland Terrapins:

WWW address: `http://`
`www.cs.fsu.edu/~smiths/`
`um.html`

Mississippi State Bulldogs:

WWW address: `http://`
`www.msstate.edu/~rdm4/`
`msubb94-95sch.html`

North Carolina Tar Heels:

WWW address: `http://`
`www.cs.fsu.edu/~smiths/`
`unc.html`

North Carolina State Wolfpack:

WWW address: `http://`
`www.cs.fsu.edu/~smiths/`
`ncst.html`

Purdue Boilermakers:

WWW address: `http://`
`meteor.atms.purdue.edu/`
`sports/basketball-95m/`

Seton Hall Pirates:

WWW address: `http://`
`www.shu.edu/html/shuinfo/`
`sports/basket/index.html`

Virginia Cavaliers:

WWW address: `http://`
`www.cs.fsu.edu/~smiths/`
`uva.html`

Wake Forest Demon Deacons:

WWW address: `http://`
`www.cs.fsu.edu/~smiths/`
`wfu.html`

UCLA Bruins:

WWW address: `http:// avicenna.icsl.ucla.edu:8001/ UCLA_Sports/mbball.html`

USC Trojans:

WWW address: `http:// cwis.usc.edu/users/rbaily/ uscsports/mbasketball/`

Utah Utes:

WWW address: `http://www/ cs.utah.edu/~msmith/WAC/ uofu.html`

Utah State Aggies:

WWW address: `http:// happy.usu.edu/~slbjb/ bbhome.html`

Villanova Wildcats:

WWW address: `http:// 153.104.58.25/sports/ bball.html`

Washington Huskies:

WWW address: `http:// lux.labmed.washington.edu/ ~shoe/uw/basketball/ bball.html`

Basketball—Women

General Sites

Home page, NCAA women's basketball:

WWW address: `http://gnn.com/ gnn/meta/sports/index.html`

Home page, Satchel Sports Women's College Basketball:

WWW address: `http:// www.starwave.com/ncw/toc.html`

Home page, women's college basketball:

WWW address: `http:// www.auburn.edu/~poperic/ wbb.html`

Polls, Top 25:

WWW address: `http:// www.nando.net/newsroom/ basketball/1994/col/feat/ wt25.html`

Schedules:

WWW address: `http:// www.nando.net/newsroom/ basketball/1994/col/feat/bkw/ wsked.html`

Team-Specific Sites

Arkansas Razorbacks:

WWW address: `http:// law.uark.edu/bball/ ladyback/ladyback.html`

Auburn Lady Tigers:

WWW address: `http:// www.auburn.edu/~poperic/ ltb/ltbmenu.html`

Florida Gators:

WWW address: `http:// www.library.health.ufl.edu/ ~bill/WBB/basketball.html`

The List

Indiana Hoosiers:

WWW address: `http://copper.ucs.indiana.edu/~wlambert/hoosiers.html`

Louisiana Tech Lady Techsters:

WWW address: `http://info.latech.edu/~wts/techsters.html`

Purdue Boilermakers:

WWW address: `http://meteor.atms.purdue.edu/sports/basketball-95w/`

Football

General Sites

Bowl games, 1994 sites:

WWW address: `http://www.nando.net/football/1994/bowls/bowl.html`

Conference, Big Eight (statistics):

WWW address: `http://www.cis.ksu.edu/~chiefs/bigeight.html`

Home page, Darryl Marsee's:

WWW address: `http://erau.db.erau.edu/~marseed/fb_page.html`

Home page, Division I-AA:

WWW address: `http://www.vt.edu:10021/bev/Users/gunner/1-aahome.html`

Home page, Gate Cybersports College Football:

WWW address: `http://sfgate.com/sports/sports/ncaa/football/index.html`

Home page, Nando X College Football:

WWW address: `http://www.nando.net/football/1994/college/college.html`

Home page, NCAA football:

WWW address: `http://www.traveller.com/sports/ncaa_fb/`

Home page, RSFC college football:

WWW address: `http://www.math.ufl.edu/~mitgardt/rsfc.html`

Home page, Satchel Sports College Football:

WWW address: `http://www.starwave.com/ncf/toc.html`

Newsgroup:

UseNet address: `rec.sport.football.college`

News stories:

UseNet address: `clari.sports.football.college`

Team-Specific Sites

Alabama Crimson Tide:

WWW address: `http:// www.traveller.com/ ~alvitar/football/index.html`

Arizona Wildcats:

WWW address: `http:// www.cs.arizona.edu/ http/html/pictorials/ wildcats.html`

Auburn Tigers:

WWW address: `http:// www.eng.auburn.edu/ network/au/ tiger_football.html`

Brigham Young Cougars:

WWW address: `http:// www.cs.byu.edu/sports/ sports.html`

Cal-Berkeley Bears:

WWW address: `http:// www.cs.cmu.edu:8001/ afs/cs.cmu.edu/user/landay/ pub/www/sports/cal/football/ football.html`

WWW address: `http:// cyber.sfgate.com/sports/ sports/ncaa/football/cal/`

Duke Blue Devils:

WWW address: `http:// www.nando.net/football/ 1994/college/duke/duke.html`

Florida Gators:

WWW address: `http:// www.library.health.ufl.edu/ ~bill/FB/football.html`

Michigan Wolverines:

WWW address: `http:// ai.eecs.umich.edu/ people/timd/ um_football94.html`

Mississippi State Bulldogs (exists only during football season):

WWW address: `http:// www2.msstate.edu/ ~rdm4/msufb94sch.html`

North Carolina Tar Heels:

WWW address: `http:// www.nando.net/football/ 1994/college/unc/unc.html`

North Carolina State Wolfpack:

WWW address: `http:// www.nando.net/football/ 1994/college/ncsu/ncsu.html`

Notre Dame Fighting Irish:

WWW address: `http:// www.nd.edu/Departments/ NDBands/season.html`

Notre Dame Fighting Irish—*Blue & Gold Illustrated*:

Gopher address: `gopher.enews.com:2100/11/ magazines/alpha/af/ bluegold_illustrated`

The List

Purdue Boilermakers:

WWW address: `http://`
`meteor.atms.purdue.edu/`
`sports/football-94/`

Stanford Cardinal:

WWW address: `http://`
`sfgate.com/sports/sports/`
`ncaa/football/stanford/`

Tennessee Volunteers:

WWW address: `http://`
`loki.ur.utk.edu/sports/`
`sports.html`

UCLA Bruins:

WWW address: `http://`
`avicenna.icsl.ucla.edu:8001/`
`UCLA_Sports/football.html`

USC Trojans:

WWW address: `http://`
`cwis.usc.edu:80/users/`
`rbaily/uscsports/football/`

Washington Huskies:

WWW address: `http://`
`lux.labmed.washington.edu/`
`~shoe/uw/uw.html`

Hockey

Information:

Gopher address: `gopher://`
`netsurf.geo.mtu.edu/11/hockey`

Computer Ratings:

WWW address: `http://`
`hydra.bgsu.edu/TCHCR/`

Swimming and Diving

Harvard men's swimming and diving:

WWW address: `http://`
`hcs.harvard.edu/~menswim/`

Volleyball

Florida State Seminoles:

WWW address: `http://`
`www.satelnet.org/`
`~msandler/fsu.vb.html`

MIT:

WWW address: `http://`
`www.mit.edu:8001/people/`
`squonk/vball/mit.html`

Delaware Blue Hens:

Gopher address:
`gopher.udel.edu/hh/.dept/`
`vball/.mosaic/vball2.htm`

Florida Gators:

WWW address: `http://`
`www.library.health.ufl.edu/`
`~bill/VB/volleyball.html`

Hawaii Rainbow Wahines:

WWW address: `http://`
`www2.hawaii.edu/`
`sports/94.wahine.html`

USC Trojans:

WWW address: `http://`
`cwis.usc.edu/users/rbaily/`
`uscsports/wvolleyball/`

Virginia Tech Lady Techsters:

WWW address: `http://www.vt.edu:10021/org/volleyball/`

Chapter 11
Hobbies and Recreational Sports

This chapter is designed for those who are actively involved in sports—rather than those who solely are fans and interested spectators.

In this chapter

- *Internet sites for information about cycling (including mountain biking)*
- *Internet sites for information about golf*
- *Internet sites for information about snow skiing*
- *Internet sites for information about sports collectibles*

In other chapters

← *If you enjoy following the PGA Tour, don't expect to find that type of information in this chapter. Instead, see Chapter 7*

← *If you're interested in information about Olympic downhill skiing, see Chapter 9*

For every fan who watches an NFL football game on television there are probably 10 people outside participating in some type of recreational sport.

Whether your interests are as intense as skydiving or as casual as collecting baseball cards, the Internet can help you enjoy your hobby to the fullest.

There are hundreds of varieties of hobbies and recreational sports, and there is no way they can all be covered here. We've done our best to compile the best list of Internet sites for a wide variety of sports.

In this chapter, we will cover some of the most popular hobbies and recreational sports and highlight some exciting places to go on the Internet. At the end of the chapter, you will find a more complete list of sites, divided alphabetically by sport/interest.

Hobbies or Passions?

For some people, recreational sports mean a weekly round of golf or a casual game of billiards. For others, it means month-long mountain bike challenges through tough terrain.

For some, a sports hobby means display cases full of autographed footballs and baseballs. Others, however, consider their occasional Rocky Mountain skiing vacations as hobbies.

That's why we've lumped together these two areas—hobbies and recreational sports—in one chapter. While there's no question that mountain bikers and baseball card collectors are participating in their areas of interest at different levels, these interests are similar in that they're participatory in nature.

The Internet is big enough to cover all of these areas.

Cycling

What running was to the 1970s and early 1980s, cycling has become to the late 1980s and mid-1990s.

More and more in America today, you hear fitness types talking about their latest mountain biking trek—not their training efforts in preparation for a marathon.

And just as running or jogging magazines were popping up all over the map in the '70s, today we see cycling or mountain biking magazines taking their place on the racks.

A big part of the surge in cycling in the United States was Greg LeMond's drive to win the Tour de France three times. But cycling encompasses a lot more than road racing.

> **TIP**
>
> Internet sites that cover cycling competitions such as the Tour de France are included in Chapter 9, "Olympic and International Sports."

Internet sites for cycling enthusiasts are wide-ranging. You can find sites that discuss equipment and manufacturers, as well as provide tips on training, stretching, and more. You can also find sites that archive the top mountain biking trails in the United States—or in a particular region within the U.S.

Whatever interest you have in cycling, the Internet probably has a home for you.

The World Wide Web is a great place to go for cycling information, although information is available from other sources as well.

The sites covered in this section are some of the top cycling sites on the Internet. In the list at the end of this chapter, you'll find plenty of sites that cover certain aspects of cycling in specific geographical regions of the U.S. and elsewhere.

 The Global Cycling Network (VeloNet)

`http://www.cycling.org/`

The Global Cycling Network (VeloNet) operates this World Wide Web home page (see fig. 11.1), which covers just about everything an avid cyclist could want. VeloNet also operates sites in FTP and Gopher.

 The Global Cycling Network (VeloNet)

`cycling.org/`

 The Global Cycling Network (VeloNet)

`gopher.cycling.org/`

VeloNet's sites are a great place to go if your interest in cycling is wide-ranging. If you're solely interested in mountain biking, for example, you might want to pick a site that is suited more directly to that interest.

Figure 11.1 `http://www.cycling.org/`
Whether it's off-road racing or road racing, this cycling page covers it all.

But the VeloNet sites do a great job covering cycling in general. There are links to everything from equipment manufacturers, to race information, to how to make your own repairs.

This site is for the fairly serious cyclist—not generally for those who take a more casual interest in the sport.

The FTP and Gopher sites include listings of support organizations available to cyclists.

 Mountain Biking Site

`http://www.cs.cmu.edu:8001/afs/`
`cs.cmu.edu/user/jake/`
`mosaic/mtb-routes.html`

It's a long address, but it's worth noting if you're a mountain bike enthusiast.

If you think you have the skills and stamina to take on some of America's top mountain-bike trails and you're looking for a great place to go, this is the site for you (see fig. 11.2).

It contains a complete listing of mountain bike routes in the Pittsburgh area, and links to San Francisco-area mountain bike routes as well. Perhaps more importantly, this site serves as a solid example of the pages that are available to people who are planning a major trek.

There are a lot of similar sites for other areas of the country. Check the list at the end of the chapter to find these addresses.

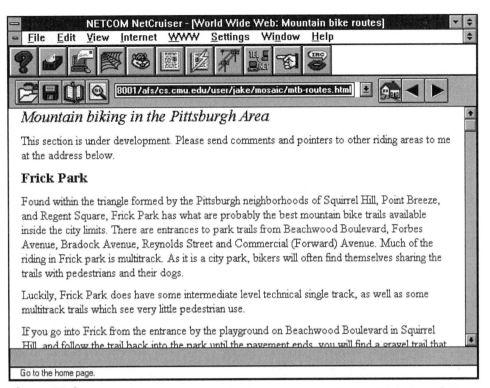

Figure 11.2 `http://www.cs.cmu.edu:8001/afs/cs.cmu.edu/user/jake/mosaic/`
`mtb-routes.html`
A good example of the type of sites that serve mountain bike enthusiasts.

 League of American Wheelmen

`draco.acs.uci.edu:1071/00/`
`law.info`

We include this site because it offers information that is general in nature, provided by a cycling advocacy group.

The League of American Wheelmen (LAW), an organization that works to improve the quality of cycling world-wide, maintains this site. It includes a newsletter-style update on the latest cycling trends and news, and offers information on issues that affect cyclists around the globe (with specific emphasis on the U.S.).

Golf

No sport has exploded in the U.S. in recent years like golf has. Courses are jam-packed on a daily basis, new courses are opening in record numbers, the cost of playing a round has risen to exorbitant levels—and people are paying it.

What used to be a casual round of golf on a public course has been turned into a test of one's survival skills—many times taking as long as six hours to get from the first tee to the 18th green.

Still, we play. Why? That's probably the best question, but the fact remains that we simply play. Sure, we do a little business out there on the course at times, but golf remains one of the top leisure activities.

The Internet has a place for you, whether you're a recreational player who tees it up a few times a month, a member of a private club who plays twice a week, or a competitor who wagers a few bucks or competes in amateur tournaments.

The Internet is loaded with information, including the following:

- Listings of courses in specific states or regions
- Scorecard archives
- Specific information about individual courses
- Travel packages

On the Internet, you can find information as specific as golf in Florida or you can find information as general as golf in America. You can find the rules of golf, the etiquette of golf, and more.

There are many, many golf pages on the Internet—as the list at the end of this chapter shows. The sites that follow are some of the best out there.

 The 19th Hole

`http://zodiac.trriscs.`
`panam.edu/golf/19thhole.html`

If you've read Chapter 7, "Other Pro Sports," you've already seen some information on this World Wide Web site (see fig. 11.3).

It's included here as well because it is a *crossover site*—it includes information on both professional golf (covered in Chapter 7) and recreational golf.

In fact, its primary strength is in the area of recreational golf. It serves the needs and desires of the avid golfer as well as any site on the Internet.

If you're trying to find a great golf course to play while you're on your next business trip, this site includes a link to a scorecard archive that lets you examine the lay of the land (so to speak) before you get on the plane.

If you're trying to find a support organization to join, this site links you to a list of golf associations in the U.S.

If you're in need of a new driver, putter, or whatever, this site includes classified advertisements for equipment.

This site also includes links to the following information:

- Frequently asked questions
- The rules of golf
- The *Golf Digest* record book
- Golf art and pictures that can be downloaded
- Recommendations on other good golf pages you can explore

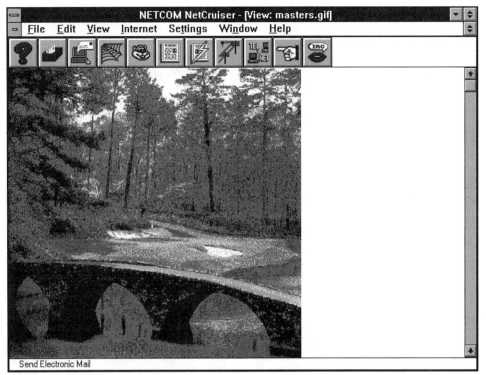

Figure 11.3 `http://zodiac.tr-riscs.panam.edu/golf/19thhole.html`
Along with a great deal of golf information, The 19th Hole contains a large selection of golf pictures—including this shot of "Amen Corner."

 The Fore Play Golf Newsletter

`http://www.deltanet.com/4play/newsltr.html`

You've just returned home from a round of golf that includes a half-dozen lost balls, three tries to get out of a single sand trap, a slew of three-putt greens and, finally, a driver wrapped around an oak tree.

You need help, and you don't want to pay your local PGA professional big bucks to cure the many things wrong with your game.

This site can help you (see fig. 11.4).

The Fore Play Golf Newsletter is more than just a clever name. It's full of useful information for the amateur golfer, both serious and not-so-serious.

The whole purpose of this site involves improving your game. It includes tips from PGA professional Steve Wolff, some advice on clubs (from what club you should buy to what club you should use from under a tree, 150 yards from the green), plus other ideas and tips to help you lower your scores.

It may not make you a scratch golfer, but it can help.

The Golf Data On-Line Home Page

`http://www.gdol.com/`

The Golf Data On-Line Home Page includes links to the following information:

- Golf publications
- An archive of golf courses
- Other course information
- Tournament and association information
- A Golf Channel update
- Notes on new equipment, including design and features

 The Golf Home Page

`http://ausg.dartmouth.edu/`
`~pete/golf/`

When it came time to build an expansion onto your home, you did it yourself. When your car's transmission went out, you fixed it yourself.

So what are you going to do when you need a new set of golf clubs?

This site (see fig. 11.5) covers just about everything you need to know in order to build yourself a set of custom irons and woods.

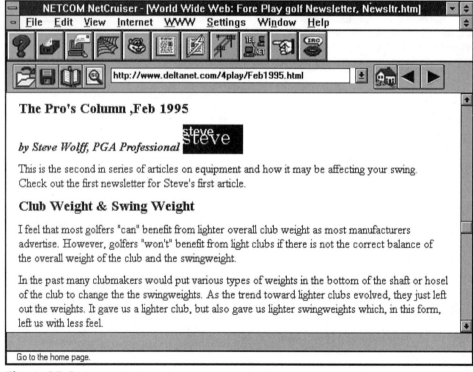

Figure 11.4 `http://www.deltanet.com/4play/newsltr.html`
The Fore Play Golf Newsletter includes tips from a PGA professional.

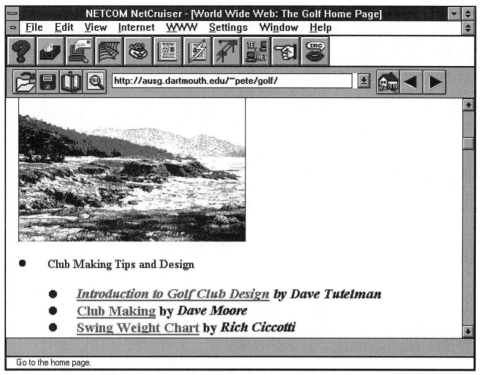

NETCOM NetCruiser - [World Wide Web: The Golf Home Page]

File   Edit   View   Internet   WWW   Settings   Window   Help

http://ausg.dartmouth.edu/~pete/golf/

- **Club Making Tips and Design**

    - *Introduction to Golf Club Design* **by Dave Tutelman**
    - *Club Making* **by Dave Moore**
    - *Swing Weight Chart* **by Rich Ciccotti**

Go to the home page.

Figure 11.5   http://ausg.dartmouth.edu/~pete/golf/
This site offers tips on designing and making clubs.

It includes an introduction to club design, an explanation of the club-making process, a swing-weight chart, and tips on how to grip and re-grip your clubs.

 America Online

Keyword: **sports**

A round of golf once was only an after-thought when you planned a vacation. Now, more and more people are plan-ning golf vacations.

With America Online, you can plan a complete golf vacation—whether it's to find great places to play (see fig. 11.6),

a professional tournament to watch, or both.

In America Online's main sports menu, click Magazines, Clubs and Info. Then double-click Golf Courses and Resorts in the menu provided.

From there, you can plan a great golf trip. America Online assembles its rec-reational golf package by combining information provided by the National Golf Course Directory and other sources.

It includes listings of courses and re-sorts from across the U.S. and covers several topics on golfing and golf travel that access a wealth of information related to the game of golf.

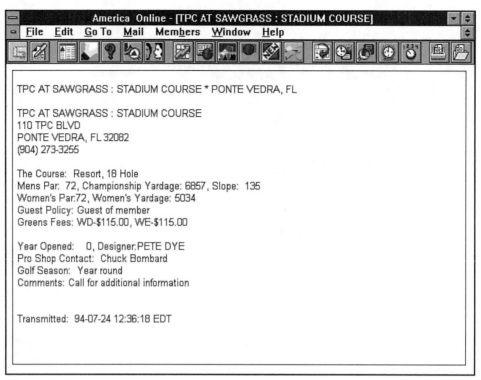

TPC AT SAWGRASS : STADIUM COURSE * PONTE VEDRA, FL

TPC AT SAWGRASS : STADIUM COURSE
110 TPC BLVD
PONTE VEDRA, FL 32082
(904) 273-3255

The Course: Resort, 18 Hole
Mens Par: 72, Championship Yardage: 6857, Slope: 135
Women's Par:72, Women's Yardage: 5034
Guest Policy: Guest of member
Greens Fees: WD-$115.00, WE-$115.00

Year Opened: 0, Designer:PETE DYE
Pro Shop Contact: Chuck Bombard
Golf Season: Year round
Comments: Call for additional information

Transmitted: 94-07-24 12:36:18 EDT

Figure 11.6 Keyword: sports
Information on nearly any course in America is available on America Online.

There is also a listing of major tournaments you may want to attend, as well as a listing of golf travel companies, associations, publishers, manufacturers, and more.

Snow Skiing

Golf vacations are becoming more common, but perhaps the most popular type of recreational sports trip is a ski vacation.

In recent years, the ski industry—which relies heavily on travellers—has found that the Internet provides a nearly endless marketplace of potential customers.

Travel brochures and other forms of traditional advertising have proven successful for ski resorts, but more and more, they are finding the Internet works just as well—and it's a much cheaper form of advertising.

For the skier, that means obtaining information on everything from the availability of inns or cabins to the depth of the snow pack.

Whether you ski downhill or cross-country, the Internet probably has a resource that will help you plan your next ski trip.

Ski destinations are available all over the Internet, but particularly on the

World Wide Web. Resorts have learned they can advertise their services through what some are calling an *online brochure*, which includes pictures of skiers in action, the chalet, and accomodations.

In this section, we'll highlight some of the top sites for obtaining general skiing information. The list at the end of the chapter includes Internet addresses for specific resorts, regions, and so on.

 The Internet Ski Guide

`http://cybil.kplus.bc.ca/www/`
`ski_net/ski_na.htm`

You just plain want to go skiing. You haven't decided yet whether you want to go to Utah, Colorado, Maine, Michigan, or Canada. All you know is you want to go skiing—and you want to go soon.

The Internet Ski Guide—North America (see fig. 11.7) is a great place to start. The site's name virtually says it all.

This is the best place to go on the Internet for skiing information anywhere in North America. It's designed to help you find a place to go, so you don't have to surf through a series of Internet pages on specific resorts while you try to make up your mind.

Use this site to narrow your focus, and then consult the list at the end of this chapter to pick out a specific resort if you want.

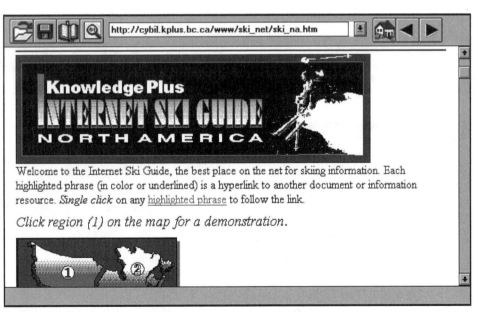

Figure 11.7 `http://cybil.kplus.bc.ca/www/ski_net/ski_na.htm`
Maps within this site provide links to ski information throughout North America.

This is a map-based graphical interface that leads the users to reports on skiing conditions, snow reports, lists of slopes and more.

Simply click a region on the map and you will get general information (for example, snow conditions) in that region. You can use this type of information to gradually narrow the focus of your trip, and then move on to the specific resort sites in that region.

 ### International Skiing Site

```
http://www.explore.com/
E_slopes.html
```

This site is also a general list of slopes, but it includes European ski areas as well.

Slopes are listed by country or state, and it includes some phone numbers for a more traditional approach—calling to find information and snow reports.

 ### Bulletin Board Site

```
http://www.cs.colorado.edu/
homes/mcbryan/public_html/bb/
ski/ski.html
```

It's certainly not surprising that one of the Internet's best skiing pages comes out of the University of Colorado.

This site takes a different approach, operating as a bulletin board for

reporting skiing conditions around the world for all types of snow skiing.

The result is an interesting site for skiers that is jam-packed with useful information.

 ### CompuServe

Go: **APO**

It wouldn't be any fun to plan a ski trip and spend thousands of dollars, only to show up on the slopes and find horrible skiing conditions.

In CompuServe's Associated Press Online section, choose Sports and then choose Olympic and Other Sports from the next menu.

The items in the menu that appears include ski reports from the main ski areas in the U.S.

Sports Collectibles

In the 1980s, the sports collectibles industry exloded—sending baby-boomers back to their parents' attics, searching for the baseball cards they collected as youths.

Several discovered that their mothers had sold them in a garage sale years ago or, worse yet, had simply thrown them away. Those who did find their cards were probably amazed at how beat up they were. After all, in the old days, we used to play games with our cards instead of putting them in protective plastic sheets.

Today sports collectibles includes balls, bats, helmets, skates—virtually any item that has anything to do with pro sports. You can spend thousands of dollars on this stuff and still come up with only a small display case of memorabilia.

The Internet has yet to catch up with the explosive growth in this industry. There are a few sites at which you can place an order or take a look at cards. But, for the most part, the best places to go for collectibles information remains within the major commercial online services.

There also are several software packages that can be purchased that are excellent sources for information on collectibles.

 Card Displays

`http://www.gems.com/ibic/`
`cards.html`

This site offers card collectors a chance to display their most-prized cards to other avid fans.

Users can display up to six cards at full size at no charge, or more cards at $5 per page. There also is a charge to have the cards scanned, if that service is needed.

Or you can simply call up this site to view others' collections.

Just For The Fun Of It

When I was a kid (and it wasn't *that* long ago, by the way), collecting baseball cards was fun. I'd take my allowance, head up to the store, and buy as many packs of Topps as my cash flow allowed.

Then I'd bring 'em home and, well, play with them. My brother had invented a game we called "Card Baseball" in which we'd use baseball cards to play a game of baseball. It's a little too involved to get into how it was played, but the point is that the cards didn't sit in three-ring binders waiting to be looked at, autographed, or sold.

I'm not saying the collecting and selling of cards is bad. In fact, I dabbled in that in recent years myself. What I am saying is that it's a shame that card collecting has become so competitive. Much of the fun of playing with the cards themselves has been lost.

I believe there's room for the more serious side of collecting *and* for the sheer fun of Card Baseball.

TIME OUT

11

HOBBIES & RECREATIONAL SPORTS

Memorabilia Lists

LISTSERV address:
cards-request@tanstaafl.uchicago.edu

This list is for those interested in collecting cards or other sports memorabilia, including those who are interested in speculating or investing.

Discussion and buy/sell advertisements are welcomed, and the list is open to anyone.

CompuServe

Go: **collect**

CompuServe's collectibles forum is a little like an online flea market (see fig. 11.8). It offers the following three discussion topics the sports hobbyist will enjoy:

- Sports Card Trading
- Sports Cards Etc.
- Sports Memorabilia

The Sports Card Trading area is full of offers to buy and sell cards of all makes and models, going far beyond the basic baseball card stuff into special sets in all sports.

Sports Cards Etc. includes some of the same, although it includes other memorabilia related to sports cards.

In the Sports Memorabilia area, you can find everything from autographed baseballs and footballs to game-worn shoes and more.

NOTE

This type of online buying and/or trading is a perfect example of *caveat emptor* (let the buyer beware). Online scam artists are still pretty few and far between, especially when the item you're buying is less than $100. I have seen some high-priced items advertised, however. It's in your best interest in these cases to arrange a meeting or some other way for you to make sure you're getting what you think you're getting—before you write the check.

Pete Rose

How the mighty have fallen.

Pete Rose is baseball's all-time hit king and a former manager of the Cincinnati Reds.

However, he has yet to be allowed back into the game he loves—let alone into the hall of fame—because he was convicted of gambling on sports games.

Rose still finds a way to be a part of the game—in a manner of speaking. Today, he hawks baseball memorabilia on home shopping television networks.

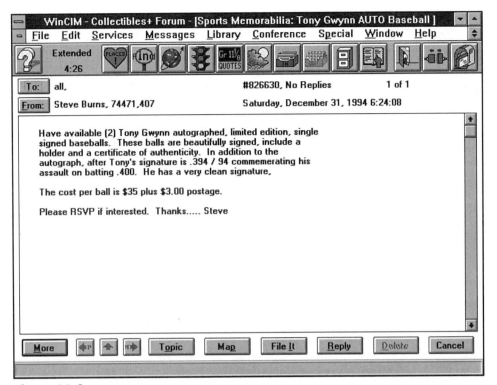

Figure 11.8 Go: `collect`
CompuServe enables you to advertise in its collectibles forum.

CompuServe allows its members to advertise items for sale, including price, and to place "wanted" ads to help fill out their collections.

 Prodigy

Jump: **collecting bb**

Much like CompuServe's offerings, Prodigy's collecting bulletin board includes sports areas. The topics in this area are every bit as lively as those in CompuServe.

Trading, buying, and selling is permitted.

Chapter Summary

In this chapter, we have covered the best places on the Internet to find information about some of the top hobbies and recreational sports. Many of these sites are designed to help those who have never tried the sport, to help them learn more about it and how to get involved.

The List

In the following list, you will find more sites on the topics we've already discussed—plus many, many more areas of interest, from air hockey to wind-surfing. If you're not sure how to use an address in this list, see Chapter 12, "Internet Basics."

Air Hockey

Events, rules, and tournament information:

WWW address: `http://www.interaccess.com/users/tweissm/ahwww.html`

Billiards

Frequently Asked Questions:

WWW address: `http://nickel.ucs.indiana.edu/~fulton/Pool/PoolFAQ.html`

Newsgroup:

UseNet address: `alt.sport.pool`

UseNet address: `rec.sport.billiards`

Boating

General Boating Info

Boating tips:

Gopher address: `gopher.internet.com:2550/11/tips`

Newsgroups:

UseNet address: `rec.boats`

UseNet address: `rec.boats.racing`

Kayaking

California Kayak Friends:

WWW address: `http://www.intelenet.com/clubs/ckf/`

Paddling

Newsgroups:

UseNet address: `rec.boats.paddling`

UseNet address: `rec.boats.paddle`

Servers:

WWW address: `http://www.recreation.com/paddling/home.html`

Wave-Length magazine:

WWW address: `http://www.intelenet.com/clubs/ckf/wavelength/`

Sailing

Aladdin sailing index:

WWW address: `http://www.aladdin.co.uk/sihe/`

Mark Rosenstein's sailing page:

WWW address: `http://community.bellcore.com/mbr/sailing-page.html`

Sailing information page:

WWW address: `http://www.armory.com/~lew/sports/sailing/`

Body Building

Female Bodybuilder home page:

> WWW address: `http://www.ama.caltech.edu/~mrm/body.html`

Photos of top bodybuilders:

> WWW address: `http://www.cs.odu.edu/~ksw/`

Climbing

Exercise information, equipment, and upcoming events:

> WWW address: `http://www.dtek.chalmers.se/Climbing/index.html`

Collectibles

Forums

Collectibles forum/bulletin board:

> CompuServe address:
> Go: `collect`

Collecting bulletin board:

> Prodigy address:
> Jump: `collecting bb`

General Info

To subscribe, send e-mail to:

> LISTSERV address: `cards-request@tanstaafl.uchicago.edu`

To post messages, send e-mail to:

> `cards@tanstaafl.uchicago.edu`

Viewing trading cards online:

> WWW address: `http://www.gems.com/ibic/cards.html`

Newsgroups

Newsgroups:

> UseNet address:
> `alt.collecting.autographs`

> UseNet address:
> `rec.collecting.cards`

Curling

General information:

> WWW address: `http://www.cs.cmu.edu:8001/afs/cs.cmm.edu/user/clamen/misc/Sports/README.html#Curling`

Cycling

Equipment

Archive of human-powered vehicles of all types:

> WWW address: `http://zippy.sonoma.edu:70/1/HPV`

Bicycle technology:

> WWW address: `http://uni.uiuc.edu/~dtucker/project.html`

Discussion of bikes and electronics:

> WWW address: `http://www.thesphere.com/bikecurrent/index.html`

General Info

Bicycling Community Page:

> WWW address: `http://www.cs.wisc.edu/~condon/sd.html`

The List

Bicycling organizations:

Gopher address: `cycling.org/11/org`

Cycling travelogues:

WWW address: `http://akebono.stanford.Edu/yahoo/Entertainment/Sports/Cycling/Travelogues/`

Cycling worldwide:

Gopher address: `draco.acs.uci.edu:1071/00/law.info`

Global Cycling Network VeloNet:

WWW address: `http://www.cycling.org/`

FTP address: `cycling.org/`

Gopher address: `gopher.cycling.org/`

Gopher server of `rec.bicycles.*`:

Gopher address: `draco.acs.uci.edu:1071/`

Information Superhighway Bike Lane:

WWW address: `http://www.fsr.com/~dearien/bike/`

Mountain bike routes throughout the United States:

WWW address: `http://www.cs.cmu.edu:8001/afs/cs.cmu.edu/user/jake/mosaic/mtb-routes.html`

Newsgroups:

UseNet address: `rec.bicycles.marketplace`

UseNet address: `rec.bicycles.misc`

UseNet address: `rec.bicycles.off-road`

UseNet address: `rec.bicycles.racing`

UseNet address: `rec.bicycles.rides`

UseNet address: `rec.bicycles.soc`

UseNet address: `rec.bicycles.tech`

Unicycling Home Page, The:

WWW address: `http://www.mcs.kent.edu/~bkonarsk/index.html`

Regional Info

Cascade Bicycle Club:

WWW address: `http://alfred1.u.washington.edu:8080/~kfink/bicycling.html`

Central NJ Bicycle Racing:

WWW address: `http://www.cs.princeton.edu/grad/cek/racing/`

Chicago-area cycling page:

WWW address: `http://www.interaccess.com/users/msanner/`

Colorado's Front-Page Cycling:

WWW address: `http://www.lance.colostate.edu/~ja740467/bike/frbike.html`

Midwest racing home page:

WWW address: `http://ids.net/`
`~bsullivan/bikeracing.html`

Mountain bike routes:

WWW address: `http://`
`www.cs.cmu.edu:8001/afs/`
`cs.cmu.edu/user/jake/mosaic/`
`mtb-routes.html`

New Jersey cycling home page:

WWW address: `http://`
`www.cs.princeton.edu/`
`grad/cek/racing`

Pittsburgh cycling home page:

WWW address: `http://`
`www.cs.cmu.edu:8001/afs/`
`cs.cmu.edu/user/jdg/www/`
`bikeFAQ.html`

The Princeton Freewheeling Club:

WWW address: `http://`
`mv2.pupress.princeton.edu/`

Equestrian

Aberdeen University Horse Riding
Club:

WWW address: `http://`
`www.abdn.ac.uk/~src011`

Fencing

Fencing club information:

WWW address: `http://`
`csclub.uwaterloo.ca/`
`u/mabuckle/fencing/`

Newsgroup:

UseNet address:
`rec.sport.fencing`

Field Hockey

Newsgroup:

UseNet address:
`rec.sport.hockey.field`

Flying Discs

Disc golf Frequently Asked Questions
and information on events:

WWW address: `http://`
`www.cqs.washington.edu/`
`~josh/discgolf.html`

Newsgroup:

UseNet address: `rec.sport.disc`

Ultimate Frisbee:

FTP address: `ftp.cs.wisc.edu/`
`pub/ultimate`

Ultimate Frisbee page:

WWW address: `http://`
`www.cs.rochester.edu/`
`u/ferguson/ultimate/`

Golf

Course Lists

Archived golf courses:

WWW address: `http://`
`dunkin.princeton.edu/.golf/`

Lanier Golf database:

CompuServe address: `Go: Lanier`

Public golf courses across the United
States:

FTP address:
`dunkin.Princeton.EDU/pub/golf`

The List

Scorecard archive:

WWW address: `http://www.traveller.com/golf/scorecards/`

Destinations

Alberta:

WWW address: `http://bear.ras.ucalgary.ca/brads_home_page/CUUG/golf.html`

Southern Utah Golf Courses:

WWW address: `http://sci.dixie.edu/StGeorge/Golf/golf.html`

Wild Dunes:

WWW address: `http://www.persimmon.com/WildDunes/`

General Info

The 19th Hole:

WWW address: `http://zodiac.tr-riscs.panam.edu/golf/19thhole.html`

Fore Play Golf Newsletter:

WWW address: `http://www.deltanet.com/4play/newsltr.html`

Golf Data Online Home Page:

WWW address: `http://www.gdol.com/`

Golf home page:

WWW address: `http://ausg.dartmouth.edu/~pete/golf/`

To subscribe, send e-mail to:

LISTSERV address: `LISTSERV@ubvm.BITNET`

To post messages, send e-mail to:

`Golf-L@UBVM.CC.BUFFALO.EDU`

Hacky Sack

Hacky sack rules, clubs, leagues, images:

WWW address: `http://www.cup.hp.com/~footbag/`

Hang Gliding

Hang Gliding Mosaic Picture server Home Page:

WWW address: `http://cougar.stanford.edu:7878/HGMPSHomePage.html`

Hiking

Equipment, clubs, trip reports, and maps:

WWW address: `http://io.datasys.swri.edu`

Hunting

To subscribe, send e-mail to:

LISTSERV address: `firearms-request@cs.cmu.EDU`

To post messages, send e-mail to:

`firearms@cs.cmu.EDU`

Martial Arts

Aikido index:

WWW address: `http://www.hal.com/~landman/Aikido/`

Aiki Jujitsu information:

WWW address: `http://www.thesphere.com/SJWC/SJWC.html`

Bay Area Wing Chun group:

WWW address: `http://www.thesphere.com/SJWC/SJWC.html`

General Martial Arts:

WWW address: `http://archie.ac.il:8001/papers/rma/rma.html`

Karate Web site, including Frequently Asked Questions:

WWW address: `http://sol45.essex.ac.uk/Web/Karate/`

Martial Arts Resource List:

WWW address: `http://www.middlebury.edu/~jswan/martial.arts/ma.html`

Newsgroup:

UseNet address: `rec.martial.arts`

Motorcycles

Reviews, images, safety, and training information:

WWW address: `http://www.halcyon.com/moto/rec_moto.html`

Outdoors

Equipment, clubs, rock climbing, paddling, caving, and skiing information:

WWW address: `http://www.princeton.edu/~rcurtis/oa.html`

Orienteering and Rogaining Home Page:

WWW address: `http://www2.aos.princeton.edu/rdslater/orienteering/`

Paintball

Newsgroups:

UseNet address: `alt.sport.paintball`

UseNet address: `rec.sport.paintball`

The Paintball Server:

WWW address: `http://warpig.cati.csufresno.edu/`

Web Paintball Field:

WWW address: `http://abacus.bates.edu/~jburke/paintball/p-ball.html`

Rowing

All rowing-related sports:

WWW address: `http://www.comlab.ox.ac.uk/archive/other/rowing.html`

The List

Running

The Dead Runners Society:

WWW address: `http://`
`www.furman.edu/drs/drs.html`

New York City marathon and others:

WWW address: `http://`
`nyweb.com/marathon.html`

The Running Page—clubs, upcoming races, and more:

WWW address: `http://`
`polar.pica.army.mil/`
`running.real/running.html`

The Running Page:

WWW address: `http://`
`sunsite.unc.edu/`
`drears/running/running.html`

Running resources:

WWW address: `http://`
`www.recreation.com/`
`running/home.html`

Scuba

Aquanaut magazine:

WWW address: `http://`
`www.opal.com/aquanaut`

Diving destinations:

WWW address: `http://`
`www.explore.com/`
`scuba/scuba_dest.html`

Internet Scuba WWW Server:

WWW address: `http://`
`www.recreation.com/scuba/`

Scuba archive at NASA-Ames:

WWW address: `http://`
`www.opal.com/aquanaut/`
`pyee.html`

Scuba forum:

WWW address: `http://`
`www.explore.com/`
`Explorer_forums.html#scuba`

Skateboarding

DansWorld of Skateboarding:

WWW address: `http://`
`web.cps.msu.edu/`
`~dunhamda/dw/dansworld.html`

Skiing—Snow

General Info

Lists of slopes by country/state:

WWW address: `http://`
`www.explore.com/E_slopes.html`

Nordic and Alpine skiing information:

WWW address: `http://`
`www.cs.colorado.edu/`
`homes/mcbryan/public_html/bb/`
`ski/ski.html`

To subscribe, send e-mail to:
LISTSERV:
`nordic-ski-request`
`@graphics.cornell.edu`

To post messages, send e-mail to:
`nordic-skiing@graphics.`
`cornell.edu`

North America

British Columbia ski page:

> WWW address: `http://www.wimsey.com/Ski/`

Colorado ski information:

> WWW address: `http://www.aescon.com/ski/index.htm`

Internet Ski Guide—North America:

> WWW address: `http://cybil.kplus.bc.ca/www/ski_net/ski_na.htm`

Michigan ski information:

> WWW address: `http://www.iquest.com/michweb/ski/`

Northwest ski report:

> WWW address: `http://www.fhcrc.org/dwaring/skipage.html`

Powder Hound ski report:

> WWW address: `http://www.icw.com/skireport.html`

Utah ski server:

> FTP address: `ski.utah.edu/skiing/`

Southland ski server:

> WWW address: `http://www.cccd.edu/ski.html`

U.S. ski reports:

> WWW address: `http://garnet.msen.com:70/1/vendor/aminews/ski-reports`

Worldwide

Australian alpine skiing information:

> WWW address: `http://www.adfa.oz.au/aais/`

European Snowboarding Network:

> WWW address: `http://www.earth.ox.ac.uk/~andyc`

Skiing—Water

Newsgroup:

> UseNet address: `rec.sport.waterski`

Skydiving

Pictures and descriptions:

> WWW address: `http://www.cis.ufl.edu/skydive`

Spelunking

Associations, equipment, and events:

> WWW address: `http://speleology.cs.yale.edu/`

Squash

Internet Squash Player's Association:

> WWW address: `http://www.ncl.ac.uk/~npb/`

Surfing

Online bodyboarding magazine:

> WWW address: `http://www.sd.monash.edu.au/~jasonl/dropin.html`

The List

Surfing conditions around the world:

WWW address: `http://sailfish.peregrine.com/surf/surf.html`

The Surfing Page:

WWW address: `http://facs.scripps.edu/surf/surfing.html`

Table Tennis

Newsgroup:

UseNet address: `rec.sport.table-tennis`

The World Wide Web of Sports—table tennis site:

WWW address: `http://peacock.tnjc.edu.tw/sports.html`

Tennis

Goddard Tennis Club home page:

WWW address: `http://epims1.gsfc.nasa.gov/tennis/GTC_homepage.html`

Online tennis shop, including equipment hints:

WWW address: `http://arganet.tenagra.com/Racquet_Workshop/Tennis.html`

Weightlifting

Frequently Asked Questions:

WWW address: `http://www.cs.odu.edu/~ksw/weightsfaq.html`

The Weightlifting Page:

WWW address: `http://www.cs.odu.edu/~ksw/weights.html`

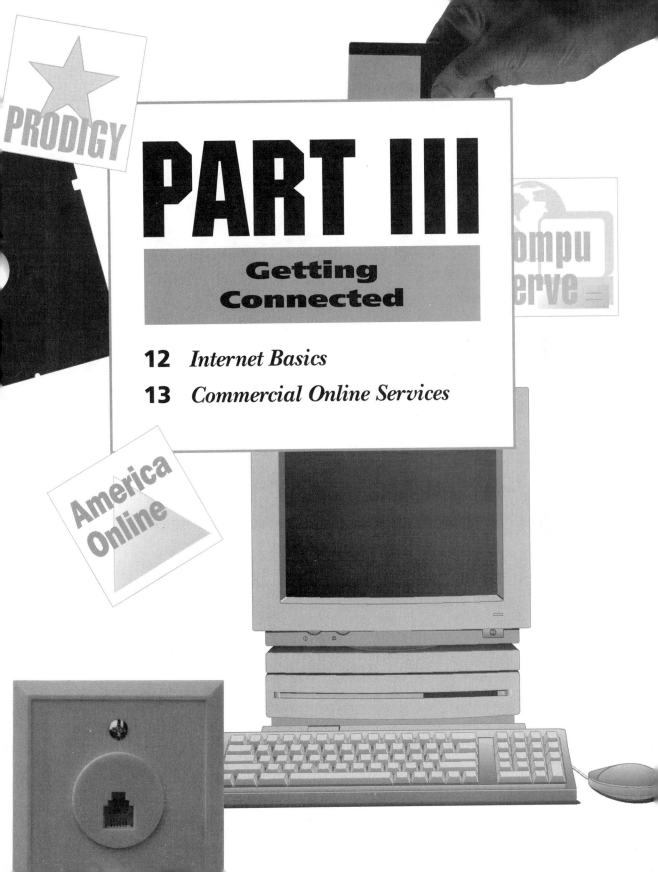

PART III

Getting Connected

Chapter 12

Internet Basics

This chapter gives you a basic understanding of some of the tools you can use when you step up to the plate.

In this chapter

- *What you need to get connected to the Internet*
- *Who provides access to the Internet*
- *How to use addresses in this book*
- *What Internet software you will need*
- *How to find other sports info on the Internet*

In other chapters

→ *For more information about commercial online services, see Chapter 13*

← *If you want addresses related to specific teams and sports, see the chapters related to specific sports in Part II*

← *If you're looking for addresses on sports talk and sports news, see Part I*

There are many ways to get sports information on the Net, and this book has provided you with many of them. However, there are some other tools available that can help you even more. Certain hardware, software, and information can make your job easier. Okay, so it doesn't sound like much fun. But that's why we've provided this chapter. It's as crucial to this book as an engine is to a car.

This chapter is designed to give you a basic understanding of some of the tools you can use when you step up the plate (provided, of course, that you're not on strike). Keep in mind that this chapter isn't designed as an exhaustive "How To." Instead, it's intended to give you a good start. The end of this chapter contains references to several books that can offer even more help.

What You Need to Get Connected to the Internet

To get connected, you need the following three basic things:

- Hardware—primarily a computer and a modem.
- Software—the kind that will connect your computer to the Internet.
- A Service Provider—whether it's a local or national provider, you'll need to get connected to the Internet to access all of the great information found in this book.

This section shows you the basics you'll need to properly locate all of these resources.

Computer

If you're the typical recreational Internet user, you will be connecting to the Internet from home using a dial-in connection. Although there are other ways to connect to the Internet, dial-in access will be the focus of this chapter.

> **NOTE**
>
> Types of Internet connections and the differences between them are discussed in the Introduction of this book. For detailed coverage, refer to Que's *Special Edition Using the Internet*, Second Edition.

There aren't many basic necessities needed to get started. To use the addresses throughout the book at the basic or intermediate level, you need the following:

- A 386 or faster computer
- 4M of RAM
- A mouse
- A modem (discussed later)
- About 10M of free hard-disk space that isn't occupied by other programs or files

While the Internet began as a text-based medium, today's Net includes graphics, video, audio, and other multimedia components. So if you want to use the Internet to its fullest, be prepared to add to your system to keep up with technology.

> **TIP**
>
> Although it's possible to use many of the resources in this book with a 286 machine without Windows or a mouse, it isn't recommended. You will eventually be frustrated by all the things you won't be able to do.

We recommend that your basic system includes the following:

- A 486 computer
- 50 MHz or higher

- At least 25-50M of free disk space and no less than a 14.4 V.32bis/V.42 modem (although 28.8 V.34 modems are already very affordable)
- At least 8M of RAM
- A sound card
- A video card that will handle at least 256 colors
- Speakers
- CD-ROM
- A mouse

If you're using a Macintosh, the aforementioned memory, hard-disk, CD-ROM, and modem requirements apply. Although you can do many things on the Net with a Mac Classic, it's recommended that you use a higher-end machine such as the Quadra or PowerMac. Many of the audio and video capabilities you need are built in to the Macintosh.

Modem

This piece of hardware affects your enjoyment of the Internet perhaps more than any other piece.

Modems can either be internal or external. Most multimedia computer systems come with an internal—or built-in—modem. For flexibility, most people buy an external modem if their machine doesn't come equipped with a modem.

If you do buy a modem, shop around. Warehouse magazines such as *Computer Shopper* or *MacMall* generally have excellent prices. Also, many of the popular retail outlets have very competitive prices on modems. 14.4 and 28.8 modems are becoming industry-standard.

Your Modem Is The Wax On Your Surfboard

When I first accessed the Internet, I was using the modem that came with my computer—a 2,400 bps fax/modem. At first, I was just messing around, and it suited my needs.

But when I really dove into the Internet, my modem was the first piece of hardware I upgraded. The faster access time my new 14.4 modem provided made "surfing" a breeze, and 28.8 modems are even better (as long as you can dial in to a line that supports 28.8—contact your local provider for this information).

TIME OUT

12

INTERNET BASICS

14.4 modems can generally be found in the $75-$200 range, while 28.8 modems are currently going for $190-$400. The highest priced modems usually come with slightly better warranties and might be manufactured with better hardware. The cheapest can often (though not always) be made with inferior products. As a rule, mid-range price modems are usually a good bet.

Software

Communications software is another indispensible element you need to connect to the Net. Like everything else, communications software can range from very basic to extremely customized and advanced.

If you're a Windows user, you can get by with the Terminal program that comes with Windows. On a Macintosh,

a shareware package such as MacKermit (available via `ftp.iastate.edu` in `/pub/mac/MacKermit.hqx`) will suffice. Also, if you purchase a modem, it usually includes some type of communication software.

More and more companies are offering dial-in Internet connections through software programs available off-the-shelf of your software retailer. Other Internet services offer prepackaged software that is already configured for use by the customer.

Service Providers

Once you have the right hardware and software, you still need one more thing—a service provider. There are hundreds of service providers—both local and national—and more spring up every day. The type of provider you choose is up to you, but getting a good one can make all the difference in your Internet experience.

What to Look for in a Service Provider

There are many things to look for in a service provider. Some considerations may be more important to you than others. When going through the following list of things to look for in a provider, prioritize each one as to how important it is to you as an individual. Is cost an overriding factor or would you rather have a more stable connection? Do you insist on having all of the services available on the Net or will just a few suffice? After considering and prioritizing, you're ready to make your decision. Perhaps the best piece of advice, as with anything else, is to shop around!

- Cost. What is the bottom line cost for the service you're looking at? A flat-rate service is often a better deal than a per-hour service. Many providers offer an attractive fee but charge extra for connect time, amount of information downloaded, higher connection speeds, and direct PPP/SLIP access. It's very important to find out all the costs—both obvious and hidden—when considering a provider.

- Company Maturity. It's also important to know how much you can rely upon a company. Find out how long it has been in business, the number of subscribers, and the number of connections. A mature company with a stable base of customers will probably be a good choice.

- Customer Support and Usability. Once you sign on the dotted line, are you on your own? Do they have online help? Do they have a toll-free service? Can you instantaneously find out how much you've used the service at any given time? Most good providers will have some degree of customer support. Also, many providers offer free initial "trial" subscriptions to see if you're happy with their services. In addition, you'll want to know how easy a system is to use. Do they provide an integrated menu that lets you access multiple functions from a central application? This can be determined when trying out their "free trial."

- Connectivity. It's very important to find out how a provider will give you access. Will you be able to dial a local number or a toll-free number?

Make sure the provider has enough lines to support the necessary users, otherwise you may end up getting busy signal after busy signal. When talking to providers, ask them what percentage of the time their users get busy signals and if it's a high percentage, ask them if they plan on adding more lines in the future. Also, what can you do once you're connected? Can you perform all the major functions of the net like Web-browsing, FTP, Gopher, and e-mail? And what type of interface does the company offer to complete these functions?

Again, you need to decide what is most important to you. If the company meets the standards in the previous list, you will probably have an enjoyable experience on the Internet.

National Providers

There are several national providers. Table 12.1 gives you the names and contact information of a few.

There's a complete list of service providers available via FTP at **is:internic.net** in the **/infoguide/getting-connected/united-states** under the document name **internic-us-provider-all**. You can also get a copy of this by calling InterNIC at 619-455-4600 or sending e-mail to **refdesk@is.internic.net**.

Table 12.1   Information on National Providers

Provider	Address & Phone Number	Services
CERFNET	P.O. Box 85608 San Diego, CA 92186 800-876-2373	14.4 Dial-up SLIP/PPP Toll-free number
JvNCnet	3 Independence Way Berkeley, CA 94704 609-897-7300	14.4 Dial-up SLIP/PPP
PINET	500 Sunnyside Blvd. Woodbury, NY 11797 800-539-3505 or 206-455-3505	14.4 Dial-up SLIP/PPP Menu
Rocky Mountain Internet	2860 S. Circle Suite 2202 Colorado Springs, CO 80906 719-576-6845	14.4 Dial-up SLIP/PPP Toll-free number Menu

Providers with Custom Software

In an attempt to keep pace with commercial services like America Online and CompuServe, some providers have developed their own interfaces to make using them easier. This section briefly looks at one such provider—The Pipeline out of New York City.

All the software needed to use The Pipeline comes on a single disk that's simple to install and get started. With The Pipeline, there's no hassle of trying to establish a special PPP or SLIP connection.

The Pipeline offers a free demo account for you to try before you decide to buy. If you decide to use it, accounts begin at about $15 per month. The Pipeline offers e-mail, FTP, online chatting, and Gopher service. Much of its interface is point-and-click and easy to use. To find out more, you can contact The Pipeline at:

> 150 Broadway
> New York, NY 10038
>
> 212-267-3636 or dial-up by modem at 212-267-6432
>
> Their WWW address is **http://www.pipeline.com** and you can also reach them via e-mail at **info@pipeline.com**

How to Use the Addresses in This Book

If you don't go with a commercial or national provider that supplies its own interface, you will need to get different pieces of software to access the type of information in this book. This section tells you what you need, where to get it, and how to use the addresses in this book with it. In addition to the locations in this section, much of the software listed here is also available via Que's FTP site at **que.mcp.com** and at several other sites such as **wuarchive.wustl.edu** and **mac.archive.umich.edu**.

 World Wide Web

The *World Wide Web* (also referred to as Web, WWW, or W3) is a hypertext system that makes jumping from link to link as easy as pointing and clicking. It's also the home for the vast majority of excellent sports information on the Internet.

The hypertext format enables you to move to more specific information on your chosen topic or you can move to another topic altogether by clicking on a line of highlighted text.

A *Web browser* is simply the tool you use to cruise the Web (see the next section). Some browsers are better than others, and it should be obvious that a good Web browser is the most important aspect of a sports fan's Internet equipment. Being a sports fan on the Net without a Web browser is like arriving at the big game without a ticket.

Web Browsers and Where to Get Them

There are many browsers available via the Internet. The two most popular browsers follow:

- NCSA Mosaic (for both Windows and Macintosh). Mosaic, the original Web browser, is an excellent choice that offers many attractive features. The Windows version is available at **ftp.cyberspace.com** in the directory **/pub/ppp/Windows/mosaic**. The Macintosh version is available at **scss3.cl.msu.edu** in the directory **/pub/mac**.
- Netscape (for both Windows and Macintosh). This is a very nice browser that's new to the scene but has a lot of people singing its praises. The Windows version is available at **ftp.halcyon.com** in the directory **/pub/slip/www/netscape**. The Macintosh version is available at **ftp.3com.com** in the directory **/netscape**.

Using a Web Browser to Find URL Addresses

Every site on the Web can be identified by its *URL* (Uniform Resource Locator). Basically, a URL tells your Web browser where to find a particular Web site. (In this book, a Web address is identified either by the World Wide Web icon or it is preceded by "WWW address:".)

Both browsers previously listed enable you to enter any URL to get to any page on the Web. Simply type the URL address and the browser takes you right to it. Another thing to remember is that URL addresses are case-sensitive. That means that if an address has capital letters, you need to use capital letters when typing it. For example, if you wanted to get to the Nando X

Baseball server, you would type **http://www.nando.net/baseball/bbserv.html** (see fig. 12.1).

TIP

Web sites aren't the only places on the Internet with URLs. You can generally use a Web browser, such as Mosaic or Netscape, to access FTP sites and other resources on the Net. For instance, if you want to FTP to **wuarchive.wustl.edu** using Netscape, type **ftp://wuarchive.wustl.edu** as the URL. If you wanted to get to Michigan State's Gopher, you would type **gopher://gopher.msu.edu**.

 FTP

File Transfer Protocol (FTP) software enables you to receive (*download*) files from another computer and send (*upload*) files to another computer. These files can be anything from documents to complex audio/video files to software programs.

FTP Clients and Where to Get Them

There are some good FTP clients for both Windows and Macintosh users. Some of the most popular are as follows:

- WS_FTP (Windows). This is probably the best Windows FTP program available. For a complete user's guide for WS_FTP, see Que's *Using*

FTP. Among many sites, WS_FTP is currently available at **ftp.halcyon.com** in the directory **/pub/slip/ftp**.

- Fetch (Macintosh). The original Macintosh FTP client, Fetch offers a good user interface along with automatic decompression and execution of downloaded files. It can be found at **bitsy.mit.edu** in the directory **/pub/mac/fetch**.

- Anarchie (Macintosh). This program allows you to first locate programs (using an FTP search client called Archie) and then instantly access the FTP site once it has been found. This is an excellent program to use if you don't know exactly where a file is located—or even if you do. It can be found at **nic.switch.ch** in the directory **/software/mac/archive**.

Using an FTP Client to Find FTP Addresses

Using FTP with the new graphical-interface clients that are available has become very, very easy. When getting a file from an FTP site, there are several things to consider.

- You should first be aware of the FTP site, or _host name_, itself. This is the place you will actually find the file.

- Know the _path_, or set of directories, that will lead you to the file. For instance, let's assume that you would like to download the NBA statistics that are available at

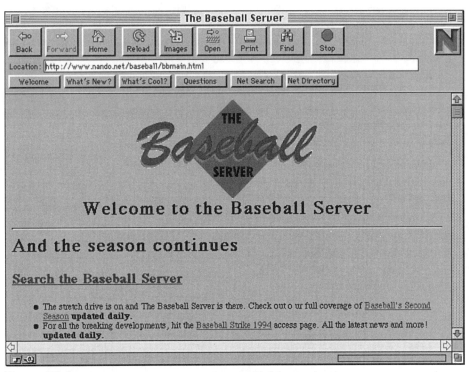

Figure 12.1 http://www.nando.net/baseball/bbserv.html
Entering Nando X's URL in Netscape instantly takes you to the Baseball Server home page.

wuarchive.wustl.edu/doc/ misc/nbastats. First, you tell your FTP client to find the host wuarchive.wustl.edu. Then you go to the directories **/doc**, **/misc**, and **/nbastats**.

- The last thing to be aware of is the file *type*. A plain text file (which often ends with **.txt** or **.doc**) can be downloaded as plain text. Most other files should be downloaded as binary data. For instance, if you see a directory with a file in it like **pub/music/ lyrics/text/highway66.txt**, the file can probably be downloaded as text. However, if a file has a different extension, such as the file found in the directory **/pub/music/ soundfiles/highway66.wav**, you should probably download the file as a binary. If you're unsure, always download as a binary, since a binary download can also handle text data. All of the FTP clients listed in the previous sections enable you to define file type automatically or manually.

NOTE

When using FTP, you're a nobody—literally. All of the FTP sites in this book are referred to as *anonymous FTP sites*. This means that when you log on to the host, you will enter **anonymous** as your user name. Also—although it isn't required—good etiquette dictates that you use your e-mail address as your password.

 # UseNet Newsgroups

Newsgroups probably contain more discussion and information than a thousand talk shows and magazines combined. They change almost constantly, with thousands of discussions occurring on hundreds of topics every day.

There are particularly active sports groups covering every sport at just about every level all over the Internet. Not only can you get current information from newsgroups, but you can also let your opinions be known as well.

Newsreaders and Where to Get Them

Newsreaders help you sort through all of the messages that are available to you on a daily basis. More than that, though, they help organize newsgroups so that you can easily pick out the topics that interest you. For complete coverage of newsgroups, see Que's *Using UseNet Newsgroups*. Some of the more common newsreaders follow:

- WinVN (Windows). This is probably the best Windows newsreader available—enabling you to do just about everything with a click of your mouse. The most recent version is available at **ftp.ksc.nasa.gov** in the directory **/pub/win3/winvn** (the most current version is **wv16_93_11.zip**).

- NewsXpress (Windows). NewsXpress is a new entry into the newsreader business. Even though it's new, it already enjoys widespread popularity. You can currently find it at `ftp.cyberspace.com` in the directory `/pub/ppp/windows/newsreaders`.

- Newswatcher (Macintosh). This is the easiest to use and most complete Macintosh newsreader. The multi-window design helps you read news quickly and easily. It can be located at `ftp.switch.ch` in the `/software/mac/news` directory.

- Nuntius (Macintosh). This is another Macintosh newsreader. It's probably not as widely used as Newswatcher, but it contains some attractive features. Nuntius is located at the same FTP site as Newswatcher (`ftp.switch.ch` in the `/software/mac/news` directory).

Using Newsreaders to Find UseNet Addresses

Once your newsreader is operational, newsgroups are very easy to locate and read. Most of the sports newsgroups reside in the `rec.*` hierarchy of UseNet. A *hierarchy* is simply a way of organizing newsgroups in UseNet. Newsgroups about recreation are in the `rec.*` hierarchy, groups about computers are in the `comp.*` hierarchy, and so on. If, for example, you wanted to read `rec.sports.football.college`, you simply tell your newsreader to go to that group, subscribe to the group, and you're off and reading.

 Gopher

No, we're not talking about the furry little animal or a certain member of the "Love Boat" crew. Gopher is a means of finding your way around the Internet. It's called Gopher because it was set up at the University of Minnesota—its mascot is the Golden Gopher—and because it's a way to *go for* files on the Internet.

Gopher was also probably the first non-command-line interface available on the Internet. Instead of using command lines to get you where you want to go, Gopher uses a menu-driven system. Getting from place to place is merely a matter of choosing a menu item.

Gopher Clients and Where to Get Them

Despite Gopher's relative ease of use, there are Gopher clients available that make "Gophering" even easier. They do so primarily through the use of a point-and-click GUI (Graphical User Interface). The two most popular Gopher clients follow:

- Hgopher (Windows). This is the most popular Gopher client for Windows. You can save electronic bookmarks and use Gopher by pointing and clicking your mouse. Hgopher is located at `ucselx.sdsu.edu` in the `/pub/ibm` directory.

- TurboGopher (Macintosh). TurboGopher is a simple Gopher client that creates separate windows for each menu. TurboGopher can be found at `bitsy.mit.edu` in the `/pub/mac/gopher` directory.

Using Gopher Clients to Find Gopher Addresses

Gopher addresses work much like FTP addresses. You need to find a Gopher address you would like to use as your "home Gopher." In other words, you want to tell your client which Gopher menu you want to appear when you first start.

Obviously, you'll want to access more than one Gopher site. There are two basic ways you can do this:

- Both Gopher clients previously mentioned enable you to start a new Gopher or go to a Gopher other than the one with which you started. When you choose the menu option that enables you to do this, simply put in the address of the Gopher site to which you'd like to go. This is the best method to use when first looking at a Gopher site. For instance, if you wanted to see what the University of Minnesota's Gopher had to offer, you would choose the menu option to start a new Gopher or go to another Gopher and type `gopher.micro.umn.edu`. You would then find yourself at the main menu of their Gopher.

- The second way to use Gopher sites is to make bookmarks in your Gopher client. Suppose you browse a Gopher site and decide you like it and will probably look at it again in the future. Instead of writing down or remembering the address for future use, let the client do it for you. The Gopher clients mentioned in the previous section enable you to set or make

bookmarks. Once a bookmark has been set, you can instantly access that Gopher site again.

 ## Mailing Lists

E-mail is probably used more than any other function on the Internet. People use e-mail to communicate, transfer files, get information, and so on. While most e-mail is transferred between two individual users privately, there are also instances in which groups use e-mail in a more public way. One of those uses, the *LISTSERV*, is mentioned in this book. LISTSERVs (sometimes referred to as mailing lists) are very similar to newsgroups, except that all LISTSERV discussion is delivered directly to your mailbox. To use a LISTSERV, you should have a good e-mail client.

E-Mail Clients and Where to Get Them

Surprisingly, there aren't many good e-mail clients out there for public use. One very good one does exist, though. Without a doubt, the most widely used e-mail client is Eudora. Although Eudora is now available commercially, there is a very functional shareware version still available. Shareware is software that you can use free on a trial basis, after which you pay a very small fee for continued use and technical support. Eudora, both the commercial and shareware version, is available for both Windows and Macintosh platforms.

The best place to get Eudora is from **ftp.qualcomm.com**. This FTP site is run by Qualcomm, the makers of Eudora. The Windows version can be found at **/quest/windows/eudora/1.4**. Version 1.4 is the latest shareware version. For the Macintosh version, go to **/quest/mac/eudora/1.5**.

Using E-Mail Clients to Find Mailing List Addresses

As previously mentioned, you will probably be accessing LISTSERVs (or mailing lists) when you use e-mail to get sports information on the Net. Using a LISTSERV is really quite easy. There are several important things to keep in mind, however.

- LISTSERVs usually have two addresses. You'll use one address to subscribe, obtain archives and help files, and so on. The other address will be where you actually send

e-mail to be posted to the rest of the subscribers.

- Always read the introductory message (and keep a copy!) that you receive when you first subscribe to a LISTSERV. It could save you a lot of hassles.

- When you join a LISTSERV for the first time, check your e-mail every day for a few days after subscribing. This way, you'll know if you've subscribed to a list that either has too much traffic, isn't interesting, or any other reason to warrant unsubscribing right away.

With these things in mind, subscribing to a LISTSERV is easy. For instance, let's say you wanted to subscribe to the Dallas Cowboys' mailing list (see fig. 12.2). Send a message to the LISTSERV's address, **cowboys-request@emmitt.dseg. ti.com** and leave the subject line blank. In the

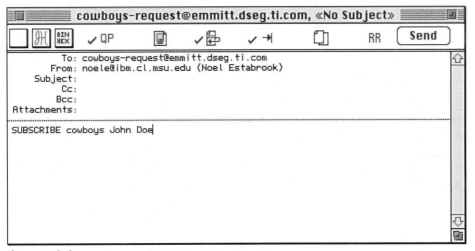

Figure 12.2 cowboys-request@emmitt.dseg.ti.com
This is an e-mail message that subscribes the user, John Doe, to the Dallas Cowboys' mailing list using Eudora.

body of the message, type **SUBSCRIBE cowboys** *Firstname Lastname.* You usually receive a message that welcomes you and provides instructions on how to send mail to the list. For more information, see "How to Find a LISTSERV" in Chapter 2.

How to Find Other Sports Info on the Internet

Although this book contains a ballpark full of information, it still doesn't exhaust all of the sports information that's available out there on the Internet. Even if it did, the available information likely will double in six months. Given this fact, it's helpful to be able to find both new and additional sources of information on the Internet. Fortunately, there are ways to do this on the Web.

Using WWW Directory Pages to Find Other Sites

There are lots of directory offerings on the Web to help you find what you're looking for. In fact, many web browsers—like Netscape—have collected a number of directory pages that are available at your fingertips.

One of the best subject directory pages is *The Whole Internet Catalog* by O'Reilly and Associates. This site offers information on What's New? What's Cool? and a host of other subjects, including—what else?—Sports! (see fig. 12.3). The Whole Internet Catalog can be accessed at the following address:

```
http://www.digital.com/gnn/
wic/index.html
```

Stanford's Yahoo Web site is another popular subject directory. If you're up for it, Yahoo even sends you to a randomly selected Web site just for you. It also offers a wide range of subjects to

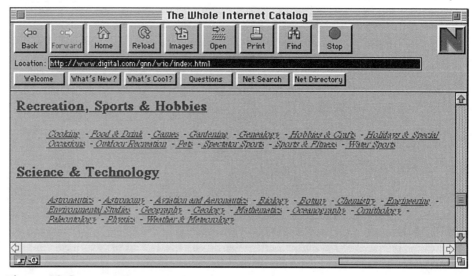

Figure 12.3 `http://www.digital.com/gnn/wic/index.html`
The Whole Internet Catalog offers directories on many subjects, including sports.

which you can get directories. You can get the Yahoo directory at the following address:

```
http://
akebono.stanford.edu/yahoo/
```

Probably the most complete directory page is the full server list available at CERN. This list gives you all of the servers by geography. Be warned! This is a big site and you may have trouble connecting. You can get this directory at the following address:

```
http://info.cern.ch/
hypertext/
DataSources/WWW/
Geographical.html
```

Using WWW Search Pages to Find Other Sites

Besides accessing directories that give you preset sites of information, you can also perform keyword searches on the Internet. There are many of these search "engines" available on the Net.

The most popular and well-known of these search engines is Carnegie Mellon's Lycos catalog (see fig. 12.4). Currently, Lycos searches more than 1.75 million documents! To use Lycos, point your Web browser to `http://lycos.cs.cmu.edu/`.

If you would like to search both documents and URL locations, perhaps the World Wide Web Worm (WWWW) would be to your liking. The Worm builds an index and then lets you effectively conduct searches to find what you need. You can access WWWW at the following address:

```
http://www.cs.colorado.edu/
mcbryan_merge/mcbryan/
WWWW.html
```

Figure 12.4 `http://lycos.cs.cmu.edu/`
The Lycos catalog at Carnegie Mellon searches nearly two million documents for what you want.

There's also a directory of search engines to help you locate even more. CUI (The Centre Universitaire d'Informatique at the University of Geneva) maintains one of the best "search for the searchers" site. Its URL follows:

```
http://cuiwww.unige.ch/
meta-index.html
```

Recommended Books on Using the Internet

- Que's *Using the Internet* is a concise, user-friendly reference to the Internet. It includes a disk with lots of Windows software for cruising the Internet.

- Que's *Special Edition Using the Internet,* Second Edition is using the Internet with guts! It includes more than 1,300 pages that tell you everything you'll ever need to know about the Internet. Also, it includes a CD with hundreds of megabytes of great software to help you along.

- Que's *Using the World Wide Web* saves you time and effort by taking you step-by-step through how to get connected and how to discover the best online resources. It's the comprehensive guide to navigating the Web on the Internet.

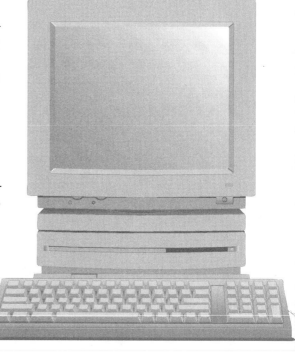

Chapter 13

Commercial Online Services

Whether you're already online or not, this chapter helps you determine the major commercial online service that's best for you.

In this chapter

- *How to subscribe to America Online, CompuServe, and Prodigy*
- *The costs of the three main commercial online services*
- *Sports information available on commerical online services*
- *Other services available on commercial online services*
- *Internet access through commerical online services*

In other chapters

← *This chapter includes general information on the sports offerings of each of these services. For specific information on a particular topic, check out the chapters in Part II*

← *If you're not sure how to use an address in this chapter, see Chapter 12*

Not everyone is fortunate enough to be able to walk into work each day and log on to a computer that is continuously linked to the Internet.

Until recently, you simply couldn't access the Internet unless you had that type of situation or enough ready cash to pay for the thick cabling necessary to wire up at home.

Historically—it's a very short history, we know—those who wanted access to bulletin boards, reference materials, or anything else online signed up with a commercial online service such as Prodigy.

Prodigy, CompuServe, and America Online soon became hugely popular for businesspeople, families, and—yes sports fans.

In the beginning, the competition between these services was based on the services they offer—what are the CompuServe bulletin boards like compared to America Online?—but in the last year or so, that has changed.

Today, with the many off-the-shelf software programs that allow dial-up access to the Internet (as discussed in Chapter 12, "Internet Basics"), anyone with a computer and a modem can get on the information superhighway.

That created a new battlefield for the commercial online services: Who could provide the best Internet access, and who could do it *fast?*

The answer, of course, is all of them.

But they have all maintained excellent offerings on their own networks, and none exists simply to provide access to the Internet—that's just the latest in a long line of services each provides.

In Part II of this book, you learned about the types of sports services each provides. There's enough sports on any of the three commercial online services to warrant subscribing to them in addition to having another type of Internet access.

This chapter is designed to give you information on the three major commercial online services—America Online, CompuServe, and Prodigy—that can help you decide which service is best for you.

Of course, there are more commercial online services than merely these three. These are, however, the three most popular networks and the three with the most complete sports packages.

 # America Online

America Online's attractive graphics and ease of use—plus the wide variety of services it offers—makes it a rising star among commercial online services.

How to Subscribe and What It Costs

America Online's start-up software is available at just about any software retailer or by calling America Online at 1-800-827-6364.

Once the software is installed on your hard drive, you're ready to go. PC systems must have at least a 386 microprocessor (preferrably better) and at least 4M of RAM.

Macintosh computers must be a Mac Plus or better with 1,200K of available memory and an operating system 6.0.5 or higher.

That software takes care of the subscription process for you. In fact, you *are* subscribing as you load the software onto your hard drive.

The sign-up process is extremely easy. The software walks you through the process on-screen at a nice pace, and everything is completely explained.

America Online's member name and password system is the best of the three. It enables you to pick your own member name (unlike the others) and password. By doing so, it makes remembering that information easier both for you and for those who might want to send you e-mail.

In most cases, you receive some sort of trial membership through the initial sign-on process. This generally includes the following features:

- Free sign-up
- Free one-month membership
- First 10 hours of connect time are free

Once you've exhausted your free first month, the monthly membership fee is $9.95 per month. That includes five hours of online time and unlimited use of the Members' Online Support department. Additional online hours cost $3.50 per hour.

These charges can be billed directly to a major credit card or deducted automatically from your checking account (the latter option brings an additional $2 service charge per month).

Sports Information

Sports is one of 14 main departments within America Online, and the emphasis on providing strong sports offerings is obvious. America Online goes the distance for sports fans by including—through one means or another—just about everything a sports fan could want.

As figure 13.1 shows, America Online's main sports menu allows members to choose a sport to look into or to pick

from one of the six icons (at left) to follow a different track.

Double-clicking any sport under Sports Categories leads you into the main menu for that particular sport. The menu includes game stories, boxscores, standings, and a notes section that is divided by team for the major pro sports. That package is provided by Sports Ticker, and it's very complete and current.

That's the guts of the America Online sports package—the basics. It's the type of information that all three of the major online services offer (although the other services get their sports news from the Associated Press). It's a thorough package, and it's presented in a very user-friendly, graphical style that makes it fun, too.

The remainder of the sports package—those icons to the left of the Sports Categories in figure 13.1—separates America Online from the others.

Sports News

Clicking this icon leads you to the top sports stories, updated on a minute-by-minute basis, from a variety of wire services. For example, this would be the place to click for the latest breaking news on the O.J. Simpson trial.

The Grandstand

This is the sports bulletin board area for America Online members. The bulletin boards are divided by topic, and they include all the big sports.

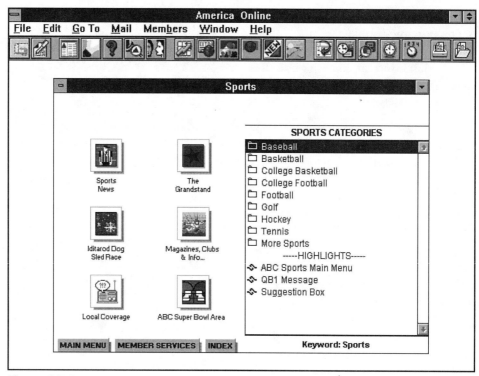

Figure 13.1 Keyword: sports
America Online's main sports menu provides sports fans just about everything they could want.

What's best about the bulletin boards is that they operate two ways:

- You can post messages and read those of others.
- You can "talk" live, online, with other members.

The latter portion of The Grandstand is probably the most fun, especially if a particularly hot debate is taking place in the one of the discussion "rooms."

Magazines, Clubs, & Info

Clicking this icon leads you to an interesting menu of options ranging from *Backpacker Magazine* to the Scuba Forum. There are regular magazines that provide their content to America Online members.

Also, available from this menu is a database of golf courses and resorts, designed to help you pick out courses or a place to set up shop for your next golf vacation.

ABC Sports

This icon, shown as ABC Super Bowl Area in figure 13.1, gives sports fans inside access to the ABC Sports operation (see fig. 13.2). The area includes pictures and video clips, message boards, an e-mail connection to ABC, and ABC Auditorium—where online discussions are held with sports personalities, and more.

Local Coverage

This icon links you to an archive of stories written by newspaper reporters around the country. You can access stories on any particular team in the major sports leagues, or you can do a search of stories by some other topic or keyword. The stories don't appear in this area until a few days after they're published in newspapers, but it does give travelers, for example, access to their hometown sports sections.

Miscellaneous

This icon, shown as Iditarod Dog Sled Race in figure 13.1, is constantly changing—thereby allowing America Online to offer special coverage of events as they warrant.

Other Important Information

In addition to sports, America Online features 13 other departments (see fig. 13.3).

The choices include the following:

- Today's News—international and domestic news stories, business, entertainment, sports, and weather.

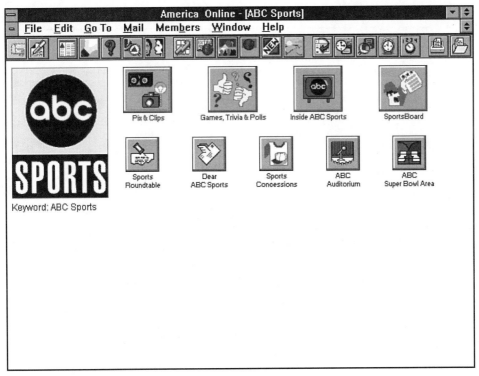

Figure 13.2 keyword: ABC
America Online's ABC Sports menu gives sports fans inside access to the ABC Sports operation.

Figure 13.3

America Online's main menu, which appears immediately after you have logged on to America Online, offers a total of 14 departments.

- Personal Finance—stock quotes and portfolios, financial news, company profiles, transactions.

- Clubs & Interests—special interest "communities."

- Computing—software center, technology news, industry connection.

- Travel—flight information, travel packages, travel advisories, accommodations.

- Marketplace—online shopping.

- People Connection—America Online's main forum area.

- Newsstand—various newspapers and magazines online.

- Entertainment—movies, games, music, television, and radio.

- Education—Smithsonian, National Geographic, Library of Congress, College Board.

- Reference Desk—Compton's Encyclopedia.

- Internet Connection—newsgroups, mail gateway, Gopher and WAIS databases, mailing lists.

- Kids Only—kids' news and sports, hobbies and clubs, search and explore, television and movies.

Internet Access

America Online was working to get its access to the World Wide Web up and running early in 1995 after promising members the Web would be available "in the winter." By the time this book reaches the shelves, that Web access will probably be in place.

To advance its Web efforts, America Online acquired BookLink Technologies and NaviSoft.

Access to the World Wide Web would round out America Online's Internet access nicely. After all, it already includes an e-mail link, UseNet Newsgroups, Gopher and WAIS databases, mailing lists, and Telnet and FTP access (see fig. 13.4).

America Online's Internet access is included with the service charge.

CompuServe

CompuServe is the least graphical of the three services, and probably the most news-oriented. It provides you with an impressive array of services without being flashy.

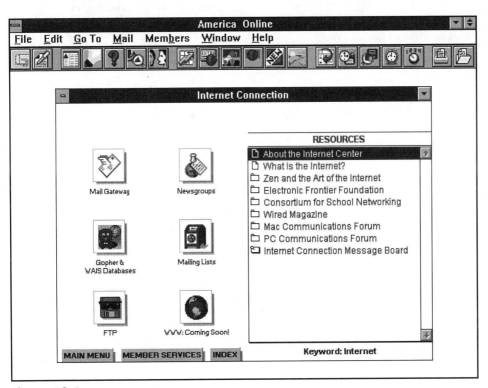

Figure 13.4 Keyword: internet
The Internet Connection on America Online.

How to Subscribe and What It Costs

CompuServe is available for DOS, Windows, and Macintosh at software retailers all over the U.S. or by calling CompuServe at 1-800-848-8990.

Like the other commercial online services, CompuServe is as easy to subscribe to as it is to install any basic software program.

As you're installing the program onto your hard drive, you will be asked (on-screen) if you would like to sign up now. If you choose to sign up immediately, it will prompt you through that process. Should you choose to sign up later, you can do so by double-clicking a sign-up icon in the CompuServe window.

CompuServe's member name system is the least user-friendly of the three; you're assigned a user *number* that can be as long as nine digits (for example, 12345,6789). It's a difficult number to remember, for both you and those who might want to send you e-mail.

CompuServe's pricing system is also markedly different from the others in that users receive unlimited online time to use CompuServe's basic services.

New subscribers usually receive their first month free, plus a $25 usage credit for extended online time. After the first month, members are charged $9.95 per month for unlimited access to CompuServe's basic services.

Extended services, which are those followed by a plus sign (+), are $4.80

per hour. Premium services—another level of services—are followed by a dollar sign ($); they're $4.80 per hour plus an additional surcharge.

Payment is typically made by automatically charging a credit card account.

While the unlimited access to basic services is great for those who are online often, it doesn't help much if the things you're interested in are extended or premium services.

For example, CompuServe's forum (bulletin boards) is an extended service.

Sports Information

To determine if the unlimited time for basic services is a good deal for you, you'll need to determine if the basic service meets your needs.

Basic Services

CompuServe's basic sports package (see fig. 13.5) is just that—basic—with one notable exception. It's a newsy package—concentrating on game stories, features, boxscores, standings, and so on—provided by the Associated Press and its sister wire services in other countries. Choosing Associated Press Online, PA News Online (UK), or Global and More Basic Sports leads you to wire-service sports copy.

If you double-click Associated Press Online, you access features such as the scoreboard shown in figure 13.6.

The lone exception is the Lanier Golf Database (see fig. 13.7), which connects you to a golf course/resort

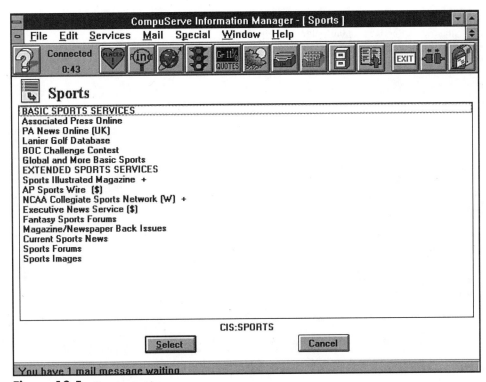

Figure 13.5 Go: sports
CompuServe's main sports menu provides a newsy package.

database that is full of information on golf courses around the world. Also, it includes some advice on how to use the database and advice on what makes a good golf course.

Extended Services

At the beginning of 1995, CompuServe announced a new addition to its family of Extended Sports Services—*Sports Illustrated* magazine.

The Sports Illustrated Magazine connection (refer to fig. 13.5) provides you with access to the magazine's content. Also, you can contact members of the *Sports Illustrated* staff and you can order *Sports Illustrated* merchandise.

Through extended services, you can also access features such as the following:

- AP Sports Wire—the most recent stories from the AP wire.
- NCAA Collegiate Sports Network— statistics, news releases, and polls.
- Executive News Service—monitors wire services based on your interests.
- Fantasy Sports Forums—play fantasy sports or talk about them online.
- Magazine/Newspaper Back Issues— an archive of past editions.
- Current Sports News—the latest sports news.

13

COMMERCIAL ONLINE SERVICES

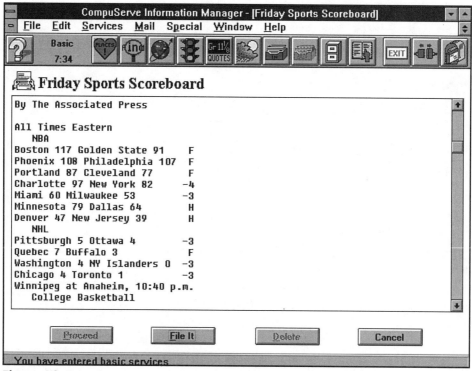

Figure 13.6 Go: APO
Associated Press Online includes an up-to-date scoreboard.

- Sports Forums—bulletin boards for sports fans.
- Sports Images—CompuServe's photo archive.

Other Important Information

As shown in figure 13.8, the CompuServe main menu includes basic and extended offerings in several categories.

- Basic Services—CompuServe's main areas.
- Computers—direct links to software and hardware companies.
- News—global news clipping service, entertainment, business, features, sports, and weather.
- Travel—flights, hotel accomodations.
- Lifestyles—personal interests and hobbies.

- Forums—bulletin boards.
- Investments—stock quotes, company profiles, buy and sell securities.
- Shopping—electronic mall.
- Professional—forums that support professionals in a variety of fields.
- Communications—information on how to communicate with other CompuServe members.
- Reference—Grolier's Academic American Encyclopedia, Peterson's College Database, HealthNet.
- Games—CastleQuest, BlackDragon, other online games.
- Member Support—support forums, practice forums, directory of members, help forum.

TIP

You'll notice the topic names shown in the CompuServe main menu (see fig. 13.8) include underlined letters. This indicates that, when you're at the CompuServe main menu screen, you simply press the letter associated with each topic to access that topic. For example, press **c** for Computers, **o** for Communications, and so on.

Internet Access

CompuServe will probably be the last of the three major commercial online services to offer access to the World

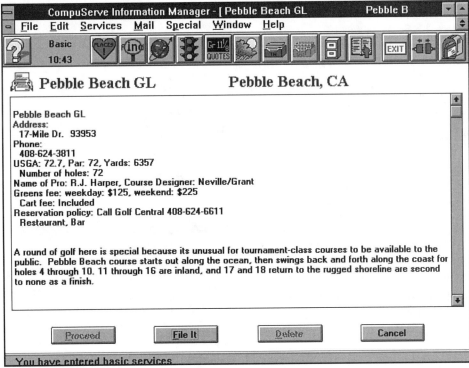

Figure 13.7 Go: lanier
The Lanier Golf Database includes information on courses throughout the country.

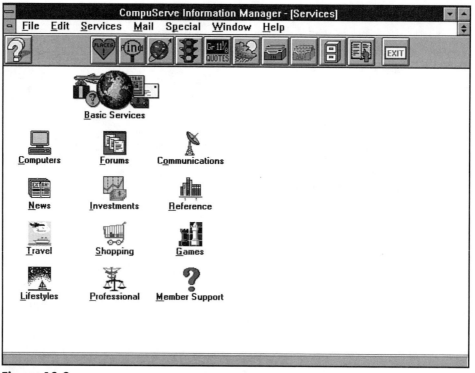

Figure 13.8
CompuServe's main menu, which appears when you log on, includes several valuable sources of information.

Wide Web, but that doesn't mean its Internet access is worse than the others.

In early 1995, CompuServe's capabilities included Internet e-mail and UseNet newsgroups, plus FTP servers and Telnet.

A press release from the company to its members indicated that the firm is committed to adding World Wide Web and Gopher access to members "in the first half of 1995."

 **Prodigy**

Prodigy is heavy on graphics and specialized areas, such as the sports services provided by ESPN.

How to Subscribe and What It Costs

Not surprisingly, joining Prodigy is no more difficult than it is with the others. Prodigy software is available—for DOS, Windows, and Macintosh—at major software retailers and, like the others, it's often preinstalled on the hard drives of new computers.

And, like the others, when you install the software on your hard drive, you're also subscribing to the Prodigy service. The prompts are clear and easy to follow.

Once you're all signed up, you receive one free month (up to 10 hours online) of Prodigy. After the first 30 days, you will be charged $9.95 per month for the right to use the service for five hours. Additional hours are the most reasonably priced of the three major services, coming in at just $2.95 per hour.

Payment is made by charging your credit card account.

Sports Information

Prodigy is the only major commercial online service to have its sports package "sponsored"—so to speak. Prodigy's sports area is called ESPNet (see fig. 13.9), although not all of the sports information is generated by ESPN.

At the main sports menu, you'll see a few numbered items that lead to coverage of breaking stories or special Prodigy offerings, like member polls or contests.

The buttons along the side of the screen (refer to fig. 13.9) link you to various sports services.

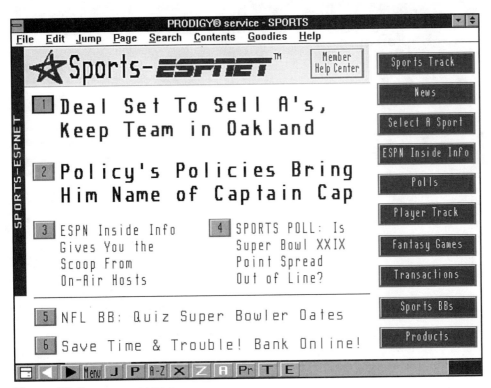

Figure 13.9 Jump: ESPNet
Prodigy's main sports menu.

Sports Track

Sports Track allows you to tailor sports scores, schedules, and such to your tastes with as many as 24 items from the NFL, NBA, Major League Baseball, NHL, college football, and college basketball. Enter the names of your favorite teams, and this area helps you follow them.

News

News links you to a menu that includes Associated Press Online, international sports, "Quick Sports" (news recaps), and other sports news.

Select A Sport

When you click Select A Sport, you can choose from a long list of sports, then choose any team—giving you information such as schedules, statistics, team reports (see fig. 13.10), standings, games stories, and so on.

ESPN Inside Info

Although the Inside Info title may make some believe they're going to get inside information about sports from ESPN's sports personalities, the truth is that most of the information in this area is actually about ESPN itself (see fig. 13.11). Information such as

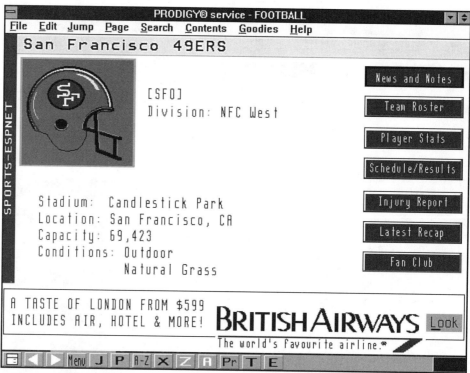

Figure 13.10 Jump: sportname
Team reports are available under the Select A Sport button in ESPNet. In this address, replace sportname *with the name of the sport in which you're interested.*

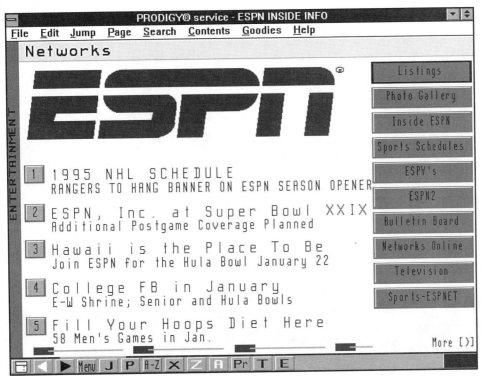

Figure 13.11 Jump: espn inside info
The ESPN Inside Info button takes you to information such as programming news and schedules for both ESPN and ESPN2.

programming news and schedules are the norm (both ESPN and ESPN2 are covered). It's a fun place to visit.

Polls

Prodigy loves its fan polls, and this is the place to find them.

Prodigy polls sports fans on all types of sports issues and honors, such as the most valuable player awards in the major sports. Because of the link with ESPN, Prodigy also allows members to vote on the annual ESPY awards.

Player Track

Player Track enables fantasy sports fans to create a list of players on their fantasy teams—or players they're considering for their teams—and the Prodigy service automatically tracks them, providing stats to help them complete their lineups.

> **NOTE**
>
> For more information on fantasy sports online, check out Chapter 8, "Fantasy Sports."

Fantasy Games

In Fantasy Games, Prodigy members can participate in online fantasy sports leagues that the service operates.

Transactions

This area includes transactions such as trades, players called up from the minor leagues, and other roster moves.

Sports BBs

Sports fans share their opinions with each other in Prodigy's sports bulletin board area.

Products

This area provides you with information about products that can be purchased online.

Other Important Information

Prodigy's other general offerings are as thorough as ESPNet. The categories include those shown in figure 13.12.

- News/Weather—AP wire service, business news, health news, international news, weather maps.

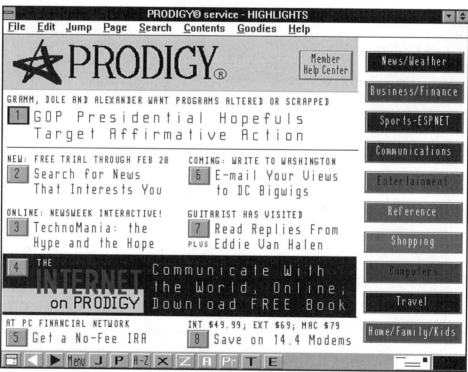

Figure 13.12 Jump: highlights
Prodigy's main menu, which appears when you log on.

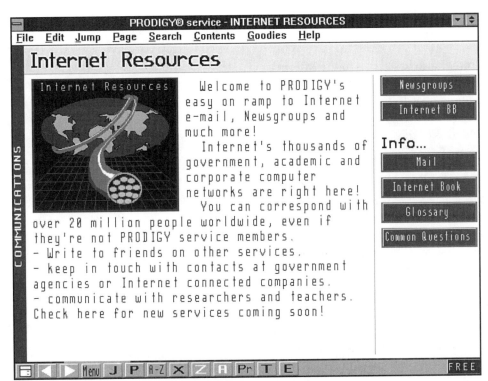

Figure 13.13 Jump: `internet`
Prodigy's Internet Resources menu leads you to the World Wide Web, newsgroups, and bulletin boards.

- Business/Finance—banking online, BillPay USA, economic indicators, investment digest.

- Communications—bulletin boards on a wide variety of topics.

- Entertainment—online games, the arts, movie guides, music, television.

- Reference—Grolier's Academic American Encyclopedia, Consumer Reports, software guides.

- Shopping—online "stores" with a wide variety of goods and services.

- Computers—software, columns related to PCs, home business information.

- Travel—flights, accomodations, Mobil Travel Guide, vacation guide.

- Home/Family/Kids—illustrated stories, Sesame Street, The Baby-Sitters' Club, Sports Illustrated for Kids, much more.

Internet Access

Prodigy was the first to give its members access to the World Wide Web— at least for those who run Prodigy through Windows.

World Wide Web (see fig. 13.13) access was added in January and, as with its

13

COMMERCIAL ONLINE SERVICES

other Internet access, Prodigy doesn't charge extra for the service.

Prodigy also has access to the Internet's UseNet newsgroups and other Internet bulletin boards, plus e-mail. Access to Gopher and FTP servers had not been added as of this writing.

Chapter Summary

This chapter contained the basic information for potential commercial online subscribers to use in deciding which of these services they would like to join. Each service has its unique advantages and disadvantages.

If you would like more information on the services they provide for specific topics, see the chapters in Part II. Each chapter includes discussion of these services.

Again, if you're not sure how to use the addresses in this chapter, see Chapter 12, "Internet Basics."

INDEX

SYMBOLS

19th Hole, The
professional golf sites, 167-169
recreational golf sites, 248-249
1994 Goodwill Games, The (international sports sites), 203-204
1994 Olympics, The (Olympic Game sites), 202
1996 Summer Games–Atlanta, GA (Olympic Game sites), 204-205
1996 Summer Olympics (OlympicGame sites), 204-205
1998 Winter Olympics (Olympic Game sites), 205-206

A

ABC Sports (Super Bowl coverage), 49
ABC Sports icon (AOL), 288-289
address lists
auto racing sites, 178-179
boxing sites, 179
fantasy sports sites, 197-198
hobby/recreational sites, 257
horse racing sites, 180
MLB sites, 95
NBA sites, 125
NFL sites, 64
NHL sites, 156-157
Olympic/international sports, 213-217
professional golf sites, 179-180
professional tennis sites, 180

school-based sites (college sports), 233, 238-241
sport-specific sites, 234
team-specific sites, 235-237
addresses, 275
FTP, 277-278
Gopher, 280
LISTSERVs, 281-282
URLs, 276
UseNet, 279
America Online, *see* **AOL**
America Online Site (fantasy sports sites), 192
Anarchie program (FTP clients), 277
AOL
auto racing sites, 165
costs, 286-287
departments, 289-290
fantasy sports sites, 193-195
Grandstand (sports talk), 36
Internet access, 291
NBA sites, 123-124
NFL sites, 63
Super Bowl information, 49
NHL sites, 153
sports packages, 287-289
Sports Ticker, 21
statistics servers, 22
subscriptions/costs, 286-287
Tour de France sites, 210-211
APO, *see* **Associated Press Online**
Arizona Cardinals (NFL address lists), 65
Associated Press Online
CompuServe, 18
MLB sites, 95
NFL sites, 63

defining, 12-13
sports resources, 15-24
sports stories, 13-14
Atlanta Braves (MLB address lists), 97
Atlanta Falcons (NFL address lists), 66
Atlanta Hawks (NBA address lists), 127
auto racing address lists, 178-179
auto racing sites, 162-163
commercial online services, 164-165
see also general auto racing sites

B

Baltimore Orioles (MLB address lists), 98
Baseball FTP Archive (MLB sites), 84
baseball sites, *see* **MLB sites, general MLB sites, 77**
Baseball Strike 1994 (Nando X Sports Server), 79
basketball
NBA (National Basketball Association), 107
NCAA (National Collegiate Athletic Association), 219
BBSs (sports talk), 26-27
LISTSERVs, 32-36
UseNet newsgroups, 28-31
Boston Bruins (NHL address lists), 157
Boston Celtics
NBA address lists, 127
Mailing List (NBA sites), 121

fantasy sports sites, 181
  commercial online services, 183-184, 195
  fantasy talk, 184-188
  leagues, 182-183
    selecting, 196
    starting, 196-197
  news/statistics, 188-193
  WWW, 188
  see also general fantasy sports sites
Fetch program (FTP clients), 277
Figure Skating Home Page (international sports sites), 211-212
figure skating sites, 211-213
File Transfer Protocol
  addresses, 277-278
  clients, 276-277
  sites, 276
files, accessing from FTP sites, 277-278
Florida Marlins (MLB address lists), 100
football
  collegiate, 219
  NFL (National Football League), 45
Fore Play Golf Newsletter, The (recreational sites), 249-250
Formula One auto racing, *see* auto racing sites
forums (CompuServe sports talk), 26, 37-38
FTP, *see* File Transfer Protocol
FTP Baseball Site (fantasy sports sites), 191
FTP Basketball Site (fantasy sports sites), 191
FTP Football Site (fantasy sports sites), 191
FTP Hockey Site (fantasy sports sites), 191-192

G

Gate Daily NBA Report, The (professional basketball sites), 111-112
Gate Sports NHL Page (professional hockey sites), 144

general auto racing sites, 178-179
general fantasy sports sites, 197-198
general golf sites, 179-180
general hobby/recreational sites, 257
  air hockey, 258
  billiards, 258
  boating, 258
  body building, 259
  climbing, 259
  collectibles, 259
  curling, 259
  cycling, 259-261
  equestrian, 261
  fencing, 261
  field hockey, 261
  flying discs, 261
  golf, 261-262
  hacky sack, 261
  hang gliding, 262
  hiking, 262
  hunting, 262
  martial arts, 263
  motorcycles, 263
  outdoors, 263
  paintball, 263
  rowing, 263
  running, 264
  scuba, 264
  skateboarding, 264
  skydiving, 265
  snow skiing, 264-265
  spelunking, 265
  squash, 265
  surfing, 265-266
  table tennis, 266
  tennis, 266
  water skiing, 265
  weightlifting, 266
General Horse Racing Sites, 175-176, 180
general international sports sites
  basketball, 214
  cricket, 214
  cycling, 214
  figure/speed skating, 215
  Goodwill Games, 214
  Olympics, 213
  rugby, 214-215
  soccer, 215-217
general men's NCAA basketball sites, 234-237
general MLB sites
  archives, 95
  discussion groups, 96

foreign-language information, 96
general information, 96
highlights, 96
home pages, 96
minor league information, 96
news stories, 96
Rotisserie League fans, 97
schedules, 97
servers, 97
statistics, 97
strike information, 97-105
general NBA sites, 126-127
general NCAA football sites, 238-240
general NFL sites, 64-65
general NHL sites, 156-157
general tennis sites, 180
general women's NCAA basketball sites, 237-238
Global Cycling Network, The (hobby/recreational sites), 245
GNN Women's Basketball Site (college sites), 225-226
Golden State Warriors (NBA address lists), 129
Golf Data On-Line Home Page, The
  professional golf sites, 169
  recreational golf sites, 250
Golf Home Page, The (recreational sites), 250-251
golf, *see* professional, recreational golf sites
Gopher
  addresses, 280
  clients, 279-280
  sites, 279-280
Grandstand (AOL), 36, 195
Grandstand icon, The (AOL), 287-288
Green Bay Packers (NFL address lists), 69

H

hardware (connection tools)
  computers, 270-271
  modems, 271-272
Hartford Whalers (NHL address lists), 157-158
Hawaii's NFL Home Page (professional football sites), 53-54

INDEX

INDEX